ST. TERESA OF AVILA

ST. TERESA OF AVILA

By
Giorgio Papàsogli

Translated from the Italian
by
Gloria Italiano Anzilotti

St. Paul Books & Media

Library of Congress Cataloging-in-Publication Data
Papàsogli, Giorgio.
    [Santi Terese d'Avila. English]
    St. Teresa of Avila / by Giorgio Papàsogli; translated from the Italian by
Gloria Italiano Anzilotti.
        p.   cm.
    Translation of: Santi Terese d'Avila.
    Bibliography: p.
    ISBN 0-8198-6879-5.   ISBN 0-8198-6880-9 (pbk.)
    1. Teresa, of Avila, Saint, 1515-1582.   2. Christian saints—Spain—
Avila—Biography. Avila (Spain)—Biography. I. Title. II. Title: Saint Teresa
of Avila.
BX4700.T4P313   1990
282'.092'4—dc19   87-30365
[B]   CIP

Printed and published in the U.S.A. by St. Paul Books & Media
50 St. Paul's Ave., Boston, MA 02130

St. Paul Books & Media is the publishing house of the Daughters of St. Paul, an
international congregation of women religous serving the Church with the
communications media.

4   5   6   7   8   9   95   94   93   92   91   90

Explanatory Note

A knowledge of the following four basic spiritual problems current in Teresa's times leads to the greater appreciation of the saint's biography:

1) The various schools of thought instituted by different "illumined persons," carry-overs of some distorted medieval ascetic-mystic movements.

2) Cardinal Ximenes de Cisneros' personal backing of the reform of religious orders and his foundation of the University of Alcalá.

3) The vast and complex influence played by the Renaissance, especially through Erasmus.

4) The almost sudden appearance of a literature of prayer.

It is in this latter category that Francisco de Osuna's influence rests, because his *Third Primer*, published about 1527, was to make a deep impression on St. Teresa. Constructed on an alphabetical basis according to the first letters of thirty-two words, he treats new and old theories of prayer and contemplation. What truly attracted young Teresa was Osuna's insistence on inner silence and solitude, for that was what Teresa needed. It was an invitation to love God according to superior spontaneity, and Teresa accepted, directing her latent immense ability to adore, love and pray to God.

Contents

INTRODUCTION

At the beginning of the sixteenth century, the city of Ávila, situated in Old Castile, consisted of perhaps two hundred families, though earlier it had been more populated. Located 3,713 feet above sea-level, overlooking vast hills, the town appeared compact and fortified within the circle of its beautiful walls—"the strongest in Europe"—so said the Avilians. Deprived as it was of mountains for protection from the north wind, it was unsheltered both from the sun's rays and the dry winter air, but in summer it was a most delightful spot.

The city was made of stone. The narrow streets wound between mansions and gray palaces as between banks of freshly cut stone. Here and there a wider facade stood out with its windows framed with smooth rock. Church portals alternated with those of the lords' mansions. But the two monuments of which the Avilians were most proud were the city walls and the cathedral.

Truly few sights impress one so deeply as do the high walls of Ávila. A certain majesty of wide line and a certain medieval hold over them arouse a feeling of intangibility. Eighty-eight huge towers, lined on the battlemented wall, form a crown over the group of roofs burnished by the centuries. Thirty towers face north, twelve west, twenty-five south, and twenty-one east. The walls between are about nine feet wide, the perimeter of the whole measuring over one and one-half miles. From a distance, this imposing mass appears as a natural complement to the airy, sloping country from which it rises.

Since it was an advance fortress of the Christian army for three hundred years of war with the Moors, the city was being fortified, demolished, pillaged, and rebuilt continually, until 1085 when the great city of Toledo, still unliberated and considered impregnable, was seized from the Moors by Alfonso VI, King of Castile. Much territory consequently returned to Christian Castilian domination.

Doña Urraca, a daughter of Alfonso VI, and her husband, Raimondo of Bourgogne, established themselves in Ávila, seeing to the restoration of the walls, the reconstruction of the cathedral, and the repopulation of the city and surrounding countryside. Much had fallen into squalor because of the long war.

People flocked from León, Asturias, Burgos, and the coast. As time passed, there rose a class of artisans, masons, stone-cutters, and blacksmiths which colonized the "arrabal," or northern section of the city. Along the banks of the river, near the bridge, were grouped the millers, tanners, and dyers; in the southern quarters lived a large number of workers and enslaved or free Moors who acknowledged Christianity. The Hebrews barricaded themselves in St. Dominic's parish down the hill on the banks of the Adaja. The city's "hidalgos" settled in St. Peter's quarters. At this time an aristocracy, characterized by the vocation of arms together with a chivalrous spirit, took root.

The city was often referred to as Avila of Knights, Avila of Saints. Each of the seven gates in the walls had a special guardian. The king, represented by the "alcaide," guarded the "Alcázar gate"; Señor Obispo y Cabildo, the bishop and the Cathedral Chapter, guarded the "gate where the flour was weighed"; the marquis de Las Navas defended the "Rastro gate"; the Aguila y Villaviciosa family watched over the "San Vicente gate"; the Polentinos family, the "Carmen gate"; the de Nunez-Vela, the "Monte Negro gate"; the City Council, called the "Ajuntamiento," protected the "bridge gate called the door of bad fortune." This powerful system increased civic-mindedness, developing a heroic and emotional localism in an already strongly individual-ized environment.

In the early part of the sixteenth century, everyone in the rest of Europe was infatuated with excessive refinement and frivolity. In contrast, the common man of Avila still spoke harshly with heavy and infrequent gestures. That typical Iberic joy seemed to have filtered through the sieve of Castilian gravity. Like their ancestors, the traditional dress worn by the women imposed a sense of careful reserve.

Manners were less severe among the aristocracy, but even in parlor talk it would have been difficult to find the poor taste of gallantry which was the vogue in France, or the broad-minded hedonism characteristic of the Italian Renaissance. Here the tone was different; a more sustained and imposing courtesy ruled over greet-ings and compliments. In fact, they tended to take common politeness too seriously. The dominating thought in the minds of both men and women, which accounted for much of their guarded mannerisms, was the ever-present concept of their "point of honor." It ruled over all as a true despot, capricious, uncompro-mising, suspicious, and irritable. No one in Castile could ignore his "point of honor."

In recompense, unlike the rest of Renaissance Europe, full of blemishes and wrongs, Castilian society was probably the least faulty of that period; rather it endured the inconveniences of its merits, as we shall see.

There are certain defects which lie in the shadows of many great virtues. It was natural that the constant search for heroism and epic deeds became tinged with exaggerated dignity and illusions. The phantom of Cid Campeador watched over every word and solemnized every action. Less important matters were neglected and the humble attractions of family life were belittled. But all this is inherent to an existence absorbed entirely in pompousness. In Avila, the call for a superior life was largely due to illustrious personalities such as Jimén Blazquez and Estéban Domingo, the founders of the two famous "Cuadrillas," and Doña Jimena Blazquez. But all of Spain was living in an era of nobility at the end of the fourteenth century and the beginning of the fifteenth, in an elated state of proud nationalism because of two glorious events—the expulsion of the Moors and the unification of the Spaniards. Every country in the civil world has, sooner or later, passed through the fiery period of unity and independence, everyone remembering with tears of rejoicing his own particular freedom. But few countries can boast memories comparable to those of Spain in this connection. Indeed, we may go so far as to say that perhaps no other country persisted as long and ended its supreme adventure of unification in such a stimulating and picturesque manner.

For seven centuries Spanish resistance against the Africans was substantially the defense of the West; and the liberation of the peninsula at the end of the fifteenth century signified the salvation of civilization. The event was of utmost importance not only to Spain and Europe, but it represented a whole Christian, human epic. Recognizing this historical significance, supported with superb stories of folklore and innumerable deeds of valor, the reader easily understands the psychology of the people who had just passed through such a period of glory.

The city of Avila with its warrior aristocracy had contributed much to the liberation. Its "hidalgos" maintained the pride and prestige of their past action. They lived in a class society within a circle of relatives and a few carefully chosen friends. Their homes were more massive than beautiful, fort-like rather than palace-like, and their names bore a long sustained cadence: Dávila, Del Aguila, Bracamontes, Barrientos, Villalobos, Villarueles, de Carvajal, de Velada, or de Navamorcuende. About ten prominent feudal families and ten others of patrician descendants (caballeros hidalgos) constituted the register of the city and surrounding country. Though none of these possessed great wealth, almost all lived in comfort.

Their mansions were solemn, lacking in imagination and harmony. Characteristic were the portals forming a halo of rays made of large chisel-smoothed rocks often placed beside two very high, thin, half-moon shaped posts. Inside, towards the courtyard, there was a less formal appearance, doors and windows becoming prominent, alternating with colonnades. The first floor was more or less considered the bottom floor of the house, serving as a cellar, storeroom, and carriage shed. After entering many homes, a guest had to climb to the second floor before meeting his hosts in the main hall, which served as a reception and banquet room. Beam-lined ceilings were high, and there were few windows. The other rooms were all built about the main hall and did not differ from one another in size or style. But here and there was a terrace or balcony which seemed to want to escape the austere structure of the house. Over tangled facades and lower roofs could be seen Amblés Valley as far as Gredos Sierra.

Many of these mansions are admired today as some of the most characteristic of Europe: for example, the "palacios" of the Del Aguilay Torre Arias, the Navamorcuende, the Las Navas (with the cozily shaded courtyard), the Nuñez-Vela palace adorned by tall, elegant posts, and then the Villaviciosa y Sofraga palace. In addition, there are the fortress-like homes (casas fuertes) belonging to the Dávila, Polentinos, Bracamontes, Henao, Velada (with its magnificent court and imposing tower), Serrano, Esquina, and other families. Also noteworthy are two small mansions, one belonging to the Valderràbanos, the other to the Counts of Superunda.

From Avila's Monte Negro gate is a panoramic view of the Amblés Valley, which seems to be created purposely for contemplation of the distant, sparkling Gredos Mountains. The Zecca palace, home of the Avilian noble family of Sánchez de Cepeda, had already been built in the late fifteenth century near the Monte Negro gate. In the early 1500's, Don Alonso Sánchez de Cepeda occupied the palace with his wife, Doña Catalina del Peso, and their two children. Sánchez, born around 1478, came from old noble stock. The Sánchez family was listed among the first "settlers" (invited by Doña Urraca and Raimondo of Bourgogne) who dared set foot in Avila in 1090. In fact, it was Sancho Sánchez Zurraquines' cry, "Avila, Caballeros!" which alone sent sixty Moors scurrying.

The Cepedas, however, came from the small castle of Cepeda, situated in the kingdom of León, near the city of Astorga.[1] An acknowledgment of nobility was

---

1. Ever since the Middle Ages, many families, probably of the same genealogical tree, took the name Cepeda. On one of these families was bestowed the coat of arms by King León. Teresa's grandfather, Juan Sánchez de Cepeda and his family who lived in Toledo and dealt with cloths and silks, renounced the Catholic religion and practiced Judaism for about five years because of economic reasons. One month after the Inquisition transferred to Toledo, Juan reentered the Church.

granted in Ciudad Real on February 5, 1500, to Juan Sánchez de Toledo, Alonso's father. Another recognition of nobility was conceeded in Valladolid on November 16, 1523, to Alonso, Pedro, Rodrigo, and Francisco Sánchez de Cepeda—all brothers—for the purpose of community tax exemption. Though not complete, their family tree was reconstructed clearly in those documents; furthermore, witnesses attested to having met the de Cepedas in other places as "fijosdalgos," or noblemen.

Alonso's family background was full of adventure, but during the early 1500's life was peaceful and plain, and Alonso de Cepeda led a family life. On November 14, 1504, Don Alonso stipulated a marriage contract with Doña Catalina del Peso, daughter of Pedro del Peso and Doña Inés de Henao, both members of the Avilian nobility. The dowry was settled at one hundred thousand "maravedis," half of which was invested in farm land in the territory of Arevalillo; the other half consisted of the bride's trousseau and cash. For his contribution to the marriage, Alonso brought money, jewels, and other objects given him by his parents, all amounting to a capital of three hundred fifty thousand "maravedis," duly listed by Gil Lopez, notary of Avila. While still a fiancé, Alonso presented his promised wife with a gold necklace, cuff links, double-stranded gold chains, six gold rings with precious stones, a "silk fawn-colored skirt with five black velvet bands," and other items.

The wedding, performed at the end of 1504, was impressive and elegant. Not possessing a house of their own, the couple looked for one. They found it nearly a year later, in 1505, and bought it by drawing up a regular contract, documented by Fernando Guillamas, for the mansion referred to as the little palace "de la Modena" in the town of Zecca near the Monte Negro gate. Several houses around it became incorporated into the main structure.

We do not know with certainty how many children were born to Don Alonso and Doña Catalina during their thirty-two months of marriage; some say three, some say two. Modern historical critics tend to believe the latter. In fact, we find mention only of Juan Vázquez de Cepeda, the first-born and heir to the illustrious family name, and Doña María Cepeda, the sister whom Teresa of Avila loved dearly. We do not know, either, the precise illness that caused Catalina del Peso's death on September 8, 1507. The young woman died in a village called Horcaiuelo, where she had probably gone to rest.

With two small children to raise, Alonso Sánchez de Cepeda fell into a state of depression, and the house became obsessed by grief. His solitude lasted two years, when it was proposed he marry young Beatriz de Ahumada.

The Ahumadas were "hidalgos" with a sonorous, mystifying name and belonged to the noble class of Avila. But why were they named Ahumada? The meaning of these few syllables has given rise to countless conjectures. Let us examine the facts. Alfonso, the Catholic King of Castile, reconquered the territories of Mave and Amaya, and toward 865, Ordone I gave orders to repopulate them. One of the towns arising then was situated north of where Villadiego is today. It was called Humada by an important family which built a house and tower there. It has been proven that an Ahumada race existed centuries later in Sandoval de la Reina in the district of Villadiego.

These Ahumadas married into powerful feudal families such as the Viscounts de la Torre de Luzón, the Marquis de las Amarillas, de Salvatierra, de Casa Tabares, and probably gave rise to the Ahumadas of Andalusia. But all this does not explain the formation of their name. A beautiful legend, dating back to the time of the Moorish invasion, explains its meaning. During the defense of Burgos—so goes the tale—a Spanish warrior called Fernando, together with his three sons, succeeded in defending a turreted bastion which had been assigned to him. He resisted attack so well that the Moors were forced to burn the whole fortification in order to win. Fernando and his sons escaped the flames and fled to the mountains of Burgos in search of Infante Don Pelagio, who, to reward such valor, decorated their shield with a tower enveloped by flames and smoke (ahumada). The coat-of-arms retained its main motif throughout all the branches of the descendants up to the time of St. Teresa.

At the transaction of his second marriage, Alonso Sánchez de Cepeda vowed to pay Beatriz de Ahumada, daughter of Juan de Ahumada and Terese de las Cuevas, "one thousand *bona fide* florins, of correct weight and value, in free and unpledged earnest money, in honor of her virginity and to increase her dowry."[2]

The wedding ceremony took place sometime in 1509 in the little town of Gotarrendura, situated fourteen miles north of Avila, where Doña Beatriz owned land. The village had ninety-five families, more or less. The place chosen would lead us to believe they wanted a quiet wedding, considering Don Alonso's widowhood; yet, in the writings of several people present, mention is made of the abundance of jewelry, expensive clothes, and much elegance. The parish sacristan, Sebastián Gutiérrez, saw "Doña Beatriz very richly attired, and had heard that her clothes and many other jewels had been given to her as gifts from Alonso Sánchez." Alonso Venegrillas wrote that "she was very richly dressed in silk and gold."

---

2. Quoted by Fr. Silverio, *Vida de Santa Teresa de Jesús*, I, III. Same for quotations immediately following.

A decorous tone prevailed in the life of the de
Cepeda couple. Don Alonso owned a noteworthy patrimony which he estimated to be worth seven hundred
forty thousand maravedis. For her part, Doña Beatriz
brought an endowment of land and cash. They settled
in Avila and in Gotarrendura, furnishing the de la Modena house with good taste.

The furnishings were as severe as the Castilian
architecture of that period. Rarely did an indentation
hint at the bizarre figures which were to characterize
the late 1500's; the figures were flat, floral geometrical
patterns with a "mudejar" (Moorish) expression of
Gothic inspiration. The large kneading-troughs and walnut chests were simple in line, and cabinets resting
over narrow, tightly twisted columns were yet to be
seen. Greater variation was revealed in the reliefs of
the silver and copper articles and water pitchers, but
even they maintained an arabesque line, full of detail.

The liveliest display of imagination was in the cloth
used for tapestries and dress. In addition to the velvets
from Toledo were the very beautifully colored, carved
leathers which were to reach the height of splendor in
the seventeenth century. However, they were already
in use in the early 1500's covering chairs, chests, and
coffers. Veiled reflections of ancient gildings put the
finishing touches to the large flowers surrounded by
arabesques, making the leathers quite fascinating.

Tapestries from Flanders were already frequent,
and in his inventory, Alonso de Cepeda listed several of
a religious nature. He also mentioned drapes on which
the family coat-of-arms was embroidered. Various "al-
fombras," or carpets with Moorish designs came from
Salamanca. He so clearly described the colors and designs on the carpets that we can easily reconstruct how
they looked—with interlacing boughs and allegorical
animals on a garnet or brick red background.

The children from Alonso's first marriage were still small when the parade of children born of the second marriage began. The first was Fernando, born in 1510. He was called Ahumada like his mother, for at that time in Spain, children could appropriate the surname of both parents, depending on the circumstances. Rodrigo de Cepeda followed after Fernando. The third child, born one morning before daybreak on March 28, 1515, was a girl.

Six days later, the baby girl was baptized Teresa in the parish church of St. John in Avila: she who was one day to become Teresa de Ahumada, Teresa of Avila, Teresa of Jesus—one of the greatest and most inimitable women of all times and all nations.

Six other children followed in the succeeding years: Lorenzo Cepeda, Antonio de Ahumada, Pedro de Ahumada, Jerónimo de Cepeda, Agustín de Ahumada and Juana de Ahumada. Among all these, it certainly cannot be said that Teresa was prey to solitude or depression during her childhood.

CHAPTER ONE

Teresa's Childhood

Passionately dominated by high ideals, speculative thoughts filled Teresa's mind when she was still very young. As a child she was keenly alert and felt everything strongly. Questions which do not normally concern children—death and the afterlife, for example—became deeply fixed in her mind and resulted in precocious meditations. She was not alone in these early spiritual explorations. Of her brothers and sisters, Rodrigo was constantly by her side, her companion in religious searches. The others quietly respected her vivaciousness which often gave rise to praiseworthy thoughts for one so young. Teresa herself said, "My brothers and sisters did not hinder my serving God in any way. I loved them all, and they loved me in return. However, I was especially fond of one of them."[1]

What was surprising was the caliber of the discussions carried on by Teresa and Rodrigo. For example, one of their favorite topics was eternity. We must not forget that these were children of seven and eleven

---

1. *Life,* I; same for the following quotations.

examining the word "always." The simple but tremendous word did not pass their minds fleetingly; instead, it fascinated and dominated them to the point of exhaustion. One of their pastimes was to repeat "forever" to each other, again and again. This was a completely intellectual and spiritual pleasure which was astounding for such young minds.

Furthermore, it was interesting to note that, for these two children, the word "always" bore a very clear meaning—it signified either paradise or hell. Firm believers, they were often startled by frequent insights. Teresa used to wonder, "Is it possible that we can obtain eternal salvation so 'cheaply' as it were?" Belonging to the hidalgos, a privileged class, their life had every promise of a happy future; yet, their minds were filled with resplendent visions of the lives of saints and martyrs. One day Teresa said that it would be worthwhile to do something wonderful for God, something tangibly certain. So she proposed going to the far land of the Moors "hoping that there they would have us decapitated. I want to see God," was what she told her brother.

How surprising this child of seven was. We cannot but wonder if she was truly convinced. Was she capable of knowing what she wanted to do? Was she not perhaps a young visionary or simply playing "martyr" as she would have played "mother"?

Years later, Teresa herself answered these questions in that outstanding clarity which is the principal characteristic of her soul as shown through her writings. True to her reputation as a woman of great sincerity, she wrote: "In my opinion, I believe God filled our young souls with so much courage that, if we had possessed but half, we would undoubtedly have carried out our project just the same."

It was a heroic motive to which history added something still more precious. Teresa's childhood resolution was probably the first serious and determined missionary idea to enter the mind of a woman. When the proposition was fully developed, the children decided to act. Teresa does not relate the second part of the episode, but we know how the story went from Ribera, an acquaintance who had spoken to her several times, and who was later to become one of Teresa's most important biographers.

One beautiful day the children ran away from home, left their city behind and crossed the Adaja bridge. Going this far, they thought innocently, was too far already, so—onward! Never looking behind, they marched toward the town where they thought the Moors lived. Just as young heroes in fairy tales—always ahead! But this was not fiction. Their escape and long walk, their anxiety were all reality—and what reality! Rodrigo was eleven and Teresa seven, but Teresa had said, "I want to see God."

When the children arrived at a curve in the road, in the middle of a large, lonely area, their mission went to pieces. Just then, an uncle of theirs, Francisco Alvarez de Cepeda, happened to be passing. He never could have expected to meet his young nephew and niece in that open country. "Where are you going?" he asked, startled. The two, denying nothing, offered a detailed explanation. Still more bewildered, he studied them breathlessly for a minute and then said, "Go home!" in such a way that left the two quite devoid of hopes of a missionary life and Moorish beheading.

At home they found Doña Beatriz crying desperately. She had searched everywhere and had sent others out after them. Finally, she believed they had fallen into some well, down one of those deep wells which are still found in the country and which were the main reserves of the city and castles. So ended an adventure which leaves us thoughtful. Underlying all was an exceptional ascetic motive grafted onto the spirit of a childish dream. It was an event which stood out like a jewel.

At the time, the delusion felt by these little would-be martyrs must have been great. Teresa said so herself, relating how she and her brother tried to console each other. "Since it was impossible to go to a country where one could die a martyr for God, we decided to lead the life of hermits...." This decision led to another poignant scene: brother and sister in the garden busily gathering small stones "to construct hermitages." But "the small stones fell almost immediately and it was continually necessary to start over from the beginning. Finally, it became evident that we had to abandon our desire for life in solitude."

Nevertheless, their games still held an almost prophetic tone of anticipation. "When I played with other little girls, our favorite game was to build convents and act as though we were nuns."

Teresa was a lively girl; nothing unbalanced or nightmarish existed in her childish mind. She acted the way she did entirely from a religious feeling already formed. In her writings, she glanced back critically and penetratingly over her childhood, unveiling her young mind before us. Referring to the Moorish incident, she writes: "It does not seem to me that this was done out of love of God, but rather out of the anxiety to enjoy as quickly as possible that heavenly bliss which I had read about." This great woman mystic used saintly severity regarding a child of seven. Please note that despite her spiritual insight (she had already seen Christ), looking down on her infant world from well-earned heights, she is not sure whether the main force driving the child was a superior hedonism or not. She writes, "It seems to me...." But even if little Teresa had truly fallen in love with paradise and wanted to hurry and get there, was not that a superior sign? This child achieved heights that showed a heart no longer satisfied by

incomplete and limited joys, but desperately wanting
perfect and infinite happiness in God.

What breadth of soul in a little round-faced, bright-
eyed girl! A pleated, starched collar formed a narrow
circle around her expressive face. Her dress was becoming, but was somewhat of a parody: an embroidered velvet bodice coming to two points over the velvet
skirt, exactly as older women's clothes. All well-dressed
children in the early part of the sixteenth century
dressed as adults, making them resemble puppets or
dolls. However, the manner of dress seemed to draw
out the charm of their age all the more.

How many of these delightful living playthings had
Doña Beatriz put together! Nine children in fourteen
years of marriage, despite her number of serious illnesses. This was her life, and she educated her children
well, making them love her intensely. Yet, she committed a slight error in Teresa's upbringing, though it in no
way lessened Teresa's veneration for her parents. "My
father was very charitable toward the poor and full of
compassion for the sick. He was truly honest." And of
her mother: "She, too, was most virtuous, always behaving with the greatest honesty. She was very lovely
but was never seen to have given much weight to that
fact. She was gentle and of great intelligence."

These two comments are enough. Teresa insisted
on honesty and charity, and since we have before us
sincere judgments made by one with a soul in the state
of grace, they can be considered complete evaluations.
But Teresa found a weakness in her mother and was
careful to explain it. So often ill, Doña Beatriz read
novels of chivalry for amusement. They were very
much the fashion in the time of Charles V. New novels
were always coming out and high society tried to keep
up-to-date. Speaking of her mother's unwariness,
Teresa said, "She enjoyed reading books on chivalry
and even encouraged me to read them; though this

pastime presented no interference with her duties, it became an impediment for me. She no doubt read those books for distraction from her daily toils and probably permitted our reading them, too, to keep us out of more unseemly occupations."

Certainly Doña Beatriz had her reasons—a bit of enjoyment for herself, an attraction for the children, perhaps preventing them from scampering about and thinking of other things, so enabling her to keep an eye on them. Her watch over them had become too tenuous during all her illnesses. Still, she showed poor judgment toward her children in this matter. The stories filled their heads with visions of greatness, violence and love. Don Alonso did not approve. "My father disapproved of this habit, and we did all we could not to be caught reading by him." For hiding their reading, they probably formed a small furtive society.

To be sure, all reading was of noble content, and if any poison lay in it, vulgarity was not a part. But in their young minds, vivid, fantastic images appeared along with heroic feats of chivalry, astonishing encounters, and valorous humane actions. Point of honor, ruling god of the fatuous, dominated the whole. This is the reason Teresa blamed Doña Beatriz. The idol of honor substituted for God. A silent, stealthy usurpation gradually grew out of that mass of adventure stories, enhanced by the multicolored epic descriptions.

Of her adolescent period, St. Teresa confessed, "My sense of honor was stronger in me than the fear of God." This revelation showed the tyranny exercised by the "point of honor," and explained the greatness and weakness of many Spaniards of the sixteenth century.

Doña Beatriz's favorite books consequently became Teresa's also. *Amadis de Guala* came out clamorously in 1508; *Caballero Gifar* was another widely proclaimed book. *Sergas de Esplandián* was present in every nobleman's library, as were *Palmarin de Inglaterra, Tirante el*

Blanco and *Don Olivante de Laura* which admirably
bore this modest subtitle: "The story of the invincible
Knight Don Olivante de Laura, Prince of Macedonia,
who, because of his extraordinary courage became Emperor of Constantinople which has just lately been re-
vivified." The frontispiece depicted Don Olivante under
an impressive crest of feathers, lance at rest and almost
sideways over his war horse in a most fear-inspiring
pose. These thick folio volumes were found lying about
in the homes of almost every well-to-do family, the
Emperor's included.

Don Alonso was evidently a stern man with a solid
foundation. He was not likely to take part in imaginative games, nor did he approve of them in others. His
severity was shown by rigid facial expressions, but his
abrupt manner often concealed a kind heart. He did not
approve of slavery and would not permit it in his
household. Teresa told that once a slave-girl belonging
to his brother came to stay a while in the "de la
Modena" house and everyone noticed how kind and
respectful Don Alonso was to her. He always acted
sympathetically toward the poor, giving them alms and
often housing them.

As all hidalgos, Don Alonso was proud of his social
position. A look at his wardrobe is enough to prove
this. He owned several crimson and black cloth capes,
gold chains, silver- and gold-buckled belts, hoods, furs,
and "terciopelo" stockings, which were made of velvet
from Toledo—all of which he considered as part of a
uniform denoting nobility. All the variety of clothing
and ornaments cannot be considered luxury because
they merely fulfilled the social tenets of the times.
However, a more strict attitude governed his intellectual trends. Don Alonso's library was composed of instructive and informative books which he carefully
read and reread. He never read fiction. There is a
valuable bound volume of *El Retablo de la Vida de*

Cristo, and *Tullio, de Officiis* with "viejo" notes. A small bound volume of *Tratado de la Misa* was found together with *Los Siete Pecados* and bound pictures by Guzmán. His interest in Christopher Columbus' great adventure accounts for *La Conquista de Ultramar.* In ancient history, this Renaissance man appreciated medieval favorites: the proverbs of Seneca and Virgil collected in Boethius' single volume. The Spanish author he seems to have enjoyed most of all was Juan de Mena, of whose works he owned *Las Trencentas* and *La Consolación.*[2]

Beside such a well-delineated figure as Don Alonso, Doña Beatriz was contrasting and more complicated. She, too, was typically Spanish, but belonging to her times and to her environment. An hidalga in a period which corresponds to full Renaissance in other parts of Europe, she reflected the cultural and social tastes of her class and nation.

Spanish nobility was then in the middle of a most interesting transition. It still lived in medieval fashion, but the heroic undertakings were only in imaginary and narrative form. Dreams took the place of reality, preceding that great ironic awakening by Don Quixote.

But imagination played only a small role in Doña Beatriz's mind, for there was no room for far-fetched stories. Keeping up with the romantic novels of the period did not in any way take her from her daily chores. She was an expert housekeeper, a faithful wife, and a self-sacrificing mother. There were two principal elements in her life: frail health which caused repeated painful illness, and the brave acceptance of the privilege of biblical fertility. She died at thirty-five, leaving nine children.

However, it was not only physiological fatigue that shortened Doña Beatriz's years. Other factors entered

---

2. Fr. Silverio, *op. cit.,* p. 84, note.

in the daily sacrificing of her life, especially anxiety over her husband's first-born child, whom she had accepted and loved as her own. Too, there was concern over her own children who left home early, called by dangerous armed adventures. On the fields of Lombardy one stormy morning in 1524, a bullet from a French harquebus killed Juan Vázquez, Don Alonso's eldest son. Later on, five of Doña Beatriz's sons were to fight in far-off Peru in the army of the Vice-king, Don Blasco Vela. Teresa's dearest brother, Rodrigo, was killed there. Two of Beatriz's brothers, Antonio and Sancho de Ahumada, fought in battles near Naples and died before 1516 while still quite young. In short, Doña Beatriz was an hidalga living in the early years of that century which was to prove to be so great for the Spanish; it was her destiny to share in the sufferings and anxieties of her class.

So much worrying undoubtedly was a bad influence on her naturally frail constitution. This well-to-do, peaceful family was forced to live in the shadow of that intensely burning Europe of the first half of the sixteenth century. That is why Teresa often wrote "of the deep sorrows her mother had borne." To compensate, however, as usually happens to those overcome by grief, came a deepened sense of religious spirituality. Family prayer became frequent in the de Cepeda household. The different, yet substantially identical, religious feelings of Don Alonso and Doña Beatriz mingled. Doña Beatriz was especially devoted to reciting the Rosary, and Teresa followed her example.

CHAPTER TWO

Adolescence and Early Youth

Teresa grew to adolescence in the midst of this strongly individualized environment. Her religious fervor had weakened, and she was the picture of a girl we would never have recognized. Carefree and likeable, with a round pleasant face, a straight nose, and laughing eyes, she was really still a child and possessed all the charms of one naïvely wishing to please. She was now without disturbing, complicated thoughts. She walked lightly, her gestures adding grace to her medium height. Her innate nobility, joined with a typical Castilian sense of security, united into ready, unrestrained manners.

Young Teresa de Ahumada's way of thinking was ruled entirely by the joy of pleasing others through cheering them. Hers was an open, sincere happiness which reflected on others, causing them to receive her just as enthusiastically. She was a most appealing adolescent, bursting with spontaneous friendliness. Teresa was a most sincere woman so this childish desire to please people when she was a girl was not an affectation, but it came from a natural generosity.

Nonetheless, this behavior was also dangerous; though the art of attracting was spontaneous and unintentional, it could have proven more harmful to oneself than to others. Whoever discovers he possesses the ability to interest and win over people is apt to rely on this privilege too much, gradually taking to flattering himself, becoming vain. Later on, he passes to an excessive self-love, inevitably a prey to egocentricity.

Teresa de Ahumada avoided this latter phase, but not the first completely. She grew proud of her capacity to please others. She dressed carefully, and complimented herself on her attributes. This was all very human and even common, but it probably wouldn't have happened to Teresa's privileged soul if there hadn't been certain particular circumstances which encouraged it.

Let us take a look in the "de la Modena" household to see how life went on there. The women of the house spent most of their time working or otherwise occupied in the large room on the first floor which opened onto the garden. Up two or three stairs were the main rooms of the house. Don Alonso's home was one of the least accessible to outsiders, but so many sons and daughters of various ages gave the house a friendly atmosphere. The numerous de Cepeda and Mejía cousins were always around also. These included the children of Don Alonso's brother, Don Francisco Alvarez de Cepeda and María de Ahumada (a cousin of Doña Beatriz), who lived next door. An inner door joined the two buildings so Don Alonso's eleven children grew up with Don Franciso's eight—five boys and three girls—named Pedro Alvarez Cimbron, Francisco Alvarez de Cepeda, Juan de Cepeda, Diego de Cepeda, Vincente de Ahumada, Inés de Cepeda, Ana de Cepeda and Jerónima de Cepeda. As though these were not enough, Don Alonso's sister, Doña Elvira de Cepeda, continually sent her children, Francisco Mejía, born in 1508, Diego Mejía, born in 1515, and Inés Mejía, born also in 1515. In addition to these came another cousin, Elvira de Cepeda, daughter of another uncle, Ruy Sánchez de Cepeda and Doña Isabella de Aguila.

Teresa spent her childhood and early youth around such pleasant company. Most of these children were typical Castilians of their period—firmly traditional, yet dreamers too, entirely taken up with big and beautiful ideals, ready to die for God and their king. But some of the girls were overly clothes-conscious. Years later, when she looked back to this time with a critical eye, Teresa of Jesus described one of her girlfriends with disapproval, proving she had reached an objective height. We do not know which, but one of her cousins then appeared conceited, empty-headed, and inclined to wasted time. The virgin of Avila scolded herself continually for lingering in this cousin's company, for imitating her, losing a great deal of time prettying herself and in talking frivolously. This was her lament, her soul's torment, if one can speak of torment in one so full of grace as she. "I am filled with remorse when I think back to the reasons why I did not live up to my childhood aims."[1]

Critics have unsuccessfully tried to individualize this "parienta." Teresa never named her, saying only that "she had such a silly way of acting that my mother, who was certainly aware of the bad influence she could be on me, tried to keep her away; but this was impossible considering the many occasions that brought her to our house. We grew to be intimate friends; she approved of my tastes and confided in me, telling me of the people she knew, describing many vain details. My favorite pastime was to be with her."[2] Charitable as Teresa was, she never mentioned the girl

---

1. *Life,* I, 6.

2. *Life,* II, 2, 3, 6, here and for following quotations.

by name. It was not an important omission, however, for she was probably the typical banal, frivolous girl who can be found in all times. The mark she caused to appear on Teresa's luminous soul was so small that it made the unknown girl appear still more insignificant.

From what Teresa wrote on another occasion, it was a slight mark indeed. "I was never tempted to commit grievous| sin, for I was repulsed naturally by dishonesty." This most sincere and summary statement traced the bounds of her confessions as well as her penance. She revealed humility when speaking of her cousins in her self-reproach. "They were about my own age, perhaps a little older. We were always together and they were very fond of me. We discussed what they wanted, and I enjoyed listening to their likes and dislikes, plans and many silly nothings. But I became so attached to these 'worthless subjects' that I did not notice that my fault lay exactly in this."

A particular fondness, perhaps even love, grew between Teresa and one of her cousins. His name is unknown, but he probably was a de Cepeda. Teresa asked advice from her confessor who said it was not harmful to speak to him since this first gleam of affection could grow into an engagement. Encouraged, Teresa did not avoid talking to him; instead she created as many opportunities as possible. Later on, she criticized herself severely, not for the affair as a whole, but for the temptations to which she exposed herself: "Once the danger was imminent, and I endangered my family's position."

Completely sincere, she wrote the aforementioned sentence in reference to this, which is an important point in our estimation of her. "However, I was never tempted to commit grievous sin for I was naturally repulsed by dishonesty. I sought only pleasant conversation." Besides, she was tormented by her sense of honor. "My fear of losing it gave me all the strength needed to safeguard it. I would never have allowed myself to lower it for anything in the world; and I believe that no human affection would have led me to lower myself but one grade."

After canonical trials full of subtle investigations, the Church established that the virgin of Avila was never blemished by grievous sin. Whoever is acquainted with Catholic morals and knows how keen the boundary is between good and evil (especially delicate in matters of purity) can view young Teresa's way of acting in its proper light, appreciating her "repentance" as a woman within dignified proper limits. An image which she herself used explained her so-called sense of remorse. "Take a glass of water and look at it: there is nothing clearer. Raise it facing the sun and there appears a whole bevy of moving dust particles." The same happened to her: raising her memories in the full light of grace, she saw shadows and imperfections crossing them. So she called herself "Teresa de Jesús, la pecadora."

Teresa was then about fourteen or fifteen. Doña Beatriz's state of health had already become progressively worse, and she felt her strength leaving her. She spent frequent periods resting on her Gottarendura farm, and she wrote her will there in 1528. The document is dated November 24, and is written in a religious manner. It started in a pleasantly dignified, solemn tone: "Let it be known to those who will see this, my last testament, that I, Doña Beatriz de Ahumada, the wife of Alonso Sánchez de Cepeda, my lord, and a citizen of the noble city of Avila, being in my right mind just as God gave it to me, firmly believing and upholding that which Holy Mother Church believes and upholds, order my testament to be in the service of God and of the Blessed Virgin Mary, His Mother, whom I call upon as my mediator in the majesty of her precious Son...."

Doña Beatriz was then thirty-three years old. Her beauty had lost the splendor of youth, but it was present in a different way. Suffering had furrowed her face, yet its pallor complemented her thick, dark hair; she had few white hairs and her eyes were gentle and thoughtful. She had cut down on her household duties some time before, and the management of the house was almost wholly in the hands of Don Alonso's eldest daughter, María de Cepeda, who was twenty-four. Teresa considered María "gifted with much goodness and modesty." This great help permitted Doña Beatriz peace of mind. It was evident to everyone that she was approaching death very well prepared. She died, with Christian serenity and piety, either at the end of 1529 or during the early months of 1530. This seems most probable, though there is no exact date, and there are many differences of opinion regarding her death.

Despite weakening strength, Doña Beatriz continued to be the pivot around which the house turned, and her death upset the whole family organization, leaving a large lacuna. Lack of maternal authority created new problems. One of these was Teresa's education. She was then an attractive teenager of fourteen or fifteen.[3] Her mother had married at her age; Teresa, instead, was still carefree and impulsive. She was a juvenile despite her airs of an elegant young lady with well-groomed hands and her use of perfume. Her natural candor was yet apparent, and that overwhelming sense of honor that fully dominated her revealed her unsophistication. We have already seen how "no human affection could make her descend but one step...." Of course, this constituted a great guarantee to her father and sister. But that girl of fourteen was nonetheless

---

3. St. Teresa says she was twelve when her mother died, but other circumstances would lead one to believe she was fifteen, as all the modern biographers agree.

human, and her attractive qualities formed a halo of danger about her. Neither could Don Alonso be satisfied with the fact that her mind and heart lived in such moral inertia. He understood what an enormous waste of intellectual and spiritual resources this would mean. Teresa was spending her time in silly talk, following the fashions and beautifying herself.

Don Alonso found support in his eldest daughter when discussing and pondering the matter. There was also another problem: María de Cepeda was now twenty-five, and for an hidalga of her time, it was getting late to marry. María had postponed marrying in consideration of her second mother's frail health, but now that things were stabilized, she needed to look after herself. It was probably more difficult to leave her father at that time, but this obstacle faded away once Teresa was settled and a good faithful "tata" had been found for little Juana, the youngest of Doña Beatriz's nine children. Her brothers, sufficiently self-reliant and headstrong, gave María small satisfaction and would certainly never obey her. Thus, she was at liberty to leave.

The solution arose naturally from the circumstances, and it could not have been a better one. Teresa was to enter a convent for some time in order to complete her education, and, above all, to revivify and direct her brilliant spiritual energies. Emotionally upset, she accepted; something had already changed in her since her mother's death, for the loss had been deeply felt. With profound and burning feelings, Teresa had accepted the death in all its finality, but her thoughts of it grew daily in intensity. At the time of the death she had immediately reacquired an unexpected worthy reaction. On the very day her mother died, she had gone to church tearfully imploring the Madonna, "O most Holy Mary, be my mother since I no longer

have my earthly one."[4] Her saddened soul somewhat
consoled by the plea, and no doubt relieved by her
complete withdrawal while invoking the Virgin, probably found another bond with the celestial Mother.

As the loss of her mother became more deeply and
steadily felt, Teresa's thoughts turned toward the
greater truths. Had she not been the pensive child both
attracted and awed by the word "always"? That same
spiritual anxiety returned now and then, but more concretely, more clearly oriented and richer in human
content. In affectionate meditation, she followed her
most beloved mother through the phases of her invisi-
ble transmigration.

The convent chosen for Teresa was one of the best
in Old Castile: that of the Augustinians of Our Mother
of Grace in Avila. She went shortly after María married
Don Martín de Guzmán y Barrientos. The marriage
probably took place in the spring of 1531 at Villatoro
where the bride and bridegroom met. Don Martín came
from Castellanos de la Cañada where he owned land,
and the de Cepedas arrived from Avila. Returning to
Ávila, the couple remained in the de la Modena house
for a month. A few more weeks passed before Teresa
left, so Don Alonso was spared the anguish of seeing
two of his beloved daughters leave home at the same
time. However, on July 31, she left.

The convent appeared severe and suffocating, and
Teresa related how she suffered much the first week.
What bothered her the most was her fear that people
would think she had entered the convent as punishment for something she had done. But after the first
few days she felt at peace. "My early restlessness diminished, and after only eight days I already felt happier there than at home."[5] Her natural need to please

---

4. *Life*, I, 7.

5. *Life*, II, 8.

helped her through the early period. After a short time, the sisters all felt favorable toward her. By unpretentiously imposing her sparkling youth on others, she went about winning their approval unconsciously and without any secret interest.

The papal foundation bull was granted by Julius II on September 28, 1508; the convent had no endowment. The building still stands southeast of the city under the heavy ancient tower of "Baluardo" on top of a steep hill going toward the Amblés Valley. But the actual convent and church are very different from those Teresa saw, for they were remodeled in the seventeenth century. The poverty of those first two decades of the institute was felt inside. During the assignment of a patronage requested by the convent in 1531, Juan de Munoherro, father of one of the nuns, said, "This convent is poor and has little income; what it has is not enough for the upkeep of the sisters if our Lord and their own manual work do not help them."[6]

There must not have been many in the convent because there were only fourteen names listed on a paper dated May 30, 1532, during Teresa's stay. Two names stand out: Doña María of St. Augustine, one of the founders, and a noted nun who was to have a determining influence on Teresa's soul, Doña María de Briceño. The latter taught the "niñas seculares," that is, the boarding-school girls (commonly called "las señoras doncellas de piso"). Fr. Varona, who knew her well, wrote, "Because of her qualities which we all admire, she was unanimously appointed the schoolgirls' teacher and she remained with them both day and night." She led them in a group to the choir for morning Mass or to a separate tribune for conventual Mass, always insisting on strict observance of the austere and formal edu-

6. Quoted by Fr. Silverio, *op. cit.* I, VI, here and for the following quotations in this chapter.

cational principles of the times. Herself a confirmed
ascetic, Sister María Briceño was the most able person
to transmit holy enthusiasm into young girls. Her countenance revealed inner conviction. Not beautiful, her
face was pleasant and truly spiritual. Most attractive in
her was the expression of a constant, undisturbed inner
meditation, not in the least diminishing her natural
vivacity. Whenever Sister María spoke of God "she was
always discreet and holy" and her eyes became very
luminous. Teresa listened to her rapturously. "I liked to
hear how well she spoke of God." Accustomed as she
was to the trivialities of the century, a whole new
unexpected world of peace, space and clarity opened
before her, bearing a resemblance to that extraordinary
horizon she had glimpsed as a child, but now having
more substantial value. So Teresa's spirit began to
change.

In her conversations, María de Briceño always related personal experiences as though she were confiding in her pupils. Her memories intermingled with her
spiritual reflections. Every now and then she would
recall her first steps toward mystic exaltation on the
road to perfection. Her early attempts were particularly
alive and suggestive of evangelical revelations. "Many
are called, but few are chosen." These words spoken by
Christ had been kindling wood to young María's mind
years before and had urged her toward her chosen
destiny. These words contained a heroic motive which
moved Teresa deeply. Indeed, no other thought could
have as effectively excited her desire for improvement.

Up until then, Teresa had always read of human,
chivalrous heroism and was prepared for an unusual
life. Her novels had pictured the call to perfection as
enveloped and overcome by a growth of human ambi-
tions, adventures and loves. Here, instead, was a clear
flame surrounded by four bare walls with its reflections
all gathering around the crucifix. Teresa's transforma-

tion began to gain ground. The abundance of ideals and daydreams which had earlier attracted her no longer appeared as an enchanted garden but as brushwood. Her change came about gradually. At first, common-place adventures and gallantries seemed insipid and vulgar. Petty pride which had occupied Teresa's soul disappeared along with pretentious elegance and excessive care of her appearance. All this parasitic vegetation dried in the sun's rays. Something evident in her manner when Teresa listened to Sister María showed the inner working of grace. Her vivid eyes would look fixedly into space and then turn to the crucifix. What did that contemplation mean? Teresa was still at the point that "to meditate on the whole passion of Christ would not have made her shed one tear." Yet she already felt the need to look at Christ.

The conversations were often held at dusk during a recreation period before the girls went to bed. It was mid-autumn and twilight lingered long, seeming to remain even longer over the high cliff of Castile where the sun left reluctantly. For some time after sundown, one could see without lights in the bare rooms of the convent. The light found no obstacles because furniture and tapestry were scarce. The oil lamp placed in the middle of a bare wall sent its pale glimmer into the shadows.

During those first encounters with the crucifix, Teresa's soul was more concerned with itself than with the contemplation of divine beauty. Just as every novice in religious life, she spoke to our Lord of herself more than of Him. She was still a long way from forgetting herself. Even so, that type of concentration was a kind of offering. Teresa was generous, and this was the note that vibrated most from her very first conversations with God. From then on, she surrendered her spirit to the divine will and was ready to follow God's decision. She even tried to hurry that

decision, she told us, reciting many prayers out loud
and asking everyone to intercede for her with God so
she might know how He wanted her to serve Him.

This was no little matter when done with Teresa's
capacity for stately sincerity. But her human nature
was still alive with its harmful tendencies. Beneath her
prayers and firm resolutions, natural inclinations acted
silently. An eagle's eye such as Teresa's—a woman and
a mystic—was needed to discover the complex weav-
ings much later. This was one of the most moving
details pointed out by this soul full of grace and wisdom. Her introspection had exactness, added to the
striking ability to discern between human and divine
motives. The first and most general lesson which we
can all (religious and laity, believers and non-believers
alike) draw from Teresa is this: to separate those aims
which are concealed from those we openly desire.

The idea of spending her entire life in the convent
entered her mind now and then, but she said that she
herself was hostile to the idea. She enjoyed the whole
impressive spiritual Augustinian convent atmosphere
and lingered with holy envy at the sight of the most
fervent sisters at prayer. Their simple, quietly meditative faces which left no doubts, their lowered eyes as if
concealing the overflow of religious effects, their lips
barely moving in audible prayer—all constituted a visible invitation to penetrate this spiritual world.

What proved even more effective to Teresa's eager
mind were the bits of light glimpsed whenever one of
the nuns confided moments of her own contemplative
life, perhaps told intentionally. So much secret beauty
served to awaken and capture her. Though no longer
"enimiguisima" (completely opposed) to the religious life
as before, she was far from inclined toward a vocation.
The idea of remaining in the convent, infrequent as it
was, persisted without causing any mental conflict.
Delightfully naïve, Teresa prayed much to know God's

will, but always hoped it would not be the monastic life. However, this has no similarity to the situation of a certain school-girl who secretly told her confessor: "I am so afraid, Father, that I will receive the religious vocation." The priest replied, "Rest assured, my child, there is no danger." Teresa's case was different; she was truly sincere. Yet, now she began to find flaws in her desire for family life which she had strongly felt a year ago. "At the same time I also feared matrimony."

What then was to be her vocation? Her ardent character could not remain uncertain much longer.

CHAPTER THREE

What Others Do Not See in a Vocation

A year and a half of convent life bore its fruit. Uncertainty about her future still persisted, but the thought of monastic life no longer frightened her.

Late in 1532 or early in 1533, Teresa became ill. Neither she nor her early biographers state the nature of her illness. She was forced to return home for several months. Having almost fully recuperated in the spring of 1533, she went to the country home of her sister, María.

On the way, she stopped at Hortigosa where an uncle, Don Pedro Sánchez de Cepeda, lived. Hortigosa, a small village spread over the mountainside, was a cluster of houses. The best-looking one belonged to Don Pedro. The villagers called it "el palacio," and Teresa's uncle led a secluded life there. Pedro loved his house mainly because it had belonged to his wife, Catalina del Aguila, who had died a few years earlier. Their marriage had been a long, happy union, and her death had left him thoroughly saddened.

His niece's arrival was a consolation to this old man accustomed to solitude. At first, Teresa thought she had entered a house that was partly closed off and neglected. The walls breathed out a stale odor and shadows and mold were everywhere. Everything in the "palacio" reflected respect for cherished memories. All the furniture, upholstery, and knick-knacks were exactly where Catalina's hands had placed them years ago.

Don Pedro promptly begged Teresa to read to him, which led to her gradual discovery of another facet to that isolated existence. They read deep devotional books which the old man enjoyed. Teresa had not planned to spend her time that way and said, "I did not enjoy doing it," but hastily added, "however, since it was a matter of pleasing someone, I was always condescending and simulated enjoyment." Without realizing it, she revealed one of the secrets of her art of pleasing: knowing how to please others by showing her approval through sacrificing her own tastes. Meanwhile, her small act of charity was being rewarded; the peculiar atmosphere of the house and Don Pedro's company made a profound impression on her. There she found the energy to free herself from the many ties which bound her imagination and heart to the world. While reading those solid books, her soul had been inadvertently conquered and led back to her prodigious meditations: forever—to live forever in happiness or in desperation.

When she left, another part of her young hidalgan levity remained at Hortigosa. She had gone one step further. Her stay at Castellanos de la Cañada was also calm and intimate. This was a little town of ten families over which the Guzmán y Barrientos homestead stood out in importance. Yet it was but a modest two-story house with thick walls made of stone from the village, small windows, and a few balconies. This small rustic building is still standing although the interior has been redecorated completely.

Teresa stayed with the Barrientos until late autumn, returning to Avila before the snow could hinder travel on the roads. There she started her life as a house-keeper, for her father left her in charge. She spent three years at this, maturing all the time. In her brief mention of this time, two determining elements stand out: her brother Rodrigo's departure for America and her inward strife for spiritual peace, which probably culminated in the three months from August to October, 1536, preceding her definite decision.

Rodrigo crossed the ocean to Peru, the land of wide-open spaces, mirages and mystery—the goal of all sixteenth-century idealists and adventure-seekers. Admirers of wandering heroes and die-hards to the cause of chivalry looked to Peru as their utopia, the "Castilla de oro." Europe was far too well-known, too cultivated and too clever. Under the Renaissance man's ironic lullaby, the Cid, was falling asleep to awaken as Don Quixote. Frightened and shamed knight-errants revived when the New World blossomed beyond the immense waters. But this was not all; other more serious ideals, both spiritual and practical, lured the Spanish to the newly-discovered lands. These were the propagation of the Christian faith, the thought of increasing Spain's influence, and the hope of personal wealth—three entirely different aims fused into one.

The Spanish colonizers were of different moral and intellectual stature. We need not go into detail over their names, for some are too well known, such as those who took part in the Pizarro expedition. Juan de Osorio of Avila took part in one of the best organized great Spanish expeditions to the "Indies" headed by Don Pedro de Mendoza. The party was made up of thirty-two hidalgos, all holders of family seniority rights, and other high-ranking men including Rodrigo de Cepeda. They left Seville on August 24, 1535, and it seems that Rodrigo helped found Santa María of Buenos Aires in 1536. He later accompanied Juan de Las Ayolas in his travels along the Paraná and Paraguay Rivers and is believed to have been present at the founding of Ascunción, Paraguay's capital. So began a most arduous period for the colonizers. Rodrigo left for Xarayes with Juan de Las Ayolas and was forced to take part in many fierce struggles with the Indians, during which a great number of the Spanish soldiers of Irala and Ayolas fell. Rodrigo escaped, only to battle against isolated bands of Indians. He and four other brothers fought in the famous battle of Inaquito.

Ten years later, Rodrigo crossed the Cordilleras to die fighting beside his brother Agustín in a skirmish with the Araucanians in Chile on August 10, 1557. It was he who had run away from home with his sister in search of martyrdom in the land of the Moors. There was a tragic fundamental similarity between his childhood dream and what actually happened! Before leaving home he had written a will full of emotional significance. Teresa was to inherit what Doña Beatriz had left him. This showed what a close bond existed between the two, a fraternity of arms it might be called. Both brother and sister fought for the same ideal— Rodrigo among bands of men, and Teresa unconsciously moving toward a more difficult apostleship.

Teresa was walking toward the goal unknowingly and without any definite decision on her part. Still bothered by uncertainty, she outwardly remained sure of herself, pleasant and joyful. She was twenty and glowing with youth. Although not beautiful, she nevertheless was well-proportioned, with lovely gestures, creating an almost perfect appearance. Her full, oval face was of a beautiful complexion, her black hair curled softly, and though not large, her eyes were most luminous with their laughing, nearly black pupils. Her nose was small, and her dark eyebrows were slightly arched. Her upper lip was thin and straight, while the lower was thicker and slightly turned down. Just above medium height, she was always well-groomed.[1] In testimonies brought before the beatification process, several remembered seeing her "in an orange-colored dress bordered with black velvet bands."

But Teresa's life had changed. Gone was every adolescent foolishness; she no longer wasted time nor sought trivial company. She was now almost indifferent toward the cousin to whom she had once felt sentimentally drawn. Her call from within was ripening. Her doubts now were of another type. "Shall I be able to endure the rigors of the religious life with my frail health?" The question kept repeating itself, but she responded vigorously: "Did not Christ suffer infinitely more?"

The saint herself relates these internal debates. It is evident that the conflict that now existed had been transferred to a very high plane. When one hears an inner voice saying, "But shall I suffer much? How shall I bear it all?" and one is able to answer with but, "And Christ?" that person is already in sight of the Divine Vision. But Teresa was not aware of this and continued to belittle herself. Another question which arose from this anxiety was one which fully demonstrates Teresa's humility. "The sufferings of the convent cannot be worse than those of purgatory. How then can I, who deserve hell, fear them?" She thought she was doing good by hedging off hell's pains by expiating those of purgatory. This type of reasoning reflects the two aspects of her spirit at that time: a deprecatory impres-

---

1. We know of this famous portrait through the testimony of Mother Mary of St. Joseph. Taking into account the difference of age, the picture greatly resembles the one drawn by Friar John of Misery, of which we shall speak later.

sion of herself, and the fear of God, which she felt more than love of Him.

Well-balanced and calm, her pessimistic view of herself was by no means due to a pathological condition. She had a quick mind, which could be witty or peacefully meditative. Her self-disapproval was entirely due to her spiritual nature, an example of humility. Remembering her glass full of dust helps us to understand her point of view.

Erroneous fear of God is a defect found in many religious novices. The mediocre and unprepared become completely exhausted at the fear stage. Teresa's state was still mediocre even though a glimpse of her gigantic Christian future had been revealed in her reply: "And Christ?" It was definitely a mediocrity which many Christians would look upon enviously, but mediocrity nevertheless.

Her inner turmoil grew to a climax between August and October in 1536. Until then her uneasiness of mind had been sporadic or latent. Now, however, a crisis had been reached. Human suffering must certainly have played no small part in encouraging profound reflections. Rodrigo's departure, with Teresa's knowing his dangers, caused her to fear she would never see him again. The affection for her dearest childhood companion had turned to a sore. Uncertainty gradually grew unbearable, and she could no longer postpone deciding between monastic and worldly life.

The religious life tended to prevail, but what would Don Alonso do without his daughter? This obstacle proved to be the most insurmountable, for not only was she the center of the whole family's affections, she was also a practical necessity in the house. A succession of unfortunate circumstances was leading the de Cepeda family to poverty. Don Alonso's patrimony at his death some years later clearly indicated decline. Even the "de la Modena" mansion, falling to ruin, was in need of repairs. Yet Teresa had succeeded in keeping within the domestic budget during those three years at home. Don Alonso and the others relied on her good sense—how then could she possibly talk to them of going into the convent?

At this point a clear, resolute inner call must have become overwhelming, forcing such a dutiful daughter as she to decide to leave home. It was one of those special moments when the soul, denuded, lies alone between the Creator and the universe just as a wing fluttering between heaven and earth. We cannot know what happened, nor can we judge what occurred. Grace prepares one for those moments long before, acting with great delicacy. The different threads long laid out are gathered together and, not knowing how, the soul is ready to comply humbly with the divine will.

Teresa was reading St. Jerome's letters at the time, and she herself says they bestowed "saintly courage" on her. No other literature could have attracted or strengthened her more. The constant, at times abrupt separation from the world which those letters described and taught was just the sign or incentive she needed at that very moment.

One October day in 1536 she went to her father telling him of her resolution to enter the convent. Don Alonso's reply was as immediate as it was clear: a brief, decisive, energetic "NO." Silence ensued, followed by reciprocal explanations. Teresa exposed the call which she had long heard without wanting to, understanding that the will of God was to have her among the religious. Don Alonso answered that if he were sure of such a truth, he would not hesitate in giving his consent. However, family circumstances, in addition to other reasons, made any thought of leaving absurd. This was the gist of their short conversation.

The two parted without settling anything; both remained steadfast. This decision which was so thoroughly religious took on human tones deep in her heart. "Such a declaration [announcement of vocation to her father] to me was equal to taking the veil, because, attached as I was to my point of honor, once spoken, never for anything in the world would I retract my decision."[2] We must not be shocked by this declaration. Teresa still belonged to the world and spoke human language because she had not yet heard that of the angels. On the other hand, we have seen how one's "point of honor" constituted the apex of human integrity and moral correctness in Spain at that time. The young Ahumada girl had a profound respect for one's word.

A battle of love began. "His love for me was so great that not even the supplications of those I had asked to intervene mattered anything. The most that we were able to obtain was his permission to do what I cared to after his death." This was no step forward, for she naturally would have been free to follow her inclination after Don Alonso's death. This paternal unwavering must have caused her a great deal of suffering during this period, which she never mentioned, leaving the details to our imaginations. The firmness of the divine command was the dominating factor, and she did not retreat despite Don Alonso's "no." Divine aid no doubt strengthened her, for we must remember that this was truly a dramatic dissension, since the two contrasting forces were unequal. Her love of God was still tepid (she herself defined it as "weak"), while love of her father and brothers seemed stronger. "My love of God was so weak that it could not succeed in overcoming my bonds with my family."[3] Her suffering at

---

2. *Life*, III, and also for the following.
3. *Life*, IV, 1, 2, here and for the following quotations.

this point must have been pitiful, yet, notwithstanding the difference in her feelings, Teresa did not hesitate. She knew she must obey God's command.

At this phase of the struggle, it was no longer a matter of a "point of honor" but was wholly religious. It was the honor of the creature before its Creator. In such deep inner anguish, purely psychological fine points were done away with; every human obstinacy evaporated before such ardor simply because, void of foundation, it meant needless suffering, and who cares to suffer needlessly?

Teresa's call became well fixed and led her on unfalteringly in spite of its being entangled in the contradictions of her heart. God was acting without imparting apparent joy; everything was entrusted to the will without the concession of feeling happiness. He was truly loved by that privileged soul, but it was almost entirely an intellectual volitive love. There was as yet no spiritual hedonism; Teresa's efforts all revolved at the top of her rational and ethic faculties.

But the most characteristic trait shown in this complexity of religious life was her ability to conceal her torment from others. "Certainly no one had suspected so much inner conflict: all that was witnessed in me was wholly attributed to the effect of a sublime resolution." From resolution to action was natural and simple. At first, Teresa tried to convince her father with every possible means. Relatives and friends alternated facing Don Alonso at the other side of his massive study table, interceding for his daughter. There was Fr. Mancho, the family confessor; Teresa's aunt, Doña Elvira de Cepeda; other aunts and uncles, especially Don Lorenzo who was a parish priest, and even Don Francisco de Pajares, a friend held in high esteem by Alonso de Cepeda. All insisted in vain, for Don Alonso, being a real old Castilian hidalgo, showed he was as strongwilled as was becoming to one with such a noble background. He is humanly understandable, and it is not up to us to criticize him. At any rate, Teresa lost hope and seriously thought over the best way to settle an unbearable situation.

She often confided to her brother Antonio who was not yet fifteen. He understood and helped her as much as he could. Rodrigo could not have done better, for Antonio was passing through a stage of believing that he, too, felt a vocation to the religious life. His feeling was perhaps the reflection of his sister's religious fervor; nevertheless, he resolved to enter the monastery.

Early one morning, brother and sister went to the Convent of the Incarnation with a well-defined program in mind. Teresa would enter there, and Antonio would ask for admission at the Dominican monastery. Why had Teresa gone there instead of to the Augustinian convent where she had spent a year and a half? There were two reasons. While with the Augustinians she had noticed acts of piety that, though most admirable, seemed excessive, and her companions in the convent had felt the same way. The other reason was that in the Incarnation Convent was a friend of hers, Doña Juana Suárez, who had often spoken to her, informing her of all the particulars of the life, zeal and serenity within those walls. From all she knew, Teresa felt as though she had already been there. Then, too, Juana's presence would be invaluable to her during her beginning months which promised to be difficult.

She had previously made arrangements with the nuns who were of divided opinion concerning her case. One group was for admitting her; the other said her request should be rejected. It seemed to the latter group that Teresa should not leave her father. It had been a mature consideration, but then, the opinion of accepting her prevailed, so preparations were made. As she stepped out the door, her suffering was poignant. Teresa later remembered, "When I left my father's house I felt such a pull at my heart that I do not believe I shall feel it so strong again, not even at death. My bones felt dislocated. My love of God was so weak that it could not overcome my family ties. The struggle was so great that, without the intervention of God's grace, my efforts would have been impotent." This is all we have that reveals Teresa's state of mind at that time. It is as a rapid ray of light over a nocturnal setting of wind-blown vegetation.

Both brother and sister runaways disappeared into the winding narrow streets of St. Dominic's parish. The doors of the cloister were open awaiting the new inhabitant. Brother and sister parted at the door of the convent; there was another pull at the heart, other stifled sobs. Then the folding doors closed behind Teresa's composed figure, and Antonio continued toward the Dominican monastery. There he asked admittance as a lifetime guest.

Let us follow this boy of fifteen who had inhaled some of the atmosphere created by a tremendous soul in whose proximity he lived. The Dominicans rejected him, and no one can blame them for having done so. Antonio was a minor without paternal consent. His father was on friendly terms with the monastery so that in return for the offering of his life, they courteously, but persuasively, replied negatively "while awaiting paternal approval." Antonio found himself once more on the street with his indomitable, unobtainable dream. He was later to be accepted by the friars of St. Jerome, but he was obliged to return home because of illness when still a novice.

Antonio's chosen path ended elsewhere. Just as his other brothers, he, too, left Spain to cross the ocean on one of those seventy- to eighty-ton caravels sailing for three, four, often five months over the great Atlantic solitude; if necessary, they would go down Magellan's Strait into the Pacific. The great lantern perched over the high bow illuminated tempests of which those navigators could have never dreamed. But the courageous sea voyage was only a prelude to the real adventures which took place on land. With cross and sword, sublime acts and cruel errors were at stake. Antonio fought several battles under the leadership of Don Blasco Nuñez-Vela, who was a very good friend of the de Cepeda family. Antonio died on a high Ecuadorian mountain in the famous battle of Inaquito that was to establish the lordship of the King of Spain over that magnificent part of American territory.

But none of this could have been foreseen that morning when brother and sister left home. Antonio returned home while Teresa was living through her new life's first impressions, which proved surprisingly calm to her. She was twenty-one, had intensively sought God and her own inner truth, had suffered through indescribable uncertainty. But now, hardly having donned the novice's habit, she felt at peace.

CHAPTER FOUR

An Unusual Novitiate

A much more attractive and important part of Teresa's life had now begun. The doors to an enchanting spirituality opened in the very first lines of her convent memoirs.

"...But as soon as I donned the holy habit, the Lord let me understand what rewards were in store for those who sacrifice themselves to follow Him. The joy I felt at seeing myself a religious has never left me to this day. God changed the mental aridity which had undermined me until then into great tenderness."[1]

It is surprising to see how this religious candidate, whom we have seen doubt, falter, and delay, suddenly became conscious of the sign of election within herself. How are we to explain this complete, joyful, uncontrasted vocation which reveals itself only after it has become a fact? The sweetness of the following words help to enlighten us:

"I delighted in the religious exercises and was especially pleased to have to sweep during those hours

---

1. *Life,* IV, 2, also for the following.

formerly dedicated to vanity. This amazed me, and I knew not how to explain its origin. I finally felt free of all my miseries.

"No matter how difficult, there is nothing today I would not do just in remembrance of this intimate satisfaction. Experience now leads me to believe that the small sacrifice I must perform before resolving certain things is always readily compensated by God with kindnesses which can be appreciated only by those who enjoy them."

Complete peace came to Teresa, which, however, was neither static nor inert, but which led to meditation.

In this way, the first segment of Teresa's life ended. Her life before entering the convent had been divided into three stages: a religious childhood, the frivolous years, and maturation. Now that the port had been reached, a second segment began in Teresa's life—one of transition that was to last seventeen years. If Teresa of Jesus were not later to reach the topmost degree in union with God, these seventeen years would have been considered as a final phase of a privileged soul which, though afflicted by contrasts and capable of contradictions, always won, triumphant in Christ. Full of love of God, certain venial weaknesses remained, causing her incessant torment, but this insignificant resistance was evident only because she was continually illuminated by flashes of light that were too bright and penetrating for human refractions. This light-giving grace gradually became a continuous vibration so that all that was left of human frailty was overcome. Teresa passed into the last period of mystical ascent which she tried her utmost to reveal to us, and certain pages of her writings are among the most beautiful humanity possesses. Only in comparison with this glorious final phase must we consider the years that precede it as a time of transition.

The first thing the nuns of the Incarnation did was to notify Teresa's father of her entrance. As was expected, Don Alonso took the news badly, but his anger did not last long, for on October 31, 1536, he already settled his daughter's dowry with the nuns. The document that was drawn up is indeed interesting and characteristic. After the toll of the bell, the "reverenda y magnifica señora" Doña Francisca del Aguila, the convent prioress, Doña María de Luna, Isabella Valla, Inés de Ceballos and all of the other nuns gathered in the community room for the signing of the contract. "Speaking for themselves, for the convent and in behalf of all the sisters therein, present and future,"[2] the religious pledged "in unanimous accord to accept Doña Teresa de Ahumada as a convent nun, seeing to her upkeep in the convent for the rest of her life." For his part, Don Alonso pledged as dowry, if in goods, the income of twenty-five bushels of bread, half wheat, half barley, from the Gotarrendura property; if in cash, two hundred gold ducats equal to seventy-five thousand maravedis.

Her trousseau was made up of one wool and two heavy cloth habits, three skirts, two capes, a worsted habit, and a fur hooded jacket.

Not satisfied with having pledged a lordly dowry, Don Alonso offered the sisters a dinner and new wimples for all.

The Incarnation Convent was the most important in Avila. Built between 1513 and 1515, one hundred fifty nuns, many of whom belonged to the first families of the region, lived there. Twenty years later, the number rose to one hundred ninety. But the building was uncomfortable. The roof was poorly constructed and snow fell on the nuns' breviaries when they were in the

---

2. *Historia del Carmel Descalzo,* T. I, book II, ch. 9, quoted by Fr. Silverio, *Life,* ch. 9.

choir. In the summer, the windows did not protect them from the hot sun so that they could read perfectly well in their rooms with the shutters closed. The food corresponded to the building: there was bread because the son of the first Duke of Alba, Don Gutierrez de Toledo, had endowed the convent with property in the diocese of Avila.

The convent garden, however, was ample and beautiful. The building was situated outside the high city walls on the Ajales cliff which begins at Las Hervencias and slopes down to the Adaja. Though certainly not sumptuous, the convent was at least spacious by the time Teresa entered, for additions had been made. Four porticos forming a square made the ground floor colonnade with stone columns supporting the low arches. The cloister today still measures 130 feet long and 120 feet wide. The archways are about thirteen feet in height and width; twenty-four stairs divide the lower and upper galleries. Tradition has it that on those steps St. Teresa, when a prioress, met a beautiful child who asked her, "Who are you?"

"I? Why, Teresa of Jesus. And who are you?"

"I, Jesus of Teresa."

What wealth of memories were to be had within these convent walls which make one relive the incredible heights of sixteenth-century Spanish holiness. Five doors leading to separate confessionals opened onto the west portico. St. John of the Cross, who was called the "doctor of divine love," had his confessional farther up.

The ceremony of admission to the novitiate took place in the autumn of 1536. The nuns gathered as a chapter while the teacher assigned to the novices led the postulant to the Mother Prioress, Doña Francisca del Aguila, who was seated in the presidential chair in the chapter hall. The girl knelt.

"What do you ask?" began the Mother Prioress.

"I ask God's mercy and shelter in your community."

The prioress asked if there was any impediment to her taking the habit of the Carmelites, to which Teresa answered negatively. The Mother Prioress then reminded her of the duties of the new state into which she was entering, of the austerity of the meals, her dress, the cloister and its regulations. Teresa replied that, confiding in the goodness of God, she desired all those things and hoped she could fulfill her duties well. The Prioress then said: "May our Lord God who gave you this desire give you the grace to succeed for Christ our Lord." To which the nuns murmered, "Amen."

The postulant then placed her hands in those of the Prioress while the latter solemnly pronounced: "We accept you into our community for love of God and His most Blessed Mother." To which Teresa answered, "Deo gratias."

On the second of November, she put on the habit. Having helped her put on the tunic of the order, the Prioress again put the question, "What do you ask?"

"The mercy of God and the community of nuns subject to perpetual cloister."

The first year passed in prayer and meditation over ascetic books, which proved to be of immense help to her. She concentrated on understanding and absorbing the spirit of the Carmelite Order, which is laid bare in the twelfth rubric of the convent constitution. The following is addressed to the teachers in charge of the novices: "They must learn to set aside and abandon the customs of the times in gesture, bearing, walk, talk, and manner of looking, according to the doctrine of the Apostle Paul who said: 'Shed the old man and old speech and put on the new man renewed in spirit according to God, full of justice and holiness, experiencing the mortification of Jesus Christ in your body.'" Moreover, if perchance some novice offended one of her fellow sisters, especially the older ones, she was to lie prostrate before the offended one until the latter helped her up.[3]

The Incarnation Convent follows the Carmelite rule of St. Albert, a patriarch of Jerusalem, and was mitigated by Eugene IV in 1432. Though several early dispositions of the rule had been abolished, the traditional Carmelites led an austere life—long fasts, frequent abstinence, discipline, poor clothing, seclusion, and infrequent communication with the outside world.

Except for three days in the week, the nuns ate once a day from the Feast of the Exaltation of the Cross until Easter. Meat was permitted three times a week if it was not Lent or Advent. The nuns disciplined themselves on Monday, Wednesday, and Friday, and it may be justly said that the Incarnation Convent still retains its old spirit of generosity and fervor.

Their dress was unflinchingly against vanity and indiscretion. According to the rule, the nuns were always to wear an ample, ankle-length, dark gray, heavy cloth tunic, tied at the waist to hold the disciplines. The sleeves were neither tight fitting nor gathered, but large and reaching the knuckles. Of the same material, the scapular was to be a hand shorter than the tunic, as was the white cloth mantle. Their loose-fitting belt was to be of no other color than black leather on which there was to be no shining metal. Their veil of common cloth was to cover the head amply on all sides.

Regarding their beds, there were to be no feathers and not even linen sheets, only wool worsted covers and simple, undecorated modest bedspreads. The rule concerning the use of their time was based on the words which St. Paul applied to the unemployed: "He who does not labor should not eat." The rule went thus: "Always do something so as to avoid the least rest....

---

3. See Fr. Silverio, I, 10, also for the following.

The prioress must see to it that each nun works at something of benefit to all." This, of course, referred to the time left over from the multiple group religious exercises, for the Carmelite Order makes much use of the choir and liturgical functions according to both ordinary and ancient ceremonial methods.

Teresa was not trained in singing or in liturgical or group prayers. Immediately studying the psychological effects of such a lacuna, she wrote, "Among my other defaults, I did not know the rubrics of the breviary, my office, or the choir ceremonies well. This was due entirely to my negligence because I used to waste time doing less useful things. There were other novices who could have taught me all these things, but I asked nothing, fearing they would notice I knew so little. I thought it was best to abstain from asking them so as not to give bad example, and this happened often. Later, however, when God deigned to open my eyes, I never hesitated to ask even the youngest whenever there was a doubt about things I knew."[4]

This is an instance of subtle inner debate which enables Teresa to penetrate deep within herself to unmask the psychological deception she was subject to. "I still could not sing well," she continued, "and I was most humiliated when I had not learned my part well. If I had felt this for want of respect toward God, it would have been a virtue, but unfortunately, I felt humiliation for those who had to listen to me. It was a question of honor and I continued singing all the worse because of my excitement. In the future, however, I resolved to confess openly when I was not well-prepared. At first it cost me a great deal of effort, but I later got to the point that I liked it. Thus, after I no longer cared if my ignorance was known, I began to sing better than ever. In short, my black point of honor

---

4. *Life*, XXXI, 23, 24, also for the following.

impeded me from performing well that which my sense of honor strove for. We all place honor where we wish."

Can one study one's own feelings with greater insight? We often refer to Teresa of Jesus as the saint of grand spiritual means as compared to Therese of the Child Jesus who was the enchanting saint of little ways. But the details cited reveal that even the great Teresa knew how to skillfully use insignificant ways. Reading on, "I do not deny that these are silly nothings which adequately demonstrate how small I am because they caused me great suffering. Yet, these little things can accustom us to acts of virtue, and, if done for love of God, can become precious though insignificant they may be. He is thus preparing us for greater deeds."

A curious similarity exists between the two saints that is brought out clearly in the following passages. In chapter VII of the *Autobiography of Therese of the Child Jesus*, we find: "Above all, I dedicated myself to insignificant humble acts of virtue; for instance, it gave me a sense of satisfaction to neatly fold my fellow sisters' mantles." Whereas Teresa of Jesus writes: "Excepting myself, I could see that all my fellow sisters were progressing in virtue, and I felt good for nothing. So I secretly began to fold their mantles when they left the choir, thus alluding myself of serving in some way those angels who praised God so well. I don't remember how, but I was discovered one day which made me become terribly confused, not out of humility, but out of fear they would laugh at me, for I was not yet so virtuous as to be pleased at being discovered."

At a distance of three hundred fifty years, a small identical gesture was repeated or transmitted as an echo repeats the voice, from the steep cliff of Castile to a serene region in France. What mysterious analogies exist between the saints! And what illumination can be gathered from these "silly nothings." To apply oneself to unseen acts of charity seems easy enough when said, but certain "silly nothings" must be felt before we can judge.

One's self-respect was indeed tried at the convent. The "chapter of faults" a common practice in many monasteries offered a "tour de force" for one's humility. Each professed nun stood in the midst of the others and outwardly confessed her infractions against the regulations. The accusation was answered with admonitions from the rule regarding the practice of charity. Novices were excluded or admitted only on condition that they accused themselves and then left immediately.

The use of the sacraments was regulated according to the custom of the times: confession once a week or at least every two weeks by the same confessor. It was the prioress' duty to see to it that this post was filled by a wise priest, whose judgment was reliable and pious, reflecting a holy and experienced life. It happened that at times the conscience of a nun was bound excessively as a result of only one confessor. Teresa later modified this in her reformed foundations and gave her daughters more complete advice.

Communion, the great moment of religious life, was distributed on the first Sunday of Advent, Christmas, the first Sunday in Lent, Holy Thursday, Easter, Ascension Day, Pentecost, Feast of Christ the King, All Saints' Day, Assumption Day, on the day someone received the religious habit, and when someone was professed. Only through recommendation of the confessor and the subsequent permission of the prioress could one receive Communion more often.

All these complex rules were distinct ascetic, ethic, and practical aspects for the development of mental prayer. The principle expression of contemplative life is exactly mental prayer—the raising of one's thoughts toward God in loving attention. Exactly in relation to the attainment of this uninterrupted spiritual orientation were the days planned with silence prevailing, and rarely did the nuns see outsiders. Their seclusion was most strict. No man could enter unless absolutely necessary: to administer the sacraments, for reasons of health, or repairs to the building. Queens, princesses, and duchesses were authorized to enter, but were to be received by at least three nuns. Conversation in the community room was rare and was prohibited to the novices without a special reason. Later, conditions changed.

There were no unfounded external coercions, but significant regulations, so Teresa remembers her novitiate period as a happy one in contrast to the years preceding it. Nonetheless, she suffered much for little things. For example, whenever she was unjustly scolded she would withdraw into herself and accept the scolding "most imperfectly and with effort." Other forms of self-respect still remained in her. She liked all of the religious practices, but she also liked to be esteemed by others, and any slight lack of esteem caused her to suffer. She acted prudently and thought all she did was virtuous and therefore fretted when she was misunderstood or scolded.

Nevertheless, she completely inhaled the convent atmosphere of spirituality. She cried often over her sins and preferred to remain alone so much that the other sisters began to feel she wanted to avoid their company—that she was unhappy in the convent. Her crying was an anticipation of that very special gift that later was to turn into tears of love. These effusions had nothing to do with human sadness, but always bore an inner delight. Her longing was already love, even though it was still overshadowed by fear. This complex state of mind described in the second "mansion" of her *Interior Castle* corresponds to a vigorous and painful climb. God's action alternates moments of overt consolation with moments of apparent numbness. The soul applies itself to prayer, to correcting its defects, and to meditation. This persevering effort is upheld by reading, the spiritual direction given and good friends. Basic to all activity is the study of Jesus through the Gospels and meditation on His sacred humanity.

The year 1536-1537 can be considered a fruitful one for Teresa since the novitiate is the foundation of the construction which the religious must offer up. Her happiness was reflected everywhere. "At the time, there was a nun who was affected by a serious illness. Because of an intestinal obstruction it was necessary to open several holes in her abdomen to let out waste, and the poor woman died after long suffering. The others were all horrified by this malady, but I instead envied the patience with which the nun bore her long suffering. I used to tell God that if I, too, had been favored with great patience, I would have been ready to accept all the illnesses He would have cared to send me. I now marvel at this inclination, and I do not know how I could have felt that way when it seems to me I did not burn with that love of God which came to me when I began mental prayer."[5]

But Teresa's inner bent for suffering was not due to platonic love because she truly sought to suffer. Many witnesses at her beatification process told of the numerous ways she physically mortified her body. Several of her convent sisters, Inés de Quesada among others, said she used to cut her innocent body with nettle gathered in the garden and perform many other similar penances. The most authoritative witness was Teresa's confidante, Mother María of St. Joseph, who declared: "Mother Teresa told me personally that at the beginning of her vocation she did such difficult and extraordinary penances that they weakened her health; yet she

---

5. *Life,* V, 2.

performed them with such fervor that she felt not even the severest of them. To the great disappointment of Mother Teresa, her superiors prohibited her from doing any type of penance other than that prescribed by the rule."[6]

And this is the period which the mature Teresa referred to as one weak in love for God! She was comparing it, naturally, to what she felt later on.

---

6. See Fr. Silverio, I, 11.

CHAPTER FIVE

Toward Becedas

On November 3, 1537, Teresa de Ahumada made her religious profession. She was forced to overcome serious inner feelings caused by her excessive humility to arrive at that holy moment. Teresa's state of mind can be defined as one of seraphic pessimism in respect to herself. She felt unworthy of uttering the three solemn vows and of donning the veil; she was going through the same feeling of humility which many of the saints have felt, St. Francis of Assisi, to name one. In her memoirs, she compares this inner resistance before professing the vows with what she had to overcome when she left her father's house to enter the convent. We already know that this pessimism is not to be in any way connected with pathological, psychological symptoms. There are no psychopathic elements; it is entirely a spiritual expression of the lowering of oneself. It could be considered as a stupendous case of timidity in certain of its aspects, but the definition would not be complete because it is an act in which both intelligence and love are in function. Through intelligence the creature knows to what heights of perfection he can aim, but it is love which is the main-spring of such profundity. In view of such a luminous ideal, then, any present state would appear unsatisfactory.

The passion of Christ and the omnipotence of His wounds is another element in her holy hesitation. "Impossible for man, all is possible to God" were the evangelical words which quieted her soul and pulled her out of the abyss of her feeling of incapacity, leading her to religious profession.

In Chapter IV of her *Life,* Teresa wrote: "The change of life and food proven ruinous to my health, and, no matter my inner delights, I fell ill again."

Of course, we know now what was implied by her "change of life and food." Her excessive penances were the chief cause of her new illness and this is proven by the testimonies of those nuns who knew Teresa as a novice. On the other hand, Teresa was going through one of the many physiological crises in store for her, for she was subject to an incompatible conflict between her body's frailness and her spirit's indomitable vigor. It is true for many saints that they should have several bodies to consume because their unyielding youth seems inadequate for physical resistance. Teresa's body was much too frail for her spiritual energy, but it bore no constitutional maladies to cause definite setbacks. Her illnesses always consisted of functional disorders which caused fatigue and disappeared whenever she put her will to it. One of the longest and most distressing afflicted her shortly after her profession. "My fainting spells increased and heart trouble set in so that those who assisted me became very frightened."[1]

The malfunction was no doubt due to physical exhaustion. In addition, she suffered from nausea. Her prodigious sensibility caused her to suffer greatly. Her

---

1. *Life*, IV, 5, 9, also for the following.

neuro-organic system was fundamentally healthy as a whole, but we must remember that her body was extremely delicate.

The nuns and members of the family were frightened by the vivacity of her sufferings, and Don Alonso decided to take his daughter home for a while. Though the convent was rigid concerning the entrance into the cloister, it did not prohibit the nuns' exit when there were serious reasons. So Teresa returned home in the company of Sister Juana Suárez. She was cared for in the de la Modena mansion by all the doctors in Avila, but still her disturbances did not diminish.

Don Alonso then decided on calling on a famous healer, thus reflecting the customs of his age. This healer had a wide reputation and was held in great esteem in the whole region, with patients flocking to her side. She was really a charlatan and lived at Becedas, a village of perhaps fifteen hundred inhabitants, forty-five miles from the capital. Don Alonso resolved to take his daughter there.

It was December, 1537, and to travel roads which went up and down three thousand feet for that long a distance over the snow and in the cold wind required courage in healthy travelers, let alone sick ones. But the de Cepedas were not strong-willed Castilians for nothing. They set out against all obstacles and went by the mule-road that passes through Hortigosa and Castellanos de la Cañada.

Teresa knew that road well and withstood the journey as did her father, Sister Juana Suárez, and a maid who accompanied them. In the evening, numb with cold, the party arrived on horseback at the home of her Uncle Pedro Sánchez, where they were warmly welcomed. The old man was putting an end to his solitary station and was soon to enter the order of the Friars of St. Jerome. He was anxious to know Teresa's state of mind, for he had noted her hidden possibilities a few years before, and now his experienced eye immediately discovered her important transformation. That girl who used to be bored at reading devotional books was now a professed nun bearing a true and serious offering to God. Again Don Pedro was able to exercise a deep influence on Teresa's soul by means of a book. He gave her a copy of Brother Francisco de Osuna's *Third Primer,* which was a treatise on prayer in solitude and on contemplation.

They took leave of Don Pedro and continued on slowly over the snow, intermittently struck by violent gusts of wind. Teresa arrived at Castellanos de la Cañada feeling miserable, and only the affectionate welcome of the Guzmán y Barrientos and the fire in the old fireplace were able to vitalize her. She felt a sense of security and enlightening conversation. Doña María comforted her especially with motherly love. María knew all of Teresa's turns of character and was now moved to compassion to see this new religious suffering so much. The evenings were intimate, with the whole family gathered around the fire. Don Alonso was now making up for his solitude with a daughter on each side, and by this time considering Sister Juana Suárez another daughter. The shutters beat louder against the windows and when the conversation fell, Teresa would let her spirit out into the vast black countryside covered with snow. Physical images became spiritual symbols and appeared to her as the world of the unbelievers, the sinners and the heretics. As soon as she was alone, she took refuge in her books. She was still in that stage when "to pray without a book was as to go to war against a formidable army. The book was not only company to me, but a shield against which my irrelevant thoughts fell."

The *Third Primer* was always at her side. In it is found the important early step of sixteenth-century Spanish mysticism.

Oechslin writes, "Teresa's encounter with this work attracted her to the general spiritual reform movement which was stirring in Spain at the beginning of the sixteenth century. Each explanation Osuna gave seemed to fit in with what was wrong with society. She did not live as a recluse, and the news of the world penetrated into the convent."[2] Her reading must have been intense as is witnessed in Mrs. Cunninghame Graham's account of her visit to St. Joseph's convent in Avila where she studied Teresa's copy of the *Third Primer*.[3] "It is evident in these yellow pages that the book was constantly used. Entire passages are heavily underlined and in the margins are frequent crosses, hearts and hands shown pointing, the latter being her favorite symbol. All point out thoughts which seem most meritorious to remember in the Gothic text." These were graphic indications of the interest and emotion which the book traced in Teresa's soul.[4]

Lepée also writes that "the Andalusian Franciscan was of capital importance to Teresa during that precious moment of her life. The solitude and silence required by Osuna in order to meditate permitted the development of her thoughts as a novice. God's transcendence, the idea of eternal realities could become more positive and act more intensively in her mind uncontaminated now by passing realities. Furthermore, Osuna's spirituality is primarily based on affection. Already joyful as Teresa was of living entirely for a God in whom lay everlasting good, she felt loving feelings of devotion and had already been rewarded with the "gift of tears," but Osuna enticed her to far greater depths in

---

2. *L'intuition mystique de Sainte Thérèse,* I, p. 12.

3. Gabriela Cunninghame Graham; *Saint Teresa of Avila,* London, 1894.

4. Fr. Silverio also attributes much influence on Teresa's soul to Osuna's book. He writes, "Certainly the *Third Primer* had the most decided influence on her mysticism." *Works of St. Teresa,* 1915, Vol. I.

her love for God. She learned that there is an art to loving, and in this lies the secret of union. Even in this life God concedes emotions, outbursts, tears and demonstrations of love to whomever can empty himself of himself.

From now on Teresa could have a taste of the promise of eternal happiness. But then, it is not only a question of acquiring eternal happiness: God is an infinite Being deserving immeasurable love. Teresa's sensitive heart had always needed to love and be loved: she would certainly love if that was all that was needed.

"Teresa owes Osuna and his school the theory and practice of humble prayer which she adhered to, denuded of all other thoughts, and which, through the grace of God, became that which she later called supernatural prayer.

"God Himself became 'sensible of heart.' For unforgettable hours Teresa reached Him, was enthralled by Him, and was lost in His infinity. This incalculable revelation never stopped acting in her subconscious even when things of the world seemed to occupy her attention. This elect soul could no longer feel inwardly balanced without God. She had to seek God because God called her and tormented her in her memories; He sought her."

Regarding the element of "silence," Lepée explains that "Osuna does not merely describe prayer of concentration, but proposes it as an art. The art of concentration requires silence in ourselves. Naturally, its counterpart consists in loving thoughts focused on God alone. One's pure intelligence fixes a very simple, alert, subtle, and penetrating look on the divine essence; knowing God is evident, the will is put to action, embraces the Supreme Being and becomes united to Him in love, tasting of His sweetness. But Osuna makes no warning of a danger which St. Teresa pointed out later (*Interior Castle*, IV Home, Ch. VII), that of suppressing all connection between active thought and love. To be aware only of God is the fixed point which is the greatest good one can derive from prayer. Even in the beginning we must jealously grasp this as God gives it to us, but when it is not given to us, it is our duty to seek it. To do this, we must insist on that type of activity which is indispensable to that silent love of God which is essentially submission. Moreover, this activity creates others which may be called points of penetration into divine influence, a certain internal disposition, an organization of ideas and impulses which renders the soul permeable to grace in subconscious depths."[5]

Yet, though Osuna's book was undeniably important, it could not have been sufficient or definite because the presentation of Osunian prayer was incomplete and in certain ways confused. Furthermore, it was difficult for an undirected soul to practice such a method. Teresa would have to appropriate other teachings and other experiences in order to achieve the fullness and efficacy of her methods of praying. Gaston Etchegoyen wrote, "The Franciscans awakened divine love in St. Teresa. The Society of Jesus fortified it through moral and intellectual discipline. Combining the two doctrines, the Dominicans favored St. Teresa's fundamental tendency, that of her apostleship. This triple initiation admirably prepares Teresa of Jesus for her mission of reform."[6]

---

5. Lepée, *Sainte Thérèse*, I, II, III.

6. Gaston Etchegoyen, *L'amour Divin, Essai sur les Sources de Sainte Thérèse*, I, II, p. 90.

CHAPTER SIX

A Famous and
Mysterious Illness

The winter frost melted and departure drew near. In April, Teresa continued her trip to Becedas accompanied by Doña María Guzmán y Barrientos. A dramatic incident occurred at the beginning of Teresa's stay in Becedas, before her health faltered again. In the renewed fervor which the *Third Primer* had brought her, Teresa went to confession as soon as she arrived in the village. She confided in a "distinguished-looking, very intelligent, though superficially cultured, priest."[1]

Her zeal desired the Sacrament of Reconciliation often, but what she had to confess was most slight. Her confessions served as outlets for her soul, duty-bound as she felt to enumerate all the particular graces God had bestowed upon her. She spoke of God already revealing a personal religious and moral experience. The way in which she thought of Him and felt Him was surprisingly original.

---

1. *Life*, V, for the whole episode.

The priest was shaken by that young voice entirely consecrated to praising the Lord. Every thought that Teresa discussed made him examine his own sinful existence. At times he wondered if that extraordinary penitent was an archangel of God announcing punishments and commanding him to cover his head with cinders. A grievous sin was destroying his life, causing his conscience to lie insensible for two years, but now he suddenly felt shaken. At other times, he saw Teresa as a messenger of peace, an angel inviting him to reconciliation.

Teresa was naturally unaware of her confessor's state of mind. For years this man had been sentimentally bound to a woman who had even resorted to witchcraft to ensnare him. He had continued to celebrate Mass in the state of mortal sin. Although his blameworthy condition was known, no one dared to reprimand him.

When Teresa found out about the priest's terrible state of conscience, she said, "I felt much compassion in my soul because I liked him." From that time began the recovery of his soul by speaking of God, awakening his slumbering faith, love and fear. One day the priest took off a copper amulet which he wore around his neck and gave it to Teresa; after that he appeared healed. His partner in sin had given him the magic charm years before, and no one had been able to make him take it off. "As soon as he had taken it off he acted as one waking from a heavy sleep; he remembered with horror what he had done during those years and began to detest his past life. Our Lady must have helped him greatly as he was very devoted to the Immaculate Conception. He stopped seeing that woman and thanked God continually for having enlightened him. He died exactly a year after I had met him."

Teresa also makes the following comment: "I don't believe in witchcraft, but I relate what I saw so that men may beware of women who try to seduce them in this way."

While this episode was drawing to a happy conclusion, the famous "cure" for Teresa's physical health was being applied, but it almost ended in disaster. Not only did Teresa feel no better, she became worse. "The remedies were so strong for my constitution that I was in continual torture. After two months of taking medicine, I was almost finished. Instead of diminishing, my heart ailment became more violent. I drank only a little, and felt repulsion for food. I had to take laxatives every day which after a month weakened me intensely. Meanwhile, I was consumed by fever." In this extreme degeneration, her whole body ached so that she never found rest. Moreover, she felt thoroughly saddened.

Seeing that the cure only made Teresa's condition become more serious, Don Alonso abruptly decided to take his daughter back to Avila in May, 1538. There, doctors were called again, and they all agreed that Teresa had a hopeless case of tuberculosis. She was so absorbed in her sufferings that the verdict failed to impress her. "I was always in a spasm from head to foot." Those about her were amazed how she could bear violent suffering for so long. Even with so much suffering, Teresa's spirit succeeded in finding an outlet and made its way toward God. She meditated on Job. "What I had read of Job in St. Gregory's *Moralia* proved of great help to me. I always thought of what Job had said: 'If we have received God's gifts, why not receive also ills,' which I repeated to myself."

Teresa asked for someone to hear her confession as Assumption Day was near. During the last three months her suffering had become so acute that all were concerned. Don Alonso had a strange feeling that Teresa had asked for a priest for fear she was about to die. He tried to overcome this imaginative fright, dissuading her from confession as a proof she was not seriously ill. Teresa insisted, but the family decided not to tell her when the priest would arrive.

A few hours later, Don Alonso repented of his error, crying bitterly. That night Teresa fell into a startling coma: in a few moments' time she lost consciousness and appeared lifeless. It was thought she had fainted, but her face did not regain color. The minutes became hours. Considering Teresa's extreme weakness, the family thought it was a mortal collapse, and as time passed, it appeared all the more probable.

A day and a night passed with no change in Teresa's condition. Although she appeared dead, her heart still continued to beat. It was not a seizure, but a death-like exhaustion. Most of the onlookers were convinced that the prostration and immobility were a long and silent, hopeless agony. Priests administered the Anointing of the Sick, and the family continually suggested she recite the Credo mentally, "just as though I could still understand something in that state." As was the custom, the nuns dug the grave and prepared the simple but moving funeral rites of the Carmelite burial.

The family took turns watching over the body and someone decided to do something to see if that apparently inanimate body would react. A lighted candle was brought to the closed lids and a few drops of wax fell on them. Teresa did not respond to the heat of the drops. The experiment convinced most of the family that Teresa was dead. This was rumored in the city, and a Carmelite monastery near Avila (no doubt San Pablo de la Moraleja) had even recited the ritual prayers for the dead. Meanwhile, that night it was the turn of Lorenzo, Teresa's brother, to watch. But he fell asleep, and the candle almost set the bed on fire. At dawn on the third day someone proposed to begin preparing for the burial. But Don Alonso, who would not stop checking Teresa's pulse, replied that his daughter was not ready for burial. The others thought he acted this way out of paternal love; they were bewildered. The sick nun's wax-like countenance persisted without change, and another person insisted that the funeral preparations be made, but Don Alonso refused again, saying it was not yet time.

Though Don Alonso maintained a calm appearance, he was desperate within. He was bitterly distressed at having prevented his daughter from receiving the Sacrament of Reconciliation and sobbed whenever he was left alone.

On the fourth day, Teresa revived. Ribera passed on the first words she uttered, which show to what unconscious depths her infirm anguish had gone. "Who called me? I was in heaven. I saw the convents I am to found, the good I shall do to my Order and the souls I shall lead to salvation. I shall die a saint, and my body shall be covered with a gold drape."[2]

Teresa's illness and her awakening after four days from the brink of death bear an inimitable mark. How this young nun, given up as hopeless by doctors and relatives, could suddenly foretell exactly what she was to do and become in the future leaves us indeed thoughtful. Those who heard her undoubtedly thought she was delirious.

But her immediate return to life was full of suffering. "After the critical four days, God only knows what indescribable pains I continued to feel. Not having taken anything during those four days added to my already weak state so that I could barely breathe. My throat was so dry I couldn't swallow even a drop of water. I felt disjointed, and a great dizziness confused me. After several spasmodic days, I found I was curled

---

2. Ribera, *Life*, I, VII. After her death Teresa actually was covered with a gold brocaded cloth.

up like a ball and almost like a dead body; I could move neither arms, hands, feet, nor head without help. I believe I could move only one finger of my right hand. Then no one knew how to touch me because my body was so sore I could not bear to be touched. In order to have me change position, they were forced to raise me on a sheet held at each end."[3]

This terrible condition lasted until Easter. Her only relief was to abandon herself in her immobility and lie completely at rest. In addition to physical relief, this also provided moral comfort because Teresa suffered spiritually during her spasms, for fear of committing acts of impatience. She wrote: "I was afraid I would lose my patience so that I was very much relieved when those acute pains stopped." But the pains returned intermittently, and she described them as unbearable, especially when the shivers of her fever returned. A strong periodical fever was still the basis of much suffering. This was no doubt caused by one of those malarial infections which were frequent around Avila in the sixteenth century.

Nevertheless, Teresa wanted to return to the convent and was brought there as soon as she felt a little better in May, 1539. There she was put in the infirmary as she could not resume normal cell life. "So," she wrote, "they received the one they thought dead—still alive and with her soul, but the body was so pitiful to behold, it looked worse than dead."

The Carmelite sisters had kept the grave dug for Teresa open for a day and a half. Now they saw her return, afflicted with momentary old age and all contracted. "I was so weak that I find no words to describe my state. I was nothing but bones and continued in that drawn condition for eight months; it took three years to

---

3. *Life*, VI, here and for the following.

recuperate slowly. When I finally began to walk on all fours, as a cat, I thanked God infinitely.''

At this point, let us reflect upon and interpret Teresa's illness. There have been many opinions on the situation. Pourrat writes, ''It has been believed to be able to classify Teresa's great illness as hysteria, but this is not possible because the word implies fundamental imbalance. It would be lasting and of both a physical and mental nature. But Teresa's illness had nothing to do with her organic constitution, and it was a passing incident of three years which never repeated itself. The immediate external causes have been proposed and set aside. Then, too, there was no chronic hereditary weakness as far as we can see. Every biographer points out Teresa's inherent good qualities and her positive sound judgment in everything. What we know of the saint's physical and mental constitution fits in with the accidental, transient quality of her illness. It may be called a neurosis inasmuch as it was a severe state of nervousness, but not due to a complete physical and mental excitement of the patient, as is more than sufficiently proved by Teresa's life after her sickness. This phenomenon can be compared to what Olier felt for two years. The founder of St. Sulpicius, with his sanguine temperament, was not predisposed to neurosis either. His, too, lasted a definite time and did not recur. The years following these phenomena were the most active and fruitful in the lives of both St. Teresa and Olier. A hereditary trait such as hysteria could never have caused anyone to do likewise.''[4]

This seems to be a balanced and true analysis of the incident. It is surprising how so many have persisted in misunderstanding Teresa's illnesses, defining them either as neuro-psychotic or entirely physical. On one

4. P. Pourrat, *Thérèse de Jesus* in *Dictionnaire de Theologie Catholique de Paris*, pp. 552-571.

side of the scale there is Charcot (who wrote of Teresa's "great hysteria"), and P. L. de San on the other. The latter affirmed that it was an acute gastritis that accounted for her coma, while Dr. Inbert Courbeire spoke only of a very strong malaria. If they had but simply followed Teresa's description of her illness, they would have found the key to the problem which, after all, was not the central point of her life since she soon passed this stage. All we must do to understand this period of her life is to remember the rigors, scourging, and garden thorns to which she used to submit herself (having already elaborated on her statement: "The change of life and food impaired my health"), the natural Carmelite convent life, added to a weakening illness such as the quartan fever, and also, the apocalyptical treatment at Becedas. This presents enough of a pathological condition in both mind and body to warrant organic malfunctioning and acute periods of pain, especially in such a sensitive person. This is all there was to it, and we must not force ourselves to read any other interpretation into the matter. Lepée writes, "The violence of the crisis attests certain organic conditions and the extraordinary force of the attack. Teresa undoubtedly possessed a rich temperament and an energetic will. Remembering her chronic ailments, it must be borne in mind that mystic life is in many ways opposed to natural life. Whatever may have been the secondary cause of her illness, it was above all due to the adaptation to a difficult life and her recovery proved her triumph over it. Thus we can explain her strange illness which cannot be well classified."[5]

---

5. Lepée adds: "It is a strange coincidence that each time she overcomes a struggle of fervor within herself, she begins to fall ill. Even Teresa noticed it because she wrote: 'In one minute God rewarded me with the freedom for which I had been unsuccessfully striving for years, often with so much effort on my part that my health was probably seriously impaired by it.' " *Op. cit.,* I, 4.

As long as we are on the subject, it is pertinent to note how strange it is that some have confused two entirely different concepts in Teresa's life: that is, her neuro-physical disturbances with her great intellectual faculties as a saint, meaning her mystical experiences. There is no affinity between the two because Teresa's illnesses in her youth clearly denoted physical and transient malfunctions of her nervous system; they were not constitutional, but with all probability, due to powerful conflicts in her personality. Teresa's case is common to many in its first stage (vivacious inner crises bearing direct exterior repercussions), and is not exceptional in its chronological development with the disappearance of the disturbances when inner peace has been established. Any physician can distinguish between nervous ailments and insanity. To suppose that this woman who was gifted with a brilliantly balanced and constructive intelligence, a reliant will, and deep, altruistic feelings, was nothing but a victim of hallucinations, constitutes a gross error.

The minor ailments which accompanied Teresa all through her life were strong palpitations, habitual vomiting and fever, which were of an interdependent nature, and did not concern Teresa's intellectual faculties in the least.

The "Teresian case" excited much sensation between 1880 and 1890, but these considerations seem superfluous today, for progress in psychology has opened new horizons to investigate those who penetrate the delicate and mysterious spiritual world.[6]

---

6. We shall conclude our discussion here with the judgments of two Protestant women. Virginia Sackville-West wrote in her book *The Eagle and the Dove:* "We must emphasize the fact that Teresa was not at all the 'malade imaginaire' type. Indeed, her bad health which forestalled her work exasperated her." After citing the saint she continues: "This is truly not the language of a hysterical woman; moreover, she never spared harsh words to those

During Teresa's great illness, certain basic elements shine out, the first of which is equilibrium. "I bore everything fully resigned to the will of God," Teresa wrote. "I felt so resigned to the will of God that if He had wished it, I would have been content to remain in that condition forever. I went to confession often and spoke much of God; everyone marveled at the patience with which God favored me. Indeed, it seemed impossible that I could bear such cruel tortures so happily."[7]

Prayer is the second element. "The grace of prayer which I received from the Lord was of great help to me. Through it I learned what it meant to love Him; it was in that short time that those virtues of which I spoke took root, though they were not yet strong enough to free me from every defect. I never spoke ill of anyone, not even in little things, and tried to evade all slander because I never wanted to say of anyone that which I did not want others to say of me.

"Whenever it happened that I offended God, I felt such acute pain that at times, I remember, I did not have the courage to pray, fearing the deep anguish I would feel as punishment for having offended Him. With time this disposition in me became so intense that there is no torment to which I can compare it. It all depended on the thought of the many favors God granted me in prayer, and therefore I could not bear to see the gratitude I owed Him repaid so poorly. The tears I shed over my sins were of no comfort because I saw that all my tears proved of little benefit to me. For as soon as the occasion arose, they could not keep me

---

who let themselves go in displays of pointless nervousness." Gabriella Cunninghame Graham wrote: "There was no one less hysterical than St. Teresa of Avila. Her life was peaceful and orderly, a model of order and discipline. She never acted hurriedly and was always keenly intelligent. These qualities are manifest when she tells of her visions as when she tells of her convents. She herself attributes her ill health to the fevers she had borne."

7. *Life*, VI, 2, also for the following quotes.

from breaking my promises or from alleviating my sorrow. They seemed to be false tears to me."

The third element was her special devotion to St. Joseph. It is at this time that love took on new forms. Analyzing this time in Teresa's life, Lepée wrote, "Thanks to constant prayer, love took on a new form. Her spirit of resignation came more from the still mercenary desire of 'eternal goods' rather than from love. But her resignation led her to modify her love profoundly, bringing about self-effacement."

Now Teresa no longer offered up her existence to attain a more beautiful one at a low price. By having dominated her pain, she understood that much more must be given in addition to one's own merits and pleasures; we must give ourselves. Her love became not only more profound, but purified. So we must not offer what is superfluous, but our basic well-being. The offering of herself was the constructive result of her crisis of health.

CHAPTER SEVEN

Inner Conflict

After so many ups and downs, Teresa's health stabilized. Her heart no longer caused sudden disturbances, and her general fatigue diminished. During that period, Don Alonso went to the convent frequently since Teresa, being in the infirmary, could converse with her father more often. The strict rules of the cloister were less strict with those nuns in the infirmary as long as they could go to the parlor. Those cherished moments were almost the only consolation left Don Alonso in his melancholy old age. His thoughts always went to his family which was breaking apart, not because of internal disharmony, but because of exterior circumstances. His daughters were either married or in the religious life, and all his sons had gone to the Indies. He knew the Indies seldom returned those who had been attracted there. On the other hand, how could he have forbidden it? The de Cepeda patrimony was barely enough to be comfortable on, and each of his progeny needed a place in the world to build a family in true hidalgan tradition. They were all so resolute in trying the great adventure! Fernando, Rodrigo, and Lorenzo were already there; Pedro and Jerónimo left on November 5, 1540, with the fleet that sailed to Peru Vaca. The last two, Antonio and Augustín, still at home, were eager to leave Avila as soon as possible.

But Teresa stayed. She, who seemed to have left first and whom he had most opposed in choosing her vocation, was the only one who stayed behind—the only one to whom he could talk openly about every member of the family.

Though Teresa still loved her family intensely, her heart was always seeking the true light, and she tried to draw her father toward that light with her. She succeeded. Don Alonso was a Christian and had lived a good life, so he was prepared to meditate on God's perfection. Teresa helped him to step over the dividing line between the common Christian and the meditative life. "To me it seemed as though there could be no greater thing on earth than to pray, and since I dearly loved my father, I wished he could enjoy what I did. Therefore, I did my best to lead him slowly to this practice, giving him books on the subject.

"As I have said, he was so virtuous and applied himself so well to this saintly exercise, that after five or six years, he was so far ahead that I was happy and thanked God. He suffered much, but he bore all with marvelous humility. He often came to see me and enjoyed speaking of God."[1]

Don Alonso's last years coincided with a very complex period in Teresa's life, years which were the most dangerous, presenting difficult contrasts for her. She was no longer a normal, graceful and simple young woman. Much painful experience had matured her in every way, making her speak with self-assurance. Her long convalescence was a rebirth, giving her renewed

---

1. *Life*, VII, 10.

life. As she regained strength, Teresa was continually drawn to her neighbor, awakening a spontaneous and affectionate bond, concealing an underlying goal.

Among all those praised throughout history, few possessed such a gift of conversation as she. If she had not become a nun, she would certainly have been the center of Spanish parlor society. Many of her contemporaries have attested to her most pleasing manner of speaking—simple, natural, but brilliant. She was always dignified but cordial. Marcelle Auclair wrote, "Avila soon learned what a pleasant conversationalist the young Carmelite nun was." Teresa forgot herself, concentrating her attention on others. Marcelle Auclair continued, "She always knew how to beautify the most insignificant of gifts by her manner of thanking; she knew how to give, compliment, sympathize and participate."[2]

She always spoke with the precise aim of diverting, consoling or edifying others. This attitude was the result of reflection and affection, always genuine and completely offered. Certainly the Marquise de Rambouillet would never have stated, "We have discovered a new pleasure—conversation," had she known that a nun in Castile had preceded and surpassed the French in that difficult art a century before.

We must bear in mind Teresa's innate cordiality in order to understand this period, 1539 to 1553. Diego de Estella defined this quality well, calling the saint of Avila "the magnet of the world." As a consequence, relatives and friends went often to the convent community room to talk with Teresa.

Conversations with outsiders were permitted in Spanish convents before the Council of Trent; naturally, all was within the bounds of the cloister rules, and the subjects discussed were devotional. The sisters talked

---

2. *La Vie de Sainte Thérèse*, part I, VII.

to their guests from the other side of the grille. The Prioress and convent directors were lenient with Teresa in allowing her to have frequent visitors because they realized what power of good Teresa's words had.

But if there was no direct reason for her visits, the time spent meant an interruption from her great desire of perfection through mental prayer. Her call to meditation and contemplation was too clear for her to keep contact with the outside world too frequently. Sometimes her visitors gossiped about mutual friends which displeased her, even though she listened courteously. Nevertheless, it was disturbing. She was not in full command of the disdain needed not to be bothered by vain triflings.

Furthermore, while conversing, she found herself inevitably approving things with her guest and enjoying the talk. Teresa was always on the alert with an inner eye which severely watched her every move, for she possessed an astounding capacity for self-analysis. She decided she must choose between being one of the many good and honest, but spiritually inefficient nuns, or undertaking the sublime task of contemplation.

The dilemma had been in the back of her mind for some time without causing any crisis, though she suffered from the compromise. Even if she enjoyed the "dissipation," as she called it, of conversation, she knew her contemplative life was injured by it. Every time she returned to her praying, she felt confused and numbed, pained that God continued to bestow His graces of prayer while she was ungrateful to Him. "It was more painful for me to receive graces rather than punishments. One grace alone afflicted me more than many illnesses and torments together. I became humble and ashamed to see I was favored after I had abused what had already been given me; this caused me unspeakable anguish." The Creator was overcoming His creature with generosity, pursuing her for years with gifts of grace. "Oh, Lord of my soul! You were preparing me to receive other gifts of grace and to taste of Your sweetness through my great repentance. There could not have been greater delicacy, but for me it was the greatest of punishments." [3]

We must remember that these words come from one who contemplated God in divine visions. "In all this period which was the most dissipated in my life, I never to my knowledge committed mortal sin. Should I have recognized such a thing, I surely could never have borne it." This statement is basic to the understanding of that contrasted period that lasted until 1553.

We know not which, but one year marked the greatest depression and the most dangerous, because of a deceit which found its way into Teresa's soul, leading her to take on a false and harmful humility. "From diversion to diversion, vanity to vanity, occasion to occasion, I began to place my poor soul in peril which, spoiled by so many distractions, was ashamed of continuing that special friendship with God that is derived from prayer. To get close to Him bothered me, since, as my sins increased, I began to lose taste for that certain sweetness which comes from the practice of virtue.

"But if this satisfaction was leaving me, O Lord, it was because I was drawing away from You, and I saw that clearly! The devil could not have done me greater harm as he tried to under the pretext of humility."

These drastic words and those to follow must not, in turn, lead us to deception because they reveal only an intense ascetic drama. "Seeing myself so lost, I began to fear prayer. Worst of all, I thought it would be better to adapt myself to what the others did, reciting what was obligatory, praying vocally and leaving mental prayer to others, for it was not right that I who

---

3. *Life,* VII, 19, also for the following.

deserved to live with the demons and did nothing but
deceive others by my usual outer conduct, should become familiar with God.''

The consequence of that false humility was entirely
negative, for Teresa no longer prayed. How much she
suffered because of this change we cannot say, but her
life became most unhappy as she herself said: ''Prayer
time had become unbearable; it consisted in concentration, but since my spirit was enslaved, all of my miseries came before me.''

A moving aspect of this state of mind was Teresa's
meetings with her father. Through his daughter's suggestion and sweet insistence, Don Alonso had become a
man of prayer and now Teresa did not have the courage
to confess to him that she no longer prayed! Sincere as
she was, she felt repugnance in deceiving her father.
On the other hand, he practiced pious meditation more
and more. ''He had reached such a high level that
when he came to see me, he stayed only briefly. He
would leave immediately after seeing me, saying that
he was wasting time if he stayed longer.''

Finally, one day, Teresa confessed to her father that
she no longer meditated, but her love kept her from
revealing everything. ''I concealed the true reason, saying that my illness prevented me from doing so.'' And
Don Alonso considered the excuse plausible enough.
''His mouth never uttered a lie, and neither should
mine have if I had been consistent with what we had
often discussed. I clearly saw that the reason I gave
was not justifiable, and to deceive him even more, I
added that it was already enough if I went to choir
functions.'' She knew that even though the reason she
adopted could well have been true, it was insufficient.
''A soul that really loves God knows there is no better
prayer than one's very sickness or work, for then it can
offer what it suffers, conforming to God's holy will.
Love only acts here, not the circumstances, and it is

inexact to believe that you cannot pray unless you have time and solitude.''

She thus felt the whole weight of her barrenness. The step backward afflicted her cruelly, but she could not overcome the deception she had fallen into; that is, wretched as she was, it was too daring for her to pray. Don Alonso believed his daughter's excuses and felt sorry for her. When he became ill, Teresa got permission to nurse him day and night in the de la Moneda house. ''Even though I was sick myself, I forced myself to serve him. I saw that if he left me, every joy and consolation would be gone. He meant everything to me. And this helped me to dissimulate my indisposition until his death, acting as though nothing bothered me. Meanwhile, to see that the end was near broke my heart, for I loved him so.''

His last illness endured for about fifteen days. Until then, Don Alonso had suffered a great deal, but the pain increased during the last two weeks. What pained him most were his shoulders, so Teresa reflected that since he was so devoted to Christ on the cross, perhaps God was permitting him to feel something of what He Himself had felt. This thought consoled the sick man immensely, and he no longer complained, but offered up his suffering to God. His approach to death glorified him. The last years' inner strivings blossomed as serenity in the dying man. He was not only serene but desired death. He welcomed the Sacrament of the Anointing of the Sick and then talked to his children; the words he uttered on the brink of death deeply impressed Teresa. ''He begged me to pray, beseeching mercy for him. He exhorted us to remain faithful to God, and to remember that all things must one day come to an end. With tears in his eyes, he said that if he felt sorry for anything, it was only because he had not served God with fervor and that at the present moment he wished he were a member of the most austere religious order."

After three days of coma, he regained consciousness on the last day and died reciting the Apostles' Creed.

Don Alonso's death deprived Teresa of her greatest human affection. After his demise a lawsuit took place between the daughter of the first marriage and the children of the second, concerning the division of the property, but Teresa did not take part in it.

Her morale was very low, but one thing enlightened her: Fr. Barrón had been Don Alonso's confessor, and Teresa went to confession to him. His advice opened the way to better spiritual living because he insisted that she continue praying no matter what her pricks of conscience might be. Teresa obeyed and never again stopped mental prayer.

However, this was not yet the decisive moment when she was to offer her life to God. She had passed, nevertheless, the greatest point of depression in her religious life and was beginning to rise slowly, regaining the means of pious meditation.

Teresa of Jesus spent almost twenty years in that mediocre state. The principal characteristic of that time lies in the absence of a great victory, and she instead was born to triumph, as she herself pointed out: "I wanted to live. I well knew that my life consisted in a struggle against some sort of death. None could give me life, and I could not gain it by myself. He alone who could have given it to me had every reason not to help me, because I had always alienated Him whenever He had welcomed me."[4]

---

4. *Life*, VIII, 12.

CHAPTER EIGHT

The Awakening
Before Christ's Passion

"My soul was tired and sought repose, but its faulty habits prevented its obtaining any. Entering church one day, my eyes fell on a statue that had been brought to the convent in preparation for a celebration about to take place. It showed our Lord covered with wounds and it inspired so much devotion that as soon as I saw it, I felt moved. It vividly demonstrated how He had suffered for us. My sorrow was so great when I thought of my ingratitude to His love that I thought my heart would break. I threw myself at His feet in tears and implored Him to give me the strength never to offend Him again."[1]

This event probably occurred in 1554 or 1555 (when Teresa was thirty-nine or forty years old), and the Ecce Homo statue still exists in the Convent of the Incarnation in Avila. Teresa truly lived through her "second conversion" before that statue when she took a definite step on her road to perfection. "Nothing

---

1. *Life,* IX, also for the following.

helped me more than to prostrate myself before God's image as described. At the time, I had no confidence in myself, so I placed all my trust in God. I told Him that I would not leave His feet until He granted me what I implored. He must certainly have fulfilled my desire because from then on I improved constantly."

Thus her praying became more intense and sincere. "This was my method of prayer: unable to discuss it with my intellect, I tried mentally to picture Jesus Christ, and I became better at it whenever I envisioned Him abandoned. I thought that if He were alone and afflicted He would be more inclined to accept me, as if He were someone who needed help. There were many simple notions in my head then."

This habit of picturing Christ in His hours of passion and solitude rather than in hours of glory softened Teresa's soul and made her realize still more what immortal affinity lies between the crucifix and any afflicted creature. Teresa, too, was suffering for herself and for others inasmuch as she was living the religious and moral problem in dramatic contradiction and would take childlike refuge in the tears and wounds of Jesus. "I was best at concentrating on Christ's passion in the garden, preferring to stay with Him there, thinking of the sweat and pain He had borne. I wanted to wipe that painful sweat myself if I could, but I remember that I never dared to do so because my sins were ever before me. So I just stayed with Him as long as my thoughts permitted, for there were many disturbing, interfering thoughts."

This admission reveals how Teresa's meditations burned with courageous love, but were chilled by her past and present distractions. "Returning to the anguish my thoughts caused me, it is necessary to know that when the soul is separated from the intellect in prayer, what follows is either profound seclusion or disorientation. If the latter happens, and the soul continues just the same, it proceeds speedily, for it is acting only from love. Before reaching its goal, however, it must try very hard, unless it is a question of those whom God wants to lead quickly to the prayer of quiet, as I have seen happen to some of my acquaintances."

Mental distraction itself became a means of advancing speedily because the will set it aside completely and the soul "acted solely out of love." What subtle insight is there in this ascetic battle, and what profound understanding of the life of prayer!

Teresa's distractions were also due to the lack of a photographic mind. "I was so poor at mentally picturing objects that if I had not seen them before with my very own eyes, I was altogether unable to envision them." This was why she could never picture the most holy humanity of Christ, try as she would. Gethsemane was her favorite meditation theme, though it must have been difficult for her with the lack of visual images. Yet, she was later to enjoy supernatural visions, further proof of her visions being supernatural gifts. For years this ascetic woman was not able to reconstruct the image of Jesus in agony, and soon marvelous apparitions which she did not even seek, came to her, and she succumbed to them through obedience!

During Teresa's period of renewed prayer, she again felt the need to consult good books, and someone gave her St. Augustine's *Confessions*. Teresa was profoundly attracted to the great work, for she had always been devoted to the saint for two reasons: she had been educated in an Augustinian convent, and most important, she was moved by the great spiritual revivers. The saints, who had lived hours and years of sublime and vehement penance, edified and encouraged her, since her burning ardor made her feel similar to them.

She became immersed in her reading of the *Confessions* while her community-room talk had already begun to diminish, and her solitude was strengthened.

One day, while reading the page which had become her mainstay, she broke into a flood of tears. It was where Augustine told of that mysterious, delicate and stupendous episode of the voice in the garden: "However when I had intensely reflected on the mysterious depth into which I had been called, I gathered all my wretchedness before my heart and then such a violent tempest burst out with an immense rain of tears that I was forced to get up and move away from Alipio in order to shed all the tears with their sobs.

"Solitude seemed more adapted for an outburst of tears, so I went still farther away, in order not to be disturbed by his presence. Such was the state I was in. He felt it, for I believe I had muttered something while I rose which revealed a hoarse voice full of tears. I got up and he remained seated in great astonishment.

"I know not how, but I fell down at the foot of a tree and loosed the tie to my tears. Rivers flowed from my eyes as a sacrifice accepted by You. Not with these exact words, but I exclaimed at length something similar to: 'And You, O Lord, till when? Till when, O Lord, will You be angry? To the end? Please don't think of my past offenses!'

"I felt as a slave and so uttered excruciating groans. 'Till when, till when? Tomorrow and still tomorrow? Why not now? Why can this not be the hour which will mark the end of my wicked life?'

"As I said these things I wept with bitter sadness of heart. Just then, I heard a child's voice from a nearby house sing repeatedly: 'Take, read; take, read.' I immediately changed and carefully began to reflect if it were common for children to sing such a refrain in their games, but I could not remember of ever having heard it.

"Having checked the impetuous tears, I got up, interpreting that voice as a divine command for me to open a book and read the first verse I fell upon. Hastily

I returned to Alipio and grasped the Apostle's book which I had laid aside upon leaving the table, opened it and silently read that verse which first caught my glance."

Teresa read these words with growing emotion and could barely finish the page when she, too, abandoned herself to a great crying spell in which she felt her past life flowing out—the time when she had been vain, weak and undecided, her love poor and incomplete, and her service mediocre. Those tears did her good, for they were genuine. This marked another decisive step, as when she fell before Christ in agony. Her external life changed rapidly; pastimes decreased, and she prayed more constantly.

Unknowingly, she was preparing a pure receptacle for the exceptional graces she was to receive from God. Years later, when she prepared her autobiography, she announced this with the following triumphant words: "From now on it will be as a new book; that is, a new life. Because if what I have described until now is mine, this that starts when I took up prayer again, is something of God that lives in me, for it seems impossible to me that I alone could have liberated myself in so little time from so many bad deeds and habits. Blessed be God who freed me from myself!"[2]

---

2. *Life,* XXIII, 1.

CHAPTER NINE

THE DEGREES OF MENTAL PRAYER

The First Water:

Beginner's Meditation

Teresa describes prayer in the context of a garden where the soul is the gardener who must water the plants. There are four ways in which the gardener can obtain water, and these symbolize the various degrees of prayer.

The first is to get it from the bottom of a well with a pail. This entails much strength and labor, the most fatiguing way to get water.

The second is to draw it by a water wheel, that is, by means of a "noria," a hydraulic machine commonly used in Europe in the sixteenth century. It consisted of a wheel made of small buckets placed in such a manner as to be easily filled.

The third method is to get the water from a stream, and this is easy, for there is an abundance of water, and the land becomes permeated with it.

The fourth is a good rain, the best way of all, because it means that God copiously pours directly on the soul the gift of prayer with no work on the soul's part.

Teresa describes the four allegories marvelously
since she talks from experience. "Those who begin
mental prayer are those who draw water from the well.
As stated, this is a laborious thing; they, in fact, must
struggle a great deal to control their feelings which are
used to roving."[1] They must gradually form a habit of
not paying attention to any other thing, not seeing or
hearing anything else and of depriving themselves of
absolutely everything while meditating. Another habit
which beginners must develop is frequent, insistent
repentance. At first it will seem as though they can
never repent enough for their sins, and they will feel
greatly afflicted. But the fact that they have resolved to
serve God truly proves that their repentance is sincere.[2]

The life of Jesus Christ must be the principal subject of their meditations.[3] With the help of the grace of
God, we can get up to this first phase of getting the
well-water by ourselves, but the water may or may not
be there. "By water I mean tears, but if these are
lacking there would be the inner sympathy and feelings
of devotion.

"But," she continues, "what must he do who after
many days of work feels nothing but aridity, disgust,
insipidness, and extreme repugnance of going to the
well for water? Certainly he would abandon the undertaking if he did not remind himself of the fact that by
doing this he is serving and pleasing the owner of the
garden, and that he might lose not only rewards already
bestowed, but also those which he hopes to gain by the
tedious task of lowering the pail into the well only to
pull it up empty. Often, moreover, after such work, he

---

1. *Life,* XI, also for the following quotations.

2. There is a parallelism between the allegory of the "first water" in the
Life and the "first three homes" of the *Interior Castle.*

3. There is some deviation from Osuna's thought concerning meditation
on the most sacred humanity of Jesus.

will not even have the strength to raise his arms and will be unable to put together a sensible thought (remember that drawing water from the well is synonymous to thought construction).

"Whatever can the gardener do at this point? Be happy and console himself in considering the fact that to be able to work in the garden of such a great Emperor is a noble honor. He also knows that he is satisfying his owner with his hard work, and the ultimate aim, after all, is to satisfy Him, not ourselves."[4]

The life of prayer must begin with meditation on the passion of Christ and in considering our ingratitude for the divine proof of love—the redemption. "Considering our wretchedness and ingratitude toward God, remembering how much the Lord has done for us, His most painful passion, His anguished life, we must earnestly contemplate His deeds, greatness and love which He bears us."[5]

Through growing grace she was nearing that state in which extraordinary favors are highly appreciated, but their absence no longer discourages. She began to understand that a soul has traveled far when it no longer becomes distressed by the absence of spiritual consolations. "At this point every fear is set aside. Even if you should stumble frequently, it is certain that you will never backslide because the edifice that has been begun stands on firm foundation."[6] This is possible because "we can serve God in any state" and perhaps the condition of inner aridity is the most advantageous.

But Teresa was still at the beginner's steps. She dedicated many pages of her autobiography to beginners in mental prayer, warning them of their depression and fear. She wanted to make clear that "it was

---

4. *Life,* XI, 9, 10.

5. *Life,* X, 2.

6. *Life,* XI, 13 and 15, here and for the following.

necessary that those who began must not be discouraged by the aridity to which they might be subject; nor should those who have already begun for some time and never succeed in finishing be likewise discouraged." She was later to explain that perhaps the reason for their defective meditation was due mostly to "not having embraced the cross with generosity from the very beginning; when they can no longer use their intellect they are grieved, for it seems they can do nothing and can no longer bear themselves. Instead, that is probably the time in which their will is unconsciously perfecting itself and gaining strength."

CHAPTER TEN

The Second Water:

Prayer of Concentration and Quiet

During the period of the "first water," extraordinary prayer was already beginning. In common prayer it is the soul which goes toward God with the help of ordinary grace; in extraordinary prayer, it is God who partially or wholly occupies the forces of the soul.

Teresa was now infused with extraordinary prayer which is true contemplation. She had spent almost twenty years in defective and incomplete prayer, and even after 1555, notwithstanding the practical transformation of her life and her greater capacity of concentration, she had been assailed by ups and downs. But the "first water" was coming along admirably. "During prayer, whenever I tried to fall at Jesus' feet, as explained before, or even when only reading, I would suddenly feel invaded by such a vivid feeling of divine presence that I could not doubt that God was in me and I in Him.

"This did not happen through any sort of vision, but I believe through that which is called 'mystical theology.'[1]

"In this case the soul remains so suspended that it seems apart from one. The will loves while the memory seems lost; the intellect takes no active part but is always present. The intellect does not operate, but it understands many things, much to its astonishment. It is God who lets it see them, conscious of its own incapability of doing so alone."[2]

She had received a foretaste of these "great delights" as a novice, but only briefly, not longer than the length of a Hail Mary. So many years of hesitation and struggle had gone between, and now the special graces appeared more often and were more important.

This is a momentous and delicate stage in the life of a mystic. Many studies have been carried out for centuries concerning this degree of prayer.[3] It is the state which crowns ascetic prayer and prepares the soul for mystical graces. It has been called pre-mystical prayer or "acquired contemplation."

Between the soul's natural activity and infused contemplation there is a pre-mystical condition which still belongs to the natural, not infused part, according to Teresa. At the beginning of the pre-mystical prayer of concentration there is meditation. "We meditate first to understand what we are saying, with whom we are speaking, and who we are to dare to address such an almighty God. To reflect on these things, on how little we have served Him, on how much we are indebted to

---

1. There are three types of visions: corporal, imaginary and intellectual, according to whether the object is seen and perceived by corporal senses, by the imagination, or purely by the intellect.

2. *Life,* X, 1.

3. As an example we cite the recently published *Contemplazione Acquisita* by Fr. Gabriel, Rome, 1950.

Him, is called prayer of concentration." This is the apex of what Teresa still calls "natural." However, she says, "The first supernatural prayer which I experienced consisted in a spiritual concentration felt in the soul." Speaking of the second water, she declared, "Here the soul starts to concentrate and already touches supernatural domain, for it could never get that far, not even with every personal effort possible."[4] It is in this zone that we can recognize an "acquired contemplation" or "pre-mystical prayer." Certainly, Teresa talks of "supernatural" often in her description of the prayer symbolizing the second water. This fact must be given considerable weight because she always uses the word in its strictest sense.

This state of prayer is, of course, difficult to prove because of its complexity and delicateness, but spiritual direction ascertains and advocates its practice constantly. The school of thought founded by St. John of the Cross upholds the reality of this intermediary state between still "natural" prayer according to St. Teresa (not infused) and truly infused contemplation. The following excerpt from the book *Acquired Contemplation,* (Chapter 1, p. 50) by Fr. Gabriel (S. M. Magdalen) helps to clear the concept in discussion: "By the teachings of St. John of the Cross, the common experience of fervent souls shows that between affective meditation and experimental infused contemplation exists a state of intermediate prayer which requires the soul's appropriate direction. That part of spiritual theology which teaches the practice of the contemplative life and forms competent spiritual directors must particularly study this phase of prayer. It must be distinguished from the two contiguous states and placed between meditation and infused contemplation as a third form of mental prayer. Its name is of secondary importance; what must

---

4. *Life,* XIV, also for the following quotations.

be remarked primarily is that it is a matter of reality and not theory."

We now ask ourselves: is that intermediary state of prayer a boundary or a point of passage? Is it a zone to be considered as a bridge between a superior state of prayer and an inferior one? In other words, can the prayer of quiet in any way "cause" infused contemplation?

Teresa insists much on the fact that infused graces cannot be "merited," even less caused. They must always be considered independent from any state of ascetic or pre-mystical prayer as from any holiness in life. God grants contemplative conditions as a pure gift not connected to moral merits or ascetic efforts. Nevertheless, St. Teresa says, when souls love God generously and act only for Him, they become predisposed to mystical graces, and God generally grants them this extraordinary sign of His love.

From Fr. Gabriel's book: *St. Teresa, Teacher of Spiritual Life* (II, pp. 60-61), we cite: "After clearly and constantly asserting that mystical graces are not necessarily connected to holiness, Teresa now states that infused contemplation is usually conceded to those who seek full and perfect holiness in order to be prepared to receive these graces. The soul's disposition is thus most important in order to acquire divine favors. What little we can do for ourselves becomes much, as she herself writes in the *Interior Castle* (Mansion V, Ch. 2, n. 1): 'Concerning what God bestows in us, we can do nothing more than prepare ourselves so that His Majesty may favor us, but this is indeed doing much.'

"God rewards even on earth, according to Teresa's *Thoughts* (Ch. 4, n. 7): 'For love of God, Christians and daughters, let us awake from this sleep and remember that God does not even await the other life to recompense us for our love. The reward begins here.'

"However, Teresa is most convinced that we can never deserve these graces: 'We must fully understand and always bear in mind that the gifts we have received from God have never been given through any merit of ours' *(Life,* X, n. 4). Indeed, she goes on to say that 'those religious who deceive themselves into believing that after many years of prayer they deserve God's favors shall never arrive at the peak of perfection' *(Autobiography,* XXXIX, n. 15). Such favors shall always remain gratuitous. Yet, it does not seem that the truly generous soul often remains without its reward: 'When God gives a soul this delicateness of avoiding the least fault, He is preparing a bed of roses as it were, and sooner or later He will certainly descend to take delight in it' *(Thoughts,* II, n. 5). Furthermore, certain expressions are most absolute: 'It is indeed certain that when we empty ourselves of everything that is created and detach ourselves for love of God, He fills us with Himself.'"

It is difficult to delineate the different phases of mental prayer, for one passes insensibly from one into the other. The second water, "prayer of concentration and quiet," has the following characteristic: the initiative of God is partially evident, occupying only the will; the intellect and memory fluctuate about it and are irresistibly drawn toward it.

The saint described this prayer in this way: "The powers of the soul gathered together to taste with greater suavity the joy which had overwhelmed them. But they were neither bewildered nor asleep. All that acted was the will, consenting to be imprisoned by Him, knowing how sweet it is to be the slave of such a Lover, and knowing how to become His prisoner."

The other two powers helped the will to become more capable of enjoying such bounty. When the will was united to God, however, their collaboration served only as a disturbance. Then the will had to ignore them in order to continue its enjoyment in silence, for it, too, would have been distracted, trying to set the others right. The powers were "as certain doves which are not content with the food they receive without toil from their owner, but go looking for it themselves. Encountering difficulty they quickly return. So they go and come, as though whetting the will to let them take part in the joy it is experiencing. They stop if God grants them a little bait, otherwise they return to the search. They think they are helping the will by doing this, but when either memory and imagination insist on wanting to represent that which the will is enjoying, they only disturb."

Everything in this degree of prayer was accompanied by great sweetness. The soul had to exert little work so that even if the meditation lasted long, it was not tiring because the intellect comported itself calmly and suavely, thus obtaining more water than when it searched for it in the well. The tears gushed out joyously without the intervention of the will.

The work of God was thus evident. The soul could never have prayed like that by itself. By means of the graces bestowed upon her she grew in her exercise of the virtues incomparably more than in the preceding period. "The soul is denuding itself of all its miseries and acquires a certain cognizance of what the delights of glory are. It seems to me that such a cognizance makes the soul progress more, always drawing nearer to that essential Virtue, God Himself, from whom all virtues proceed. In fact, His Majesty is starting to communicate to this soul and wants it to understand in what way this is done."

When she began to taste of the delights of extraordinary prayer, she completely detached herself from all human desires. "When you get to this point you lose attraction for worldly things and find no satisfaction in them. You clearly see that they can never make you enjoy, not even for an instant, what you are enjoying then. Wealth, power, honors and pleasures are incapable of furnishing similar joys. The happiness which those things produce cannot be compared to that true and complete happiness with which the soul is wholly overwhelmed. I am convinced it is impossible to feel so much happiness from terrestrial joys because there is always some contrast present in them, whereas here reigns pure contentedness. The pain comes later when we realize that it has passed without knowing how, or we are unable to recapture such bliss. Even if we would tear ourselves to pieces by dint of penances and prayers, we could never receive it again if the Lord did not will to restore it to us.

"Our Lord God acts in us in a very special manner; while He grants delightful external and internal joys, He has us understand what great difference exists between those and worldly joys. It seems as though the hole which our sins had formed in us has become filled."

But in what way does the soul perceive these delights that have nothing to do with the senses? "It perceives them in the innermost part of its being without knowing how or in what manner it does so. At times the soul knows not what to do, what to wish for or ask. It seems to have found all, but does not know how to describe it." It was a sublime gratification that can only be described as "quiet" in this particular state of prayer. The body had nothing to do with it, established as it was in the depths of the soul where the senses of the body could not reach. Teresa expressed it beautifully by saying: "You seem to have found everything."

When this state would cease, great grief would set in. Frigid hours would replace solar happiness, and the "gardener" would contemplate the garden of her soul without finding a flower. She wrote that in those moments she could not even remember the beautiful hours. The garden appeared dry, and she could not find water for it, as though she had never borne any seed of virtue. She was tempted to consider all her labor of cultivation and irrigation lost. All was dead and desolate within her.

But precisely in those hours of trial did she learn to react with the best means at her defense. She applied herself energetically to self-betterment, forcing herself to file down and consume the remains of the bad part of her human nature. "It is time to remove and tear up the very roots of the remaining bad weeds, small as they may be, and to realize that our efforts mean nothing if God denies us the water of His grace. We must not bother about our troubles which are less than nothing, for then the soul will progress in humility and the flowers will reappear."

Teresa's prayer of concentration and quiet became steadily more frequent, tending to remain constant, and the "third water" gleamed through from time to time.

CHAPTER ELEVEN

The Third Water:

Prayer of Quiet, Distressing Doubts

The "third type" or "third water" which is true "prayer of quiet" consists of different degrees forming a gradual ascent. There is very little work required here for all that is needed is to direct the water, but there are three distinct ways to do this.

In the first, the will is a prisoner of God, while the intellect and memory are free to attend to external matters. However, this is not the same as during the second water. There is a difference in intensity, and God's action is still more direct and predominating, becoming the principal cause and the soul the instrumental cause. The mystic bond is more intense, and moral effects are richer. The virtues are more firmly rooted than in the preceding phase. The soul is aware of this and knows it has changed. The flowers in the garden are in full bloom. This full devotion to God turns words into songs: "to become completely abandoned in God's arms. Does He wish to take my soul into heaven? There could be nothing better. To hell? My soul is not afraid as long as it is with its Love. Does He wish to take it forever from this world? That is what it desires. Does He want it to live long? Let it. My soul no longer belongs to itself, but entirely to God. He may do with it what He wills because it cares nothing."[1]

Teresa also reached the second degree of this type of prayer in those years from 1555 to 1558. Here God occupies the intellect along with the soul, making it become totally absorbed in His possession. However, memory and imagination are not yet irresistibly attracted, continuing to move freely, provoking distractions from the contemplative act. These disturbances tired Teresa. "Feeling itself alone, imagination sets up an unbelievable struggle to upset everything; it has been detestably tiring. I often pray to God to suspend my contemplation rather than be so disturbed.... O Lord, when will the powers of my soul be united to sing Your praises? When will my soul cease to be so divided it cannot even control itself?"

Teresa later reached the fullness of this third type in which all three of the soul's powers are occupied by God. The powers seem to act while dozing because they know not how they are acting, but they are not altogether asleep. The supreme degree of sweetness which the soul feels as entirely spiritual and insensible is incomparably greater than in the preceding stages. The body is non-existent while the soul is transformed into a part of paradise. "The water of grace here gets as far as the throat, and the immersed soul knows not how to advance or recede; it would continue forever in that bliss. It experiences such a great happiness in that agony that it is indescribable. It seems to be a state of complete death to the things of the world in order to be immersed in the enjoyment of God.

"The soul knows not whether to talk or keep silent, whether to cry or laugh. It has plunged into a glorious

---

1. *Life*, XVII, also for the following quotations.

delirium which is celestial abandon, but all the while it is learning true wisdom."

These words represent an elevated condition, and yet Teresa is to reach still greater horizons. It is as though we were being led by her hand in the discovery of a series of concentric horizons, one more vast than the other. Whenever we feel as though we could not witness anything greater, to our astonishment, there she clears the clouds to present a still more luminous horizon.

However, since 1554, contemporaneous to Teresa's progress in mystical graces, a new psychological drama arose in her which lasted several years. In Spain at that time, the case of Magdalen of the Cross, "the devil-deceived," was very famous. Teresa referred to this in her autobiography when she said, "I was shaken by great fears because in those days women had been discovered who had been deceived by the devil through grand illusions."

She most certainly was referring to Magdalen of the Cross who had become a nun of the order of St. Clare in Córdoba and had astounded Spain with her miracles, prophecies, and knowledge in all matters. She foretold the imprisonment of Francis I and the sack of Rome. On the most important feast days she could be seen raised from the earth holding a beautiful child in her arms, and her hair visibly grew down to her feet. Emperors, kings, queens, and princesses all tried to be in her graces; Isabella of Portugal insisted that she bless the swaddling-bands of the future Philip II. But it was later discovered that she dealt with the devil and was banished from the convent to end her days in obscurity.

The situation caused much scandal, producing a wave of terror to sweep over ascetic, believing Spain; the most sensitive began to fear diabolical arts and illusions everywhere. Receptive as Teresa was, she began fearing if she, too, were not an object of diabolical deceits. The world of mystical revelations which had opened before her made her grow suspicious. Were all those lofty contemplations perhaps tricks of the devil because she well knew that theologians referred to the devil as "God's monkey," capable of deceiving pious souls with artificial mysticism. "On the other hand," she wrote, "I felt firmly persuaded that those delights came from God, especially during meditation times, and all the more so because I felt better and stronger after them. But as soon as I became disturbed, my fears would return, suspecting a devil's trick which would deprive me of my mental praying by prohibiting my intellect to think on the passion or to act intelligently in any way."[2]

Her fears became so vivid that she began looking for spiritual directors in whom to confide and from whom to ask advice. She had heard of the priests of the Society of Jesus, who had founded the College of St. Giles in Avila in 1553, Juan de Pradavos and Fernando Alvarez. Having heard of the saintly reputation of the institution, she felt strongly attracted to going to confession there to seek enlightenment. But she did not feel worthy of dealing with the followers of St. Ignatius whom she considered heroes far out of her ascetic range.

She hesitated until she could bear it no longer and decided to confide in Fr. Gaspar Daza of Avila. She knew who he was, for many had spoken to her of this priest who seemed to be an apostle initiating many holy functions, such as forming a sort of organization for priests. Daza was truly a follower of Christ and spent all of his time arousing people to the imitation of the Savior. Teresa was introduced to Daza by Francisco de Salcedo who belonged to Daza's Confraternity even

---

2. *Life,* XXIII, also for the following quotations.

though he was a layman and married. Teresa wrote this description of Salcedo: "He leads such an exemplary and virtuous life, full of prayer and charity that you can see he is perfectly good. I say this because I know he has brought many souls to perfection. The Lord has given him special talents which he constantly uses even if he is hindered by his status. He directs everything to the good of the souls of his fellow men and seems to care only about doing good to those he sees fit."

Salcedo was very happy to bring Gaspar Daza to the convent, and Teresa went to confession, confiding in him the degree of her meditations. Daza was definitely struck by her revelations, and counterbalancing the small defects still discerned in Teresa with the extraordinary gifts she received, "with saintly courage he began treating me as a great soul, demanding that I no longer offend God."

Overtaken by his zeal, he rushed things, for suddenly to require perfection of one is a difficult task which cannot always succeed. Teresa became affected by this seemingly unattainable goal and wept. "His demand was most reasonable considering the degree of prayer he noted in me. But when I saw that he was so resolute in having me immediately do away with my small shortcomings, from which I did not feel strong enough to withdraw so perfectly, I became terribly saddened. He considered my soul's travail as work that had to be accomplished immediately, while I felt the need to be guided more patiently."

She realized that Fr. Daza's direction was not adaptable to her, and instead sought comfort in discussing asceticism with Salcedo who was more indulgent.

"He used to encourage me during his visits, telling me not to detach myself from everything in one day, for God would have withdrawn me a little at a time; he, too, had been unable to break definitely with certain frivolities for several years."

Teresa gradually told him of her special graces and in addition, revealed what imperfections remained in her. Salcedo remarked that these two things could not go together because such special graces were for more humble people closer to perfection. He added that Teresa should be careful because he could see the marks of a bad spirit. He did not pronounce a definite opinion, but told her to study closely her meditation in every aspect and then refer to him.

His words saddened Teresa for she was already afraid that her inner visions were due to a malignant spirit, so her anguish grew. "I was greatly grieved and began to cry. I definitely wanted to please God and could not believe I was a victim of the devil. Yet I feared lest He deny me His light as punishment for my sins so that I could not comprehend my condition."

It was at this time that she happened to come upon *The Ascent to Mount Sion* by Bernardino de Laredo who had been the physician assigned to Juan II of Portugal and had become a Franciscan lay-brother. In a chapter on the soul's union with God, she found the same state of intellectual repose, the impossibility to think of anything that she felt during contemplation which bothered her, described by Laredo. She was comforted, and having underlined the passage with a pencil, she sent the book to de Salcedo, begging him to examine it well and to seek Gaspar Daza's counsel on what she was to do; she was even disposed to make the greatest sacrifice of renouncing contemplation. In order to further better judgment, she also sent a written report of her life as complete as possible, stating her sins.

Gaspar Daza and Francisco de Salcedo studied the manuscript carefully, reflecting on the true necessities of that tested soul. Teresa spent several days in solitude praying and having others pray for her. The answer finally came. Francisco de Salcedo came to the speaking grate with a desolated expression and declared, according to them, Teresa was a victim of the devil, and that she should treat the matter with a priest of the Society of Jesus. She was to make a clear general confession to him and by virtue of the Sacrament of Reconciliation the Lord would give the priest greater lucidity. "Do not in any way disregard these suggestions for anything in the world," he warned, "because your soul is in great danger if you are not guided."

This threw Teresa into such an anguished state of tribulation that she could do nothing but cry. While she was in the oratory one day her hands opened a book and she read, "God is very true and does not permit those who love Him to be deceived by the devil."

She felt consoled and prepared for her general confession putting down in writing the good and the bad in her life in the most sincere and complete manner. She later wrote that, rereading what she had written, she saw "so much bad and almost nothing good," which grieved her. She then requested that a Jesuit father be called to hear her confession.

One March day, probably in 1555 or 1556, Father Diego de Cetina went from the College of St. Giles to the Incarnation Convent to speak to Teresa. After she had described all her soul's wanderings, he reassured her. He said that it was evident that the spirit of God was acting in her and that she certainly should not stop mental prayer. He said that her spiritual structure was not on firm foundation because she did not yet understand humility, but this was no reason to give up pious meditation. Indeed, she should practice it with greater care: how did she know the designs of God, and whether the Lord wished to use her to do good?

Fr. de Cetina added other reflections which seem prophetic concerning what happened later. Leaving him, Teresa was altogether consoled as though transformed. "Those words became so profoundly impressed in my soul that they seemed to be dictated by the Holy Spirit for my spiritual recovery...."

The Jesuit also gave her detailed instructions. Every day she was to meditate on one particular phase of Christ's passion, seeking to gain profit by it, never allowing her thoughts to stray from the most holy humanity of Christ. But she was to avoid solitude and mystical states until further orders. These directions left Teresa "full of joy and courage," and full of a feeling of obedience which never left her. From that time on, she faithfully followed instructions and felt herself become steadily better.

CHAPTER TWELVE

Jesuit Directives

"The affection I felt imbued with at that time would have led me to do anything. Without pressure from my confessor, I slowly began to reform my life in many respects. He seemed not to notice my efforts which encouraged me all the more. He guided me on the road of loving God, leaving me free to follow my own loving inclinations."[1]

It is paradoxical that Teresa's enriched and experienced, yet anguished, soul should have been entrusted to a young priest of twenty-three who was not particularly extraordinary in any way. He was considered a mediocre preacher and confessor, unable to do more. Yet Fr. Cetina indicated the spiritual steps that were to lead Teresa so high. He, too, spent much time in mental prayer so that his advice produced effective benefits. For two months Teresa did all she could to obey. In her obedience she was to resist the graces and favors of God; she became visibly better because she could even

---

1. *Life,* XXIV, 1.

do certain deeds which appeared heroic to those around her.

But graces and favors followed her. "The more I tried to be distracted, the more the Lord poured down spiritual messages and happy moments. I felt surrounded by them and unable to escape. This impossibility tormented me, but the Lord continued to send His graces to my soul more frequently for two months. In short, He wanted me to understand that I could not resist Him."

St. Francis Borgia came to Avila for the second time in 1557. He was at the center of the episode which involved some of the leading personalities of the sixteenth century. Francis was the Marquis of Lombay, Duke of Gandia and a powerful minister of Emperor Charles V. In 1550, however, he left the world to enter the Society of Jesus after long years of thought had preceded his decision. He was probably first driven in that direction by the Empress Isabella of Portugal who stayed overnight in Toledo in 1539 as the guest of a count. Married to Charles V, she was the young and beautiful first lady of the land, and Spain was most enthusiastic over her. Titian's portrait of her depicts a thin face of a pallid complexion and a sweet profile; she had almond-shaped eyes and a reposing look with a straight harmonious nose.

But at the time of her trip the Empress was very tired due to her fifth pregnancy, and a premature birth took place which ended her life. Her body was carried across Castile and Andalusia to the royal cemetery in Granada. Much mourning surrounded the richly decorated coffin as it passed on its way.

The numerous companies of honor guards which escorted the body were led by the Marquis of Lombay, Francis Borgia, who followed in a carriage behind the hearse as the representative of the Emperor. He had been almost as a brother to the royal couple, and his wife, Doña Leonor de Castro was considered the Empress' dearest friend.

At the burial a few days later, the Archbishop of Granada gave the funeral sermon, and after having ordered the cover of the coffin raised, asked: "Do you all swear to recognize our beloved Empress Doña Isabella in this body?" Everyone answered yes except the Duke of Gandia who did not reply. When the Archbishop asked why he was silent, Borgia answered: "Ask me what you wish, but I cannot recognize the beautiful face of our late Empress in this disfigured one."

Those present could not imagine what deep significance lay behind this response. When Borgia returned to the Emperor and minutely related the funeral, the minister spoke of human greatness which passes as the wind; of beauty, power and prestige which are worth less than a grain of dust. He was pale and had a fixed gaze, revealing a new and heavy burden. Was it only sorrow, or had he changed? Francis had thought a great deal in those few days about the simple and fundamental theme of life and death, and those hours spent beside the dead queen had transformed his soul. He was no longer a formal courtier of the world but a new man; he had seen the "nothingness" of all human things.

The Emperor understood because he, too, had been pondering the higher truths since he was sated with power and bitter grief. Now while Borgia spoke of human "nothingness," the Emperor had the impression that Borgia was drawing those words from his own heart. He said to him, "Friend, we shall leave the world!"

But their duties were too great to permit their breaking away from one day to the next. However, Borgia became solitary and thought only of God, even though he remained among men.

The years of waiting went by, and Borgia's resolution had matured; he would enter the Society of Jesus. But Ignatius of Loyola, to whom he wrote of his anxiousness to leave worldly affairs, answered, "First settle your family affairs; the world is not yet mature to accept this innovation." Francis bowed his head in obedience, which became part of his preparation. It cost him more to renounce that luminous world which he had recently discovered than it had to renounce human greatness. But divine grace helped him, and he became humble and penitent. He was an ascetic before becoming a Jesuit. When, in 1550, he entered the Society, his spiritual preparation made him ready for important assignments. Ignatius saw this and had him tour the various Society houses in Spain.

A moving episode happened before Fr. Borgia went to Avila. He paid a visit to Juana of Castile, an old insane woman mad about Charles V. The insane queen lived at Tordesillas in a huge, gloomy castle-fortress. Here she sat on the floor of a large, dim room absorbed in memories of her youth; she would not receive anyone and ate very little. A small court in the function of custodians was about her, but she cared for no one. Only the visits of Fr. Borgia animated her, and she spent many hours conversing with him. As long as he remained in Tordesillas, the queen changed, smiling and talking sanely.

Meanwhile, the most powerful man of modern history, Charles V, was getting ready to follow out the words he had uttered years before. Two years later he entered a monastery at Yuste and from there observed the vicissitudes of the world over which he had been sovereign.

But let us return to Teresa's encounter with Borgia which took place in the convent probably in 1557, because he returned to Avila again in 1557 to talk with Teresa. She unfolded her soul to him at their first meeting, and he told her that the spirit of God was acting in her. He said she should lay aside every fear, and that even if she had done well to resist divine favors for some time, it was better that she no longer resist them. He advised her to meditate on one moment of Christ's passion; then if God wished to elevate her soul she was not to oppose Him, but was to submit entirely because it would be an error to continue renouncing Him.

Teresa considered Fr. Borgia an advanced man of prayer, someone truly experienced. She was immensely consoled, and Francisco de Salcedo also rejoiced with her even though he could not always understand the favorable conclusions of others. Teresa corresponded with Borgia all her life, though not frequently. Mother Isabella of St. Dominic, Prioress of the Carmelite Convent at Saragossa, was an eyewitness at the beatification processes and attested to having seen "many papers" which were letters that Teresa wrote Borgia, but none exist to reveal new aspects of the two great saints and to bring to light reciprocal influences. The Duchess of Gandia, Borgia's daughter-in-law, testified at the beatification processes of 1609 that she had repeatedly heard Borgia speak of the greatness of spirit and lofty holiness of Teresa of Jesus.

Meanwhile, Fr. Cetina had been transferred, and Teresa again felt deprived of a director and under menace of being considered deceived by the devil. "My soul was so disconsolate and disheartened, I felt as though I were in a desert."

But a relative invited her to her home, and she took the occasion to look for another Jesuit confessor. It was then that she met someone who was to bear an important influence on her life.

A certain Doña Jerónima, commonly called Guiomár, from Ulloa, who was the daughter of Toro's governor, lived in Avila. She had married Don Francisco Dávila, lord of Salobralejo and a descendent of the old noble Villatoro family, and had borne him several children. Left a widow between 1552 and 1554 at the age of twenty-five, instead of thinking of remarriage, she dedicated herself entirely to God and to educating her children. She was very well off because Salobralejo had left her a great deal of property, and in addition, she herself owned a lot of land. Her home was a typical palace of the time situated near the Jesuit College of St. Giles so that she went to confession in the Jesuit church.

She was an unpretentious, truly pious woman. When she met Teresa she immediately felt the importance of the encounter and took a great liking to the Carmelite nun. She invited Teresa to her home and counseled her to be directed by Fr. Juan de Prádanos who had been sent in Fr. Cetina's place.

Teresa's stay in the Salobralejo home probably lasted until 1558 allowing Fr. Prádanos' directions to act profoundly. Concerning him Teresa wrote, "This priest began to guide me toward greater perfection. He would say that I had to do all to satisfy God in every way. He acted very prudently and politely, for my soul was still far from strong especially regarding those friendships which were dear to me and which did not offend God. I felt I would show ingratitude by breaking them and used to ask my confessor why I should show myself ungrateful if there was no offense to God. He then ordered me to commit myself to the Lord and to recite the 'Veni Creator' so that He might enlighten me on what was best to do.

"One day, when I had been supplicating God to help me please Him in every way, I began to recite the prayer, and before I had finished it I was caught by such a sudden rapture that I almost fainted. It was the first time the Lord granted me this grace, but it was so evident I could not doubt it. I then heard these words:

'I do not want you to converse any longer with humans, but only with angels.'"

She was afraid because the transport had been violent and the words uttered at the bottom of her soul. But great consolation accompanied the fear and remained after the fear had subsided. The words she had heard came true because "from then on I have not been able to feel consolation, friendship or special affection for anyone who does not love and serve God. I absolutely cannot do otherwise, be they relatives or friends. It is painful for me to deal with people whom I do not see burning with love of God, or who do not practice mental prayer."

It was a true transformation, and Teresa felt ready to undergo any kind of sacrifice for God. Every hesitation and attachment had fallen. Even those old friendships which were without offense to God no longer had any hold over her. At times she had forced herself to counteract her naturally social and cordial nature to the point of becoming sad and ill; now she suddenly felt freed from human bonds.

From those who knew Teresa during her three-year stay with the Salobralejo family, we know what type of life she led. On August 19, 1585, Doña Guiomár told Fr. Ribera, "Mother Teresa remained with me for three consecutive years because she did not feel well and desired to be where she could unfold her soul to theologians who were servants of God. This was why she remained so long. Mother Maridíaz stayed with me for the same period. Mother Teresa was very detached, clear, disciplined; she wore a hair shirt and prayed so much that I could enjoy her company only a short while after lunch and after supper. She was in very poor health, habitually vomiting twice daily, once in the morning and once at night, but our Lord relieved her of the morning attack so that she might receive Communion."[2]

Those had been the first words God had let her understand from within, and this occurred several times. In connection with this, Teresa wrote, "His words are very distinct; the corporal ears cannot hear them, but they are heard more clearly than if they had been perceived by the ears. It would be useless to try not to hear them. Among people, if you don't want to pay attention to what someone is saying, you can always stuff your ears or do something else in order not to hear, but in this case it is absolutely impossible. You must listen even if you don't want to because the intellect becomes almost obliged to understand what the Lord wants it to understand. There is no use wanting or not wanting. He who is Almighty reveals Himself as our real Master and makes us see that, in spite of all, we must do what He wills. This is something I know from experience because my fears led me to try to resist Him for almost two years.

"I would furthermore like to expose the difference that lies between words that come from a holy spirit and those from an evil one, and also how oftentimes they are only impressions the intellect receives (something that can easily happen), or words which we utter to ourselves. I don't know if the latter is possible, but it seems to be so."[3]

The analysis which follows in her *Life* indicates different characteristics which distinguish words of divine origin. There are two which she experienced. One was an objective sign and the other intrinsic. For the first she states, "I can truly say it was God who spoke to me because after repeated experiences I saw how all

---

2. Royal Academy of History manuscript quoted by Fr. Silverio, *op. cit.*, I, XXI.

3. *Life*, XXV, 1, 2.

that had been told to me two or three years earlier had come true without even one having been false."

The second is explained thus: "Another more evident sign is that the words that come from the intellect do not generate any activity in the soul, whereas those from God are both words and actions. Even if they are reprimanding and not devotional, they immediately cause the soul to change, enabling it to undertake all for the service of God. The soul is illuminated, moved to pity and overcome with joy. If it should be arid or disturbed, it suddenly feels something like a hand dissipating its ills and doing even more. God wants it to know that He is all powerful and that His words are deeds.... For my part, the same difference lies between these different types of words as between talking and listening. When I talk it is my intellect that understands what I say, but when others talk to me, I only listen and no work is implied."

Thus the action-producing characteristic of the word of God is one of the most important signs. And the words of God create an incomparable tenderness which Teresa defines as "real suavity; sweet, strong, penetrating, delightful and calm which has nothing to do with certain superficial devotions which should not even be called so, that are made up of tears and shallow feelings which, like delicate flowers, fall at the first breath of persecution."

If the visions or internal words are divine, they should be accompanied by obvious spiritual advantage; otherwise, they are suspicious and should be shunned.

The word "rapture" sums up the state Teresa felt at the fourth type of prayer, the highest, which is ecstatic contemplation.

This occurred to her during her stay in the home of Doña Guiomár. The environment was adapted to her efforts of ascent because Doña Guiomár had transformed her palace into a home for great believers who

were advanced in mental prayer. Mother Maridíaz
was also a guest along with Teresa, and the two became
close friends. María Diaz del Vivar was pure and charitable and had dedicated herself to a life of mortifications. She dressed very poorly, and the little food she
took that was so poor in content greatly impressed
those who saw her. But happiness and friendship
reigned in the house. Ten years later, in 1568, Teresa
still mentioned her fervent companion in her letters.
The bond continued for both so that when Mother
Maridíaz drew up her will, she left the only important object she owned, her tunic, to the Convent of
St. Joseph, which Teresa had founded.

Teresa left Doña Guiomár in 1558 and returned to
the Incarnation Convent.

CHAPTER THIRTEEN

Deep Anguish
and Celestial Favors

Fr. Prádanos was transferred at the end of 1558, and again Teresa felt desolate at the departure of her spiritual guide. The most profound souls often feel the greatest need of a guide. Their very humility, fervor, and complexity of aspirations, the terrifying tempests which menace them, the anxious delicacy of their feelings are forces which make them giants and yet children desirous of a leading hand.

That year Baltasar Alvarez was ordained a Jesuit priest in Avila. Born in Cervera in 1534, he became famous because "in him God wished to show His magnificence." [1]

Most of Fr. Prádanos' penitents passed to Fr. Alvarez' guidance; among these were Guiomár de Ulloa, Maridíaz, Anna Reyes, Francisco de Salcedo, and Teresa de Ahumada. The effect of his direction on Teresa was complex and disturbing. Very intelligent, careful, and exceptionally brilliant, he nevertheless was subject to

---

1. Fr. La Fuente, *Life of V. P. Baltasar Alvarez, S.J.*

incomprehension of others because, young as he was,
he was intimidated by the judgments of his elders, who
contributed in disorientating him concerning such a
difficult case as Teresa's. Moreover, the burning atmosphere over Spain at that time caused by illusioned or
false prophets helps to explain the error still further.
St. John of the Cross depicted this period when he said,
"What happens in these days surprises me very much;
if some souls, after a four-cent meditation, hear words,
they immediately refer to them as God's, saying 'God
has told me so' or 'God answered me thus.' They cannot
hear those words without repeating them to everyone,
while their desire for this grows so that they answer
themselves and think that God has answered them. In
this way they go into a frenzy and can no longer control
themselves, and He who governs over these souls does
not interfere to stop these words."[2]

To discern spirits was arduous, and a sense of prudence was common to all the conscientious spiritual
directors of the time due to the great delusions experienced by several mystic illusionists. This explains the
attitude many of the learned and fervent religious of
Avila took regarding Teresa of Jesus. She was really
completely understood by two saints alone, Francis
Borgia and Peter of Alcántara. They resemble two doctors who, years apart, went to the same patient after
many doctors had treated her. But they alone immediately recognized what type of illness was involved. It
was a divine infirmity which caused life on earth to be
difficult since it rendered the creature more celestial
than human.

It was probably in early 1559 that several learned
and religious men, both ecclesiastics and laymen, met
to consider Teresa's exceptional spiritual life and to

---

2. *Subida del Monte Carmelo,* II-XXVII (XXIX); *Works,* S.E.F.

decide whether those mystic favors were of human or demoniacal origin.

Gaspar Daza, Francisco de Salcedo and Gonzalo de Aranda were included in the group, and the meeting coincided with one of the most intense periods of special graces conceded to Teresa. Internal locutions alternated with rapture. The question of judging her spirit had been brought up exactly because those men of prayer had noticed the increasing intensity of supernatural favors which were showered upon her. Three of the men had never met her; Gaspar Daza had not kept up with her after his unsuccessful spiritual direction, leaving Francisco de Salcedo the only one who had always followed her and who referred to the others what Teresa told him. But though de Salcedo was a most fervent and strictly honest man, he had a preconceived notion of perfection which Teresa did not entirely fulfill.

The conclusion this group reached was certainly a sad and dramatic verdict for Teresa and her confessor, Fr. Alvarez, who both had placed great faith in these five men since they represented a sort of multiple consultation which was to emit a definite diagnosis. De Salcedo referred the verdict to Fr. Alvarez instead of to Teresa directly. He, in turn, rather indelicately told her exactly what he had been told. All five of them agreed that Teresa was a victim of the devil and insisted that she not receive Communion often and should try to be distracted so as not to be left in solitude.

Teresa's grief was immeasurable. Considering her sensitivity and love for God, it is almost miraculous that her mind remained balanced through so much anguish at different periods in her life. The following excerpt pictures her state of mind thus: "I was extremely terrified, so much so that I dared not remain alone in a room, not even in the daytime. My heart trouble increased my fears. Seeing, therefore, that so many affirmed what I could not admit, I was over-whelmed by many scruples fearing I was not humble enough. Those men, in fact, were learned and of an incomparably holier life than mine—why should I not have believed their judgment?"[3]

One day, at the height of her affliction, Teresa went to the church of St. Giles and took refuge in an oratory. It was already some time that she had been forbidden to go to Communion and to remain in solitude, the only two things which could comfort her. She had no one in whom she could confide because everyone was against her. Whenever she spoke of her anguish, some would make fun of her, calling her fears self-induced, while others warned her confessor to be careful, subject as she was to the devil.

"I was alone in that oratory without anyone to con-sole me, unable to pray or read because I was op-pressed by my tribulations with a desolate soul over-come by bitterness, and so tormented by the fear of being a victim of the devil that I knew not what to do. I remained in this state for four or five hours without heavenly or earthly consolation. My Lord had aban-doned me in my anguish, prey to a thousand perils."

Just then she clearly heard the following divine words: "Do not fear, daughter, for it is I and I will never abandon you. Do not fear!"

At these words her calmness was restored; she felt courage, security and illumination. Her soul was trans-formed and "ready to uphold the divine source of her grace to the whole world."

Time passed and one day Teresa had a special vi-sion, different from the corporal and imaginary ones contemplated with the eye of the body or with the eye of the imagination. This type of vision could be called intellectual in that it is witnessed wholly by the intel-

---

3. *Life*, XXV and XXVII here and for the following quotations.

lect. "While praying on the feast of St. Peter, I saw, or rather felt, Jesus Christ close to me. I say this because I saw nothing, not with my bodily eyes nor with my soul's eyes.

"It became evident that Christ was near me, and I saw that whoever was talking to me could be no one else. I did not know that one could have such visions, so I began to cry at first from fright. But only one word from this gentle Man sufficed to reassure me, and I again became calm and content as usual. It seemed as though He walked by my side constantly, though I cannot say in what form for it was not one of those which are called images. He always stayed to my right; there was no mistaking the fact. He witnessed whatever I did. Unless I was distracted, there was no time that I did not feel Him near me when I meditated.

"I went to my confessor and told him how things were. He asked under what form I saw Him, and I answered that I did not see Him at all.

"'Then how can you say it is Jesus Christ?' he asked.

"I answered that I did not know, but I could not doubt that He was at my side; it was clear to me, and I simultaneously felt that my pious meditation was much more profound, as in a prolonged prayer in silence, while its effects were very different from usual. I sought to explain it with comparisons but could find none for this type of vision. A very holy man, Fr. Peter of Alcántara, whom I shall later mention, said that this was one of the most sublime visions; other learned men added that it was one of those visions in which the action of the devil is least possible. That is why women of little learning such as I cannot find words to explain ourselves. But the learned will know how to do so.

"I speak of seeing the Lord neither with bodily eyes nor with those of the soul because this vision is not imaginary. Then how can I explain my affirmation that

He is beside me in a more evident manner than if I saw Him with my eyes? To say that the soul is blind, or as one surrounded by darkness, is not exact; a slight similarity exists, but that person can always feel with his senses. There is nothing like that here, and far from being in darkness, it is as though we are flooded by a light clearer than the sun. I do not mean that the sun or any light is seen, yet an unseen light illuminates the intelligence and immerses the soul in exquisite joy, and wonderful advantages are received.

"This presence of God is not like that felt by many during the prayer of quiet or of union. In these it seems at times that when beginning to meditate, we find someone to whom we can speak, and because of our deep religious sense, great faith and love and other tender resolutions, it seems that someone is really listening to us. This is a great grace of God, and whoever is favored with it must hold it in esteem because it is an elevated prayer. But it is not yet a vision. No matter how we understand that God is present, it is possible only through the effects He causes in us that He shows Himself. Here, instead, we see clearly that we are close to Jesus, the Son of the Virgin, in person. In the former, divine influence alone acts, but here we can see even the blessed humanity of Christ accompanying and enriching us."

She continues, explaining, "Let us suppose I were blind or surrounded by darkness, and someone I have never seen before, but of whom I have heard, comes to me. I believe it is he because he tells me so, but I could not affirm it with the same certainty as I could if I had seen him. Here, instead, even without seeing, we are so certain and have such a clear conception of Him that there can be no doubt. The Lord remains so profoundly impressed in us that we are as sure of it as though we had seen Him, even more so, because in this case we could harbor the doubt of having been a victim of some illusion. Such a fear immediately presents itself, even in the graces of which I speak, but the soul is so sure that the doubt quickly vanishes.

"In this favor, God instructs the soul by talking to it without actually talking. It is an absolutely celestial language which could never be taught, no matter how much we tried, unless God Himself taught it by experience.

"He places what He wants to be known in the innermost part of our soul without image or word form, but in the manner of the vision I am talking of."

The soul finds the words of the Lord in it without knowing how they got there and never having been conscious of hearing them. It is as though someone who had never studied and could not write, all at once found he was an erudite person. Teresa also makes an earthy comparison the better to explain the infusion of the divine language in the soul: it is as though the stomach found digested food in it without the mouth ever having swallowed it.

She further explains that it is through these locutions that the soul learns lofty truths of faith. "The soul instantly finds it is wise, clearly seeing into the mystery of the Holy Trinity and other mysteries, ready to discuss with any theologian.

"One of these graces is enough to revivify the soul; it is no longer able to love anything other than Him who showers such favors on it, revealing secrets and showing ineffable proofs of love and friendship."

CHAPTER FOURTEEN

Visions

The "intellectual" vision of which we have been talking lasted continuously for a few days; it was so intense and precious that Teresa hardly ever stopped praying. She applied herself "to perform every action in such a way that could not in the least displease Him who clearly could be seen near."[1]

Still all this could not prevent the momentary fears of deception, but Teresa felt the Lord Himself "bow to reassure her."

Meanwhile, a new series of splendid visions were conceded to her which were to culminate with the famous vision of June 29, 1560, and with the piercing of her heart wrought by the angel.

"One day while I was praying, the Lord deigned to show me His hands. They were of such extraordinary beauty that I could never describe them.

"I always feel disturbed at first whenever there is something new in these supernatural matters, and this

---

1. *Life,* XXVIII, also for the following quotations.

happened again. But after a few days I saw His divine face, and I became completely enraptured.

"I could not understand why the Lord showed Himself to me a little at a time, supposing that He would later let me see Him entirely. But I understood that He did this so my weak nature could adapt itself. May He be blessed forever because such a weak, miserable creature as I could never have resisted such an accumulation of glory. That was the reason the God of goodness prepared me by degrees.

"It may seem not much effort is needed to contemplate such beautiful hands and face, but glorified bodies are of such elevated supernatural beauty and reflect so much glory, we are awestruck. Afraid and disturbed at first, I would become reassured by the effects produced in me."

On January 25, 1558, the feast of St. Paul's conversion, Teresa had one of the loftiest and most complete visions contained in mystical history. "The entire sacred humanity of Christ appeared to me on the Feast of St. Paul while I was at Mass. Jesus looked as He is usually depicted at the resurrection, but of incomparable beauty and majesty. To relate these things spoils them; I shall only say that if heaven be nothing but the enjoyment of seeing the sublime beauty of glorified bodies and especially the body of our Lord, the pleasure will be truly immense."

This vision belongs to the imaginary category because she saw the apparition through the eyes of her soul. According to theologians consulted by Teresa, this type of vision is less perfect than the one described just before which is intellectual, but it is superior to those seen with the physical eyes. Though those seen with bodily eyes were the least perfect, Teresa desired to see that celestial apparition physically so that her confessor could no longer say she was dreaming. Besides, the fear of having dreamed arose in her as soon as the vision vanished.

She would confide these apprehensions to her confessor. He would ask if she were not trying to deceive him, and Teresa would answer that she had spoken the truth in everything and would never speak insincerely to him. Then the confessor would try to calm her, believing all she had told him.

It was a great effort for her to tell of the graces she had received, but she realized that her imagination could never have conceived anything similar to the apparitions. She explained: "The brightness of the light which adorns our Lord surpasses human imagination. It is not glaring, but brightly pleasing, of a glorious splendor which delightfully enchants the eye without fatiguing it. The clarity of that celestial beauty is superior to any terrestrial clarity. Compared to it, the sun seems so faded we would never want to see it again. It is like seeing very limpid water flowing over crystal reflecting the sun's rays, compared to very torpid water flowing through dirt under a cloudy sky. What we see is a natural light which makes the sun's light appear artificial. It is clearness that never diminishes, and since it is eternal nothing will ever cloud it. In short, it is so above everything that even if a highly intelligent person spent his life trying to imagine it, he would not be able to do so. God puts it before us so rapidly that if it were necessary to open our eyes to see it, we would not be quick enough. But it does not matter whether the eyes are closed or open, for when God wishes it, we see even if we don't want to. No distraction can prevent it, nor any power resist it, nor is there any diligence that can find enough obstacles. I have experienced this very well."

After having described certain aspects of the vision in detail, she pointed out other notable characteristics. "At times the Lord shows Himself so majestically that we cannot doubt it is He, especially when the grace is granted after Holy Communion when we know by faith that He is present. He then lets us behold Him as our Master and the soul is entirely absorbed by Him. O my God, who could make others understand the majesty with which You show Yourself, and how You prove You are the absolute Master of the earth, heaven and of all the earths and heavens You could create and of a thousand other worlds!"

She then insisted on a point which is important for a complete evaluation of these visions: that is, the impossibility for the soul to provoke, multiply or prevent them. They do not occur when the soul desires it, but they depend on an external divine force. This also holds true for the passing of it. The soul is completely passive and does nothing but receive the divine gift. This is a very distinctive characteristic and explains the genuine value of the supernatural visions.

Another characteristic is that the soul emerges from the visions remarkably strengthened, more courageous, and more limpid. Teresa does not tire of insisting on this which is basic to distinguish divine visions from diabolical deceptions or natural illusions. The latter, for example, are hallucinations which can be more or less caused by the will and have totally different effects from the supernatural visions. "If we could do something in this vision of divine origin, picturing it to ourselves with our intellect, not only would we not have the effects of the true vision, but no other effect, either, so that we would resemble someone who does everything in order to sleep but still remains awake because sleep does not come. He desires it because he feels he needs it and his head is tired: he gathers all his faculties together, does all to fall asleep, and at times seems almost to drop off, but since it is not a true sleep, he gets no advantage from it; it leaves his head as tired as before or even more so. The same partly happens in hallucinations caused by efforts of the will or otherwise. The soul is exhausted and instead of becoming stronger, feels annoyed and unhappy. Instead, the treasures which are heaped upon it when the vision comes from God cannot be magnified enough. Even the body participates, drawing increased vigor and health."

CHAPTER FIFTEEN

Great Seraphic Joys

For two and one half years the Lord appeared to Teresa often. "At times I notice that He looks upon me most kindly, and His look is so penetrating that my soul can only be absorbed in such great rapture, and when it tries to enjoy the bliss still more, the vision disappears. The will has no strength, which proves that God wishes only humility and surrender, and we are happy with what He gives us and can only deeply thank Him.

"This happens in all visions. We can do absolutely nothing, either to see less or more. It is the will of God, and we are convinced that this grace is not due to any merit of ours, but His. To keep us from becoming proud He lets us understand that just as He can prevent us from seeing what we want to, He can totally suspend His favors, leaving us completely miserable. Naturally we are kept humble and fearful.

"I've seen Him on the cross and in the garden as well as under the weight of the cross; occasionally, with His crown of thorns. He always conformed Himself to my needs or to those of others, but even then His flesh was always glorified."[1]

Teresa's counselors, or judges, became increasingly impressed by this intensifying of her visions. Fr. Alvarez was slowly caught in the wave of fear. Some of Teresa's friends even thought she should be exorcised.

"Notwithstanding such persecutions, I was never displeased to have those divine spectacles. I would never trade one for all the wealth and happiness of the world. I felt my love for God grow daily and confided all my troubles to Him so that I always left prayer-time full of love, consoled and heartened. Seeing that I made matters worse if I answered my opposers by appearing to lack humility, I decided to speak of those things only to my confessor. The latter tried his best to console me in my grief.

"Yet I could not prevent those visions from coming, and I was commanded to make the Sign of the Cross as soon as I saw one coming on, repudiating the vision with scornful gestures. Meanwhile, I was not to fear, for God would surely watch over me and have me liberated."[2]

Teresa's suffering reached its apex. Profoundly convinced as she was that those apparitions came from God, she nevertheless obeyed. She tried to fight them back, and once even went so far as to fork her fingers at one. The sorrow she felt in those moments was ineffable. "At the thought of those actions which Jesus had to bear from the Jews, I begged Him to pardon me for those I performed in obedience to those He had placed in His Church. He would then tell me not to despair because I acted rightly to obey and He would have the truth be seen."

---

1. *Life,* 1, 2, 3, 4, here and for the following.
2. *Life,* XXIX, also for the following quotations.

Christ once answered in a most beautiful and consoling manner. In her obedience, Teresa was to make the sign of the cross continually when a vision appeared. Since this lasted quite a while, she would hold a crucifix in her hands in order not to repeat the Sign of the Cross so often. "Once while I was holding the cross of the rosary in my hands, the Lord took it, and when He returned it to me, there were five large stones on it which were more precious than diamonds. Diamonds seem false and of no value next to them because there is no comparison between earthly and supernatural things. The five wounds of the Lord were finely engraved in them, and He said I would henceforth always see them there. His words came true, for in the cross I no longer saw the wood of which it was made, only the five precious stones, but I alone could see them."

Meanwhile, a grandiose event was taking place in Teresa's soul. Celestial favors showered down upon her with increasing frequency. Even though she wished to be distracted, she was no longer able to suspend prayer, and she felt immersed in it all day long. She never ceased to lovingly tell God her troubles, saying she could no longer bear that torture. No matter how she tried, it was impossible for her not to think of God. She tried to obey as best she could, but to no avail.

Though the Lord continued to appear before her, He always advised her to obey, assuring her that He was God and telling her how she should answer her opposers. From then on, He had her understand still better how those visions came from Him. Teresa's soul began to glow with such ardent love for God "that I knew not whence it came. It was so very supernatural that I had no part in it. I burned in my yearning to see God. He was my life, and I could not seek Him anywhere except in death. The emotion caused by this love became increasingly violent so that I knew not what to do. Nothing could calm me. I was no longer myself, and it seemed as though my soul was being drawn from my body. O the sublime workings of my Lord! What gentle, cunning devices You did use on such a wretched slave! You hid from my sight, yet Your love penetrated every fiber, plunging me into a sweet agony from which I would never have departed.

"The emotions of which I speak are altogether different from those derived from devotions of the senses. Here we do not kindle the fire, for the fire seems already lighted, and we seem to be thrown into it, too, so that we may be burned up. The creature sighs for God's presence, but the pain is caused by an arrow which pierces the heart and entrails so deeply that the creature is left incapable of doing or desiring anything. It understands only that it wants God. The arrow which pierces it seems moistened with an herb juice which goads it still more to hate itself and to love God for whom it would die.

"The way such wounds are made is inexpressible. They are so tortuous that at first the soul is beside itself with pain, but at the same time so sublime as not to be compared to any earthly joy. This is why the soul would always rather die as the result of these wounds.

"So much torment united to so much joy greatly stupefied me, and I could not understand how this all happened.

"How amazed the soul is to see these wounds. It can certainly say it has been wounded because of what it feels, but all is due to the great love of God which the soul did nothing to attract, but with which it is now consumed. How often do I remember David's passage which fits me exactly when I am in this state: 'Just as the stag sighs for water at the fountain, so does my heart sigh for You, O my Lord.'

"Meanwhile, not knowing what else to do, the soul searches for a remedy. When that ecstatic bliss is not so violent, it seems that acts of penance can calm it down.

But the body seems inanimate and feels no pain even if blood flows. In any way it wants to suffer for God, but that first torment is so great that no bodily pain can calm it. No remedy or medicine can help whatsoever. Only God can give us the remedy to mitigate the torture, rendering it bearable. There is nothing left for the soul but death, for only then can it totally enjoy His bliss.

"At times the emotion is so violent that nothing can be done, not even call for help from God. The body seems dead, unable to move. If the person is standing, the body slumps heavily on itself without even the strength to breathe. Unable to bear more, a sort of weak groan escapes, stifled by the great feeling.

"Several times it pleased the Lord to favor me with the following vision: to my left I would see an angel in bodily form. It was rare for me to see angels so, because I had hitherto always seen them with the intellect alone. This time it pleased God to have me see the angel thus; he was not large, but small and very beautiful. His glowing face resembled those sublime spirits which seem to be full of love—I believe they are called cherubs. They never tell me what they are called, but there is such a great difference between certain angels and others and between themselves that I would not know how to explain this.

"The cherub held a long golden arrow in his hand. A small fire seemed to burn at the arrow's iron tip, and it was as though he pierced my heart with it several times, going deep inside my body, leaving me enveloped in a furnace of love when he pulled out the arrow. The spasm due to the wound overwhelmed me so that I uttered groans, yet the feeling was so elevated that I did not wish it to end, and I could think of nothing else except God.

"Even though this is not a physical but a spiritual pain, the body participates, too. Then the sweetest contentment takes place; I pray divine goodness to permit those who do not believe me to have the same happen to them.

"I was beside myself whenever this occurred, and I would see or talk to no one, preferring to remain alone in my torment, which to me seemed the greatest joy that could ever exist.

"This was the grace God deigned to grant me several times before it pleased Him to send me those raptures which were so great that they even spread over me in the presence of others, unable as I was to resist them, but I was extremely delighted.

"Now this agony of desire has become somewhat mitigated, but I feel that other loftier one which I have already mentioned: the Lord ravishes the soul with delight, engulfing it with a glory saturated with joy, when there is no longer pain or the possibility of pain. Blessed be God who exchanges such favors for the ingratitude of those who reciprocate His immense benefits so poorly!"

CHAPTER SIXTEEN

Peter of Alcántara

Toward the middle of August in 1560, Teresa was consoled regarding her secret fears of diabolical delusions.

At that time, a tall, thin friar, whose eyes always bore an expression of ascetic defense, and whose name was Peter of Alcántara, came to Avila. He was one of the greatest saints of Spain.

When Teresa saw him, she said he gave her the impression of being made of tree roots: he was so bony and thin. But she found him extraordinarily affable. He spoke little, then only to answer questions asked of him, but his words were very appropriate and penetrating.

Doña Guiomár de Ulloa planned the meeting. Knowing how Teresa suffered, she thought the friar could help her friend. Friar Peter was well known in Spain, for his penances were famous, his mystic exaltation stupefying and edifying, notwithstanding that the highest details were secret. So Doña Guiomár obtained permission for Teresa to spend eight days in her home where the two met.[1] Teresa had been informed of his life so that she could appreciate him. She even traced a brief biography of him. Born in Alcántara d'Estremadura in 1499, at seventeen he entered the Franciscan Order. At Pedroso in 1540 he initiated a reform which was named after him: the "Alcantarian" reform.[2]

The two spoke uninhibited by human fears. They talked openly of God, each informing the other about details of their exceptional lives without bothering about vanity. "He told me that for forty years he has been sleeping an hour and a half out of twenty-four. He said that in the beginning his most arduous penance was this one of overcoming sleepiness; to fight it off he would remain standing or kneeling. That little rest which he granted himself was taken sitting with his head resting against a peg he had fixed in the wall. Besides, he couldn't have lain down even if he had wanted to because his cell, as is well known, was no more than four and one-half feet long. In all this time, he has never covered his head with his hood, no matter how the sun burned or how hard it rained. He has never worn shoes, and he has only a habit of sackcloth with a cloak of the same material to wear over it. He said that when winter was at its coldest, he would take off his cloak and open the door and window of his cell so that he could later satisfy his body a little by putting his cloak back on to rest in that bit of warmth. He was accustomed to eating every three days. When I marveled at this, he said that this is most possible once the habit is formed. A companion of his assured me that at times he went eight days without food. I believe this

---

1. See Fr. Silverio I, 24, for the conversations with Friar Peter.

2. Peers writes: "Except for two young contemporaries, St. John of the Cross and Fr. Jerónimo Gracián, no man influenced her personality so much as this old Franciscan Friar who met her near the end of his long religious life" [Studies of Spanish Mystics].

occurred when he was immersed in prayer because I know he was subject to raptures and great ecstatic exaltations with love of God, and I once had the good fortune of witnessing one of these periods.

"His poverty is extreme. He has been mortifying himself from the time he was a youth. He told me that he never raised his eyes from the ground. In fact, after three years in a monastery, he recognized his fellow friars by their voices. Whenever he was to go to another monastery he did so by following the others, for he would never have succeeded alone. When he traveled, it was the same. He had not looked a woman in the face for many years. Indeed, he said that to see or not to see was the same thing to him. When he realized he was about to die, he recited the Psalm, 'I rejoiced for the things that were said to me,' then knelt and died." [3]

These two great saints facing each other were a contrast. The Franciscan represented the apex of reserve and mortification, a true personification of superhuman austerity. On the other hand, the Carmelite maintained a natural vivaciousness that pertained to her character. A curious testimony was given by a nun who was one of Teresa's nieces: "My aunt was so full of life and free in her ways that most people could not believe how much of a saint she was!" Yet the same grace filled both, calling them to be reformers.

Friar Peter's example no doubt incited her on her way to a more austere life. But for the moment, Teresa was still a soul in need of help. She was wounded by an insatiable love, brooding over a nightmarish suspicion and was bruised by an obedience which forced her to struggle against God whom she loved. She spoke to the friar openly, telling both the good and the bad about herself. She was seeking the truth even if it should throw her into a barren desert if deprived of prayer.

---

3. *Life,* XXVII, 17.

"I told him all my secret thoughts without dissimu-
lation. From the very beginning I knew that he understood me from personal experience. This was exactly
what I needed because I did not yet have that enlightenment which I now possess to explain what happened
in me. It was later that God gave me the grace to
understand and to have others understand what favors
He granted me. Thus, it was necessary that one had
personally experienced the same things in order to
understand me.

"I was not yet ready to perceive the visions in
which there were no images, and this saint helped me
greatly on this point. Similarly, he set me straight regarding what I saw with the soul's eyes, since I thought
I should give importance only to those visions which
were imaginable, and which permit the eyes of the
body to see. I had never been thus favored.

"He explained and elucidated everything, telling
me to stop fearing, but to thank God because, leaving
aside the truths of the faith, there could be nothing to
believe more securely than that the Spirit of God
worked in me. He congratulated me, showing kindness
and esteem toward me. Even later he always treated
me with respect, telling me of his thoughts and plans;
seeing that the Lord had infused such courageous
thoughts in me to do as he had done, he would talk to
me visibly satisfied."[4]

Those talks which took place in Doña Guiomár's
home or in the Mosén Rubi Chapel were probably the
most important in Teresa's life, impressing their mark
on her work.

Friar Peter's response reflected the intellectual
comprehension and human sympathy which she
needed. "He felt deep sympathy for me and told me
that the most serious trial of my life was what I had

---

4. *Life,* XXX, here and for the following.

just suffered—that of contradiction of rights. He prophesied that I still had much to suffer, for needful as I was of continuous assistance, there was no one in the city who could understand me. At any rate, he would talk to my confessor and to that married man who oppressed me the most." Friar Peter spoke to Fr. Alvarez and to Don Francisco de Salcedo. "My confessor did not need it as much as did the other one who was still not entirely convinced. Ever since then, however, he has no longer tormented me as much as before."

Peter of Alcántara left Avila with Teresa profoundly relieved and reassured. She was to notify him of anything important or new happening to her, and they promised to pray for each other.

CHAPTER SEVENTEEN

The Darkness of the Spirit

Teresa was still not at the end of her marvelous repertoire of spiritual suffering. There approached a period of barrenness and of moral and physical agonies. After Peter of Alcántara left her "fully comforted," she found herself in frail health and again alone in the midst of friends who did not understand her. Her human fears again returned sporadically, and there were hours of desert dullness.

It was true martyrdom when both her spiritual tortures and physical ailments came at the same time. "Then I would forget the favors I had received, remembering only a distant dream which increased my suffering. My mind would become clouded and a thousand doubts and anxieties would envelop me. It seemed as though I could not understand what was happening in me, and I wondered if it were all in my imagination. And then I would think, 'Why draw others into this delusion? Wasn't it enough that I alone be deceived?' I would become so pessimistic with myself that I would begin to think that all the evil and heresy in the world were due to my sins."[1]

Once, two days before the Feast of Corpus Christi, she underwent a temptation that lasted until the feast day. Her mind became suddenly filled with frivolous thoughts which would have made her laugh at other times. Her soul seemed clouded over, clogged up and disturbed by a heap of silly deformities. "Demons seemed to be playing ball with my soul, and I could not free myself from their hands."

It is impossible to explain such suffering. She sought aid everywhere while God permitted her not to find it. All that was left was the will which was weak. The soul felt blindfolded as though walking down a well-known path on a dark night; the only reason it did not fall was that it remembered where the obstacles were. "This is our case because if we don't commit sin, it is that we act according to habit, taking for granted, of course, the continual assistance of God."

In this state of darkness, faith and the other virtues remain. The soul is attached to the Church's teachings. Faith, however, is weakened and very drowsy; the acts of faith are nothing but sounds on the lips. The soul feels chained down, tired, and the very meaning of God is vague and distant. Love for God has become so lukewarm that the soul admits what is said of God because it is faith taught by the Church, but no longer remembers that which it had once felt. If it tries to meditate or go into seclusion, the difficulties become still greater. "The indefinite pain felt deep within us is truly unbearable and seems to be one of hell's torments; it is that because God deigned to let me see this in a vision later. The soul feels a devouring fire within itself. Not knowing from where it came or who lit it, we are unable to escape or extinguish it. If we seek

---

1. *Life,* XXX, here and for the following.

comfort in reading, it seems as though we cannot read. Once when I wanted to divert my thoughts from these pains, I wanted to read the life of a saint to see if I could be consoled. It was written in Castilian, and I read several lines over four or five times but understood less of the contents each time so that I had to give it up. This occurred to me quite often, but I only remember this incident distinctly."

Yet this was not all. Other trials came upon Teresa. One involved the rebellion of her intellect and imagination. They rebelled against the will which was peaceful and well-disposed. They were as violent, mad men who could not be chained down. The will could not control them, not even for the length of time it took to recite the Credo.

At other times, a terrible spiritual nausea would come over Teresa and everything disgusted her. Then she would busy herself with some external good work, much as she knew that a soul can do little without the grace of God. "When, O Lord, will I see my soul taken up entirely with Your praises? When will my faculties be able to enjoy You in unison? O my Lord, do not permit my soul to be so divided within itself. I feel it is all in tatters, separately falling apart."

Another negative state was that one which she called her "spiritual numbness." "I do neither good nor evil, but follow others without pain or consolation. Life, death, joy, suffering are all indifferent to me for the soul has no feeling. It is as an ass which grazes without realizing it and is thus nourished. No effect or inner feeling is perceived. Yet, unawares to the soul, God is maintaining it with sublime grace in reward for such calm resignation to this wretched life. In this way the soul greatly advances."

Horrible visions complicated her spiritual night, but Teresa showed herself courageous before them. They were external temptations that corresponded to the internal ones which were directed at frightening the soul.

"Once in an oratory, a devil with a horrible appearance became visible to my left. His mouth drew my attention particularly because he spoke to me. He was absolutely abominable. A great flame seemed to project itself out which illuminated him without casting a shadow. In a terrifying voice he said that if I had escaped his hands once he would catch me another time. I was terrified and made the Sign of the Cross the best I could. He disappeared, but he returned almost immediately. This went on for two or three times so I did not know how to free myself. I then took holy water and sprinkled it all about the oratory, and the devil never returned." [2]

Teresa underwent several demoniacal apparitions, but she succeeded in being impassive to them so the devil was staggered by this. The cross and the holy water were her weapons of defense. "These cursed spirits torment me often, but they hardly frighten me now, for I see that they cannot even move without God's permission. All this should help true Christians to disdain the phantasms with which the demons try to frighten them. We know that each time we despise them, their vigor is diminished, and the soul acquires an increasingly strong dominion over them."

---

2. *Life*, XXXI, here and for the following.

CHAPTER EIGHTEEN

A Song of Simplicity

There is another chapter in Teresa's life which may be called the "song of simplicity." Throughout her entire life, Teresa was subject to worries dictated by a most simplified humility.

"It was a cruel torment for me at times and still is, to see myself esteemed and praised by important people. It has made me suffer much. Turning to the life of Jesus or of a saint, I felt I was walking down an opposite road because they were surrounded by insults and affronts. Fear would overcome me so that I dared not raise my head, wishing to hide myself from all eyes.

"I was different, however, during my persecutions. Though my body felt them and was grieved, the soul became so elevated that not even I could understand how this could be. The soul seemed to reign supreme."[1] The mark of a direct and immense experience is evident in these words because only someone who had profoundly lived through it could explain the concept so skillfully.

---

1. *Life,* XXX and XXXI for all the quotations in this chapter.

Her fear of being esteemed, praised, and even venerated assailed her, and she believed that her distress
derived from a virtuous feeling of humility, only later
seeing it in its true light.

"Meanwhile, the thought of making public God's
favors to me made me feel miserable, preferring to be
buried alive rather than be present when the news
spread. Later, when my pious concentration and raptures became so violent that I was unable to conceal
them from the public eye, I became so embarrassed I
would never see anyone again if that were possible."

She would go so far as to entreat God to enlighten
those who had faith in her, beseeching Him to show
them her faults so that they could judge her accord-
ingly. Yet she felt a growing wave of interest and stupor
about her which caused her to be exasperated. She
probably felt imprisoned by everyone's esteem and
sought a way out. Gradually, the idea of leaving the
Incarnation Convent and the people of Avila who were
beginning to know too much about her took hold more
and more. "The temptation was so strong that I had
decided to leave the city with my dowry for another
convent where I had heard there were more severe
cloister rules. It was of the same Order, but quite
distant so that no one would know me. But my confessor never consented to this." The reason for this denial
is clear. Teresa's need for concealment was excessive
and reflected inner misgivings. Evidently, her act of
humility was defective and resembled temptation
which proved she was lacking in simplicity. To submit
to her inner desire for satisfaction and calm would have
meant following a false humility. Christ Himself gave
her the best explanation of this when He appeared to
her one day. "What do you fear? Either of two things
can happen: slander against you or glory toward me."
He let her understand that those who believed in her
divine favors would glorify Him, whereas the others

would unjustly condemn Teresa. Since either way she lost nothing, there was no reason to be distressed. "The Lord let me see that all those graces which I possessed came only from Him, without my having merited them. Therefore, just as I did not become saddened to hear other people praised, but rather rejoiced to see the gifts of God shine forth from them, I was to stop being sad if those gifts shone in me."

She then realized how all her fears had revealed imperfect humility and not enough mortification. "When a soul submits itself entirely to God, it should no longer worry about what is said concerning it, be it good or bad, knowing as it does that all comes from God. We must trust in Him, who, having filled us with His grace, knows why He wants to render them (God's gifts) public."

The triumph of Teresa's struggle for simplicity signifies another step toward perfection. At this point, Teresa realized how the world is indulgent to the mediocre, but exacting to the great. Whoever resolves to walk on the road of perfection is closely watched for a false move. "The only merit the world has to my eyes is that of not permitting the good to have faults and obliging them to correct themselves by murmuring against them. According to the world, those who strive for perfection should neither eat nor sleep, nor even breathe for that matter. The higher we are esteemed, the more they forget we are still made of flesh. No matter the degree of perfection reached, as long as one remains on earth he is subject to its miseries."

There is one conclusion to draw from all this: if you wish to become perfect without severing the world completely, it will surely trample over you with its blows. That is why a soul that is not yet free of every defect needs more courage to travel the road of perfection than it does to undergo quick martyrdom. We must avoid excessive depression and presumption. We must simply, totally and actively accept what God sends us. Never trust in yourself. We can practice the virtue of detachment for years, believing we have acquired it. Then one fine day we realize we don't possess it at all. Some family affection turns up, some interest, or dominating bent. Above all, we must escape from our "point of honor," for it only serves to break up the whole harmony of things. "First we try to unite ourselves intimately with God and follow Christ's advice after He was slandered and spit upon...and then we pretend to preserve our own honor and reputation whole. These roads are too different, and we shall never get to our goal. God unites Himself only with those who deny themselves and who do not fear losing their own rights frequently.

"For the love of God, I beseech you to take heed of these words which come from an ant whom God has commanded to speak."

CHAPTER NINETEEN

The Beginning of the Reform

There is a moment in all great lives which marks the full maturation of the capacities needed to create new things. It usually comes after long years of preparation and resembles "noon" in the personality.

Prayer, solitude, austerity, and a zeal for souls were the four aspects in which Teresa's Carmelite soul glowed.

But in Teresa's religious elevation the Carmelite spirit as she saw it in the sixteenth century was no longer sufficient for her. The Convent of the Incarnation was good enough and housed many fervent souls, but its habits were now deprived of that austere and penitential vigor which the Carmelite Order had had in the beginning. Teresa was not the only one to feel this, for there were many inconveniences. First of all, there were too many nuns—almost one hundred and eighty; consequently it was impossible to avoid bustle and fuss. There were no strict cloister rules; the nuns could leave the convent for lengthy periods of time. This disturbed concentration and the development of unison of spirituality which, when mastered, constitutes a single sigh of love toward God.

The beginnings of the Order had been indeed different. About 1100 A.D., there were several monasteries on Mount Carmel dedicated to the Blessed Virgin Mary. During the first crusade, Bertoldo of Malafaida, a beggar of noble birth, became a member of that hermit community and was elected general. Toward 1205, St. Albert, Archbishop of Jerusalem, wrote the rule by which the hermits of Mount Carmel were to live. Under Pope Innocent IV this rule became modified on behalf of St. Simon Stock even though it still maintained its original characteristic of austerity.

But many events had altered the rule from then until Teresa's times. The black plague had ravaged Europe repeatedly in the fourteenth and fifteenth centuries and had ruined the health of three generations. The effects of the plague were felt within monastery walls because it seemed impossible for such weakened bodies to maintain the strict observances. This is how the movement to lighten the original austerity developed into a "Mitigation Bull" granted by Eugene IV on February 15, 1432. It permitted meat to be eaten three days a week, and Pope Pius II later added a fourth. Greater liberty was permitted regarding solitude and silence. In addition to physical mitigation, the rule continually underwent a spiritual weakening in cloistered principles.

This was the situation when Teresa began to feel her environment insufficient for her need for mortification. One evening several nuns were gathered in Teresa's cell: Juana Suárez, Inés and Ana de Tapia, Leonora de Ocampo, and young María de Ocampo, a boarding-school girl. The latter two were daughters of Teresa's cousin, Diego. The conversation fell on the religious life led by the Discalced Franciscans who had left the mitigated convent of Avila for the one in Madrid to live the rule in its original vigor. By analogy, they discussed how simple, austere, and delightful life must have been on Mount Carmel, so different from the distraction that reigned presently in the Carmelite Convents.

Young María de Ocampo then exclaimed: "If a house could be established for living according to the original rules, I would offer my thousand ducats inheritance." The others turned to her, stunned and filled with admiration. María was smiling and her eyes shone brightly. Teresa sensed how serious the words had been and thought the sum of money would be enough to found the house. That evening's conversational hour was to become historical because the founding of one of the most serious movements of religious life was then laid down.

Teresa told Doña Guiomár about it, who said she was willing to do all she could to help such a saintly project and immediately began to collect funds for the future convent.

The project was only at the beginning stage, and a strange inner conflict began to take hold of Teresa. From a human point of view she was well off at the Incarnation Convent; she had become accustomed to the place and was loved by her convent sisters. Teresa's spirit desired a more elevated place, but her sensibility for human things was still alive in spite of her lofty visions. She was attached to her cell, for she liked that big room which looked out over the garden, the hills, and wide valley.

Arguments such as these did not count, of course, when it was a question of deciding. Then she thought only of the spiritual ones which were in the interest of God. But what would the reaction be in the city? One day our Lord appeared to her and "ordered me decidedly to work with all my might to put our plan into action, assuring me that the convent would be founded and He would look upon it kindly. He wished it to be dedicated to St. Joseph who would stand guard at one door, the Madonna at the other, and Jesus with us, so that the convent would become a resplendent star."[1]

She realized that a number of contrasting and inevitable difficulties awaited whoever undertook such a project and therefore had no illusions concerning the problem. Yet it was clear that God was commanding her to get to work on it because the vision was repeated. Teresa decided to talk to Fr. Alvarez about it.

As usual he was very prudent. He did not prohibit it, but neither did he nurture illusions concerning human possibilities. The financial problem appeared to be a great obstacle. Doña Guiomár had little at her disposal. Her children had a right to the Salobralejo patrimony, and she neither could nor wished to impoverish them. Her own income barely covered the expenses of her hospitable house which was always open to the religious and to the God-loving. Young María's thousand ducats would be slow in coming and several differences had to be settled before the payment could be effected. Then, too, how could the nuns live after the convent had been built?

Before acting in any direction, Teresa and Guiomár consulted Peter of Alcántara and Luis Beltran. They both encouraged the two women so they decided to ask permission from the Carmelite superiors. Guiomár spoke to the provincial, Fr. Gregory Fernández, obtaining his permission.

The practical necessities were to be settled now. The established number of nuns was thirteen. But just then, the most difficult obstacle began to be felt— persecution. "As soon as our plans were known in the city, a violent persecution, which would be too long to

---

1. *Life*, XXXII, here and for the following.

tell, fell upon us. There was gossip and laughter everywhere. Our project was termed mad, and they said I
was well off where I was. This abuse grieved my companion immensely. I knew not what to do because I
saw that they were partly right."

If that happened outside the convent, what then
happened inside? It was like a revolution. After twenty-
five years there, one of the best known among them
wished to leave everything and everyone and even
thought of starting a reform in the Order! Didn't the
convent seem regulated enough for her? Was the religious spirit in it insufficient for her? Did she mean then
that all the others there were apathetic and lukewarm
toward God?

Guiomár decided the best thing to do would be to
ask the most highly esteemed theologian of the city,
Fr. Pedro Ibañez, for advice. When she and Teresa
disclosed their problem to him, he asked for eight days
to think the matter over.

He later told Teresa what surprising changes in
thought he had undergone during that week. Having
examined the matter in all its aspects, he felt bound by
duty to reply "no" to the project. So he set about
finding the most adaptable words with which to state
his verdict. They were difficult to find; the more
Fr. Ibañez reflected, the more difficult it became to put
down the reasons for his "no." In reality, all those two
women were asking was to live more intimately united
with God in a very saintly manner. Why go against
them so? Indeed, they were but two creatures of God
who had offered themselves to God. And gradually,
Fr. Ibañez's "no" became "yes." In fact, when they
came for his answer he told them to hurry. "If there is
little income, all you will need to do is have more faith
in the Providence of God." He also added that if anyone had anything to say against this undertaking, just

send them to him, and he would put them in their place.[2]

They were relieved and overjoyed with Fr. Ibañez's assuring answer. One consolation led to another. Even Gaspar Daza and Francisco de Salcedo had deeply pondered the matter and came out realizing that it was a means to higher perfection. Spiritual difficulties cleared up, they set out to find a solution to their financial problem.

---

2. See Fr. Silverio II, 2, for Fr. Ibañez's reply.

CHAPTER TWENTY

External Oppositions and Grand Internal Elevations

Contrary to all expectations, Fr. Fernández, the provincial, who was therefore Teresa's direct superior, changed his mind. He didn't feel like combating a host of enemies to the new foundation, so he called Doña Guiomár to tell her that the income was not secure and was definitely not enough. How was it possible to live on alms when the entire city was against them? The whole thing appeared much too absurd for him. Hearing that this was the Provincial's opinion, Teresa's confessor, Fr. Alvarez, also prohibited her from going on with the project. "I gave the thing up, notwithstanding the trials and opposition I had borne."

Their adversaries rejoiced, terming the event a "woman's dream." Almost all the nuns considered the attempted reform as an affront and felt that punishment was in order. Though imprisonment in the convent cell for that purpose was spoken of, Teresa was not led there because no matter how heated the reaction was, charity reigned over the convent, and Teresa was too respected and loved to receive such punishment.

Oddly enough, Teresa felt calm through it all. "The Lord granted me the famous grace of remaining calm so I abandoned everything easily and happily, as though getting that far had cost me nothing. But no one would believe that I was serene, thinking I should be deeply upset. My confessor used to encourage me endlessly. But I felt I had done all I was able to and was no longer obliged to carry out God's command, so I simply lived my quiet, relatively leisurely life in the convent. Yet I was always certain that the foundation would be made, but I knew not when or where."[1]

During this interim, "those great transports of love, followed by most elevated raptures, awoke in my soul." At times it seemed as though her soul would rise away from itself as a great fire flaming high. We have now entered the most stupendously exciting degree of prayer named the "fourth water." It is surprising to find these contemplative jewels in the midst of an active and obstacle-laden life such as Teresa led to bring about the Carmelite reform. We shall now penetrate the "ecstatic union" which is subdivided into three types: simple ecstasy, which comes on slowly and gradually, not at all violent; rapture, which is sudden and violent; and the spirit's flight, when the rapture is so overwhelming the soul seems to leave the body.

"While the creature is seeking God, it seems to lose its senses because of a powerfully sweet spiritual happiness; breathing becomes difficult, physical movements are at a standstill, so much so that to move the hands entails deep suffering; the eyes close automatically, but if they are kept open, almost nothing is discernable. If one is reading, not only is it impossible to pronounce a word, but the word cannot even be distinguished. One

---

1. *Life*, XXXIII, here and for the following.

hears, but what is heard cannot be understood. The senses do not function. It is impossible to utter a word, both for incapability of forming it and for lack of strength to pronounce it. All physical powers are concentrated in the soul, enriching its energy to make it happier.

"No matter how long this prayer lasts, no harm can be done. If the Lord takes away our strength during that excessive joy, He gives us more when the vision has passed. At first this favor lasts but a short time, so it was for me in any case. When it is so fleeting it is not very strong, sensibility is not suspended, nor are there any outward signs. Superabundant grace fills the soul after a very brilliant streak of light has passed over it.

"In my estimation the vision must never last very long, never exceeding a half hour, and I don't believe mine were ever that long. Since there is no perception, it is impossible to measure the time, but all one's faculties remain suspended for only a short time because one or the other comes to intermittently. The will alone remains absorbed, while the other two disturb it from time to time. However, if the will remains steadfastly quiet, it succeeds in suspending the other two again. These remain quiet until they again succumb to their natural mobility."

This is one of the most complete and accurate descriptions of mystical phenomena. Teresa continues to analyze and describe all the details, aspects, and developments of the loftiest degrees of mental prayer with perspicacious intelligence. "When this union and prayer end, the soul remains filled with a great tenderness that makes it want to annihilate itself, crying tears of joy which fall bounteously and unnoticed. The soul leaves this prayer full of courage, ready to joyfully accept being torn to pieces for God. This is the hour of great promises and heroic resolutions. The world is seen in all its vanity, and we abhor it."[2] Teresa is stupendously penetrating in her study of the difference between union and rapture. "The rapture far surpasses union in grand effects and other ways. To me, union is the beginning, the middle and the end of the rapture which develops entirely in the soul. The rapture is of a very elevated order which operates both in the soul and body.

"It seems as though the soul detaches itself from the body during these raptures. In fact, the body perceptibly loses its natural bodily heat, becoming gradually cooler, yet there is unspeakable joy and happiness. In union we can still resist even if it costs pain and violence because we can master ourselves; here, however, it is not usually possible. Oftentimes, the rapture prevents any thought or cooperation whatsoever, for it assails us so violently that we suddenly feel lifted by that cloud[3] and are carried on the wings of that powerful eagle.

"I say you notice, or feel rather, that you are being carried, but you don't know where. At first we are a bit afraid for our nature is weak; that is why we must have a more resolute and courageous soul here than in the preceding states. We must risk everything in the hands of God; since He even takes us against our will, no matter what happens, we must let ourselves be led willingly.

"When I felt such great violence, especially in public or even alone, I used to wonder if I were not the victim of some illusion and, therefore, resisted with all my strength. If I succeeded, I became so exhausted as though having battled with a giant. When my efforts

---

2. *Life,* XIX, 1, 2.

3. She has already referred to the image of the cloud to indicate God.

availed nothing, my soul was carried away; my head fell back without my being able to control it, while even my body would rise into the air.

"But this did not occur many times.

"One day this rapture overcame me while I was kneeling together with the other nuns ready to receive Holy Communion. This troubled me greatly because I knew it was too extraordinary for the matter not to cause a stir. The same thing happens to me yet, but since I am the Prioress, I have forbidden the nuns to speak of it.

"At other times when I realized that the Lord was about to grant me this grace, I would prostrate myself on the floor. Once, when I did this on the feast of the Epiphany while listening to the sermon together with many women of high society, they ran to help me up. The vision came over me anyway."[4]

An eyewitness, Sr. Petronia of St. John the Baptist related that once a rapturous vision overcame Teresa while she was listening to Fr. Domingo Báñez, who was talking to the community of St. Joseph's Convent in Avila. The priest uncovered his head and remained in devout silence until the vision passed.

Many times she sought to resist the rapture, but whenever she did this, she felt lifted off her feet with an impetuosity that far surpassed her former visions, and she came out of it torn to pieces. Her great battle for humility made her well aware of the fact that when God wishes, our efforts avail nothing. So Teresa begged the Lord not to grant her any more favors which bore external manifestations, and her prayer seemed to be answered, for it never happened again.

---

4. *Life,* XX, 1, 3, 4, 5.

Important moral effects occurred in connection with those splendid favors. First of all was the certainty of God's omnipotence. She saw that when God willed it, she had no command over either body or soul. In this manner, an ever deeper humility took root in her. Another effect was the extraordinary, indescribable detachment which overcame her.

CHAPTER TWENTY-ONE

Persecution

All through these sublime favors, Teresa continued to obey. She maintained absolute silence for five or six months and never worried about her unfinished project, nor did she hear any more commands from God about it. She could not understand the absence of inspiration, but was still sure the foundation would be established. Not much later, divine communications favoring the foundation started again, and even Teresa's confessor, St. Gile's new rector, Fr. Gaspar de Salazar, permitted her to dedicate herself wholeheartedly to the undertaking. With renewed vigor, she picked up the threads where she had dropped them. She worked cautiously, fully conscious of the impossibility of overcoming the opposition. The only feasible thing to do was to work secretly so that Avila would wake up some morning to find the foundation already there.

Teresa went to see her sister Juana who had married Juan de Ovalle in 1553, and who was now living in Alba de Tormes. "Why don't we put your name to the house I shall buy so that you and your husband could do the remodeling as though for yourselves? What can the people find to say against your wanting to settle in Avila, and preparing your home!" Juana hesitated at first, but ended by smiling at the idea of the adventure. Not long after, Juana and her husband moved into the small house Teresa had bought. Masons and carpenters were called to transform the house into a convent. Since the de Ovalles lived there directing the workers, Teresa could go there often with the pretext of visiting her sister. That was when two splendid visions came to console her.

The visions of St. Clare came to her on August 12, 1561, and on August 15; during this latter one the Madonna, who was accompanied by St. Joseph, put a luminous cloak and gold chain on her. The Madonna also said that the convent would be founded and that her Son would live there between her and St. Joseph.

But worldly persecution was still rampant. Some preachers discussed the problem in the pulpit as though referring to a public calamity. One evening in the church of St. Thomas a crowd, including important members of the town, was gathered to hear the sermon. Teresa, too, was present with her sister Juana and her husband. The preacher began by condemning certain projects of reform which seemed to lead nowhere as far as he could see. "There are some nuns," he said, "who want to leave the convent they are in and so jump at this pretext." He forcefully explained how these ideas were based on nothing but vanity and pride.

Needless to say, a general excitement ran through the crowd, all the more because Teresa was there even though she listened impassively, as if nothing unusual were going on. Those who could see her noted that she was serene and looked as happy as usual. But Juana was most annoyed, and upon returning home, she insisted that Teresa go back to her tranquil convent life and give up those thoughts of reform which put everyone in a dither. Teresa only smiled, feeling better after being publicly humiliated than if she had been crowned. As she later wrote, the soul elevates itself when persecuted and considers all worldly things beneath it.

Work on the foundation continued slowly and secretly. A request had been sent to Rome for the foundation brief.

In November, 1561, a son of the de Ovalles, Gonzalo, who was five or six years old, remained at home while his parents went out with Teresa. On their return, Juana stopped in an anteroom to receive a woman who had come to call on her. In another room Juan, her husband, saw his son lying on the floor lifeless. His father tried desperately to revive him, but the child remained motionless and deathly white. Juan then took the boy to Teresa, placing him in her arms. Meanwhile, the visiting woman was notified to keep the boy's mother busy for some time for fear the shock would harm Juana who was with child.

Teresa, Juan and servants were in the next room silent with anguish. What had happened? Had he perhaps struck his temple while playing? Teresa held him tightly to her, covering him with her veil and inwardly crying to the Lord to spare such terrible pain to the child's parents. At that moment Juana entered and, instantly excited, asked what had happened. Teresa signaled to her to keep calm, as did the others. Juana thought that a momentary disturbance had come over the child and so remained still and silent with the others in hopeful expectation.

After a few moments the child began to breathe and extended his hand to caress his aunt's face in a deeply significant manner. Then Teresa, giving thanks to God, handed the child to his mother.

CHAPTER TWENTY-TWO

Toledo

At this point, the action transfers to Toledo. Though work on the foundation was carried on secretly, a certain amount of curiosity arose, and there were doubts about the true nature of the remodeling; furthermore, the situation was complicated by an unforeseen event.

A widow, Luisa de la Cerda, who was the daughter of the second Duke of Medinaceli who belonged to one of the most aristocratic families of Spain, lived in the "imperial city." Her late husband, Don Antonio Arias Pardo de Saavedra, was considered the richest and the most titled man of New Castile. Upon his death, Doña Luisa isolated herself in her grief. It was then that she had the inspiration to ask permission from the Carmelite Provincial, Fr. Angel de Salazar, to have Teresa de Ahumada visit her for some time in Toledo. She had heard of Teresa and hoped her inspired company would raise her spirits.

At first the Provincial hesitated, but it was difficult to say no to Doña Luisa, and he ended by calling Teresa to come to Toledo with another nun, explaining the matter. The order arrived on Christmas night at the beginning of choir prayer.

Teresa spent that evening in intensive prayer. The Lord then told her to go and not to worry about contrary events. In the interests of the future convent, it was wise that she keep out of the city until the papal brief arrived. The Jesuit rector, Fr. Gaspar de Salazar, also advised her to go, so she left.

Her old friend, Sr. Juana Suárez, and her brother-in-law, Juan de Ovalle, accompanied her to Toledo. The long trip was undergone partly on horseback and partly in cart-carriage combination and even on foot through strong winds.

Toledo held an immense attraction for Teresa, for it was the spiritual and aristocratic center of Spain. In the sixteenth century, feudal lords left their fortress-castles and settled within Toledo's walls, attracted by a monarchy which had strengthened and had become a way of life. Toledo was the political and military center. Quarrelsome dukes, marquises, counts and others had become generals, admirals, military mission heads, and ambassadors. Contacts with the Crown increased and regal cordiality was returned with high caliber loyalty.

This took place about the thrones of Charles V and Philip II after Isabel and Ferdinand had strongly renovated the monarchy, and Cisneros had reigned so genially. A century later, France went through the same political-social evolution which Louis XIII and Richelieu had prepared for Louis XIV. Indeed, in France the consequences were more definite because feudalism was strangled and much of the old nobility was reduced to parlor nobility. The important Castilian landowners followed the King and built sumptuous palaces around the royal palace. At one time there were as many as sixty family heads, each disposing of an income of 3,000 ducats.

Those sumptuous palaces were enjoyed by the women, for the men were usually away in other regions of the Empire. Spain was a world in itself, but her possessions across the ocean were even more immensely vast. Then there was Flanders, the Milanese Region, and the Kingdom of Naples, so it is easily understood how many different missions and positions were at the disposal of the King. His dignitaries, chosen from the most important families, had to obey, going to distant lands to govern peoples they did not know. The sea, too, needed faithful leaders, for Spain was still the greatest naval nation.

While the men were out performing their duties and acquiring honors, the women lived an inimitable life in their palaces. Each palace became a small court with all the complications of caste in their guests so that the hosts appeared as little kings and queens. One's "social position" regulated habits, hours, greetings, dress and food. The authority of etiquette was rigorously felt every minute. As a consequence, there was much elegance of speech, so much so that there was the saying, "A Toledan woman says more in one word than a Greek philosopher in an entire book."

But Toledan life was based on an inner value, on a tutored nobility of ascetic intentions which in some represented profound sacred love. Greco's paintings serve to describe the Toledo to which Teresa went. In his art, Greco mirrored the great reawakening of Catholicism that was alive in Spain then. Ignatius of Loyola, Teresa of Avila, Peter of Alcántara, Francis Borgia, and John of the Cross all belonged to this movement.

CHAPTER TWENTY-THREE

At the Home of
Doña Luisa de la Cerda

Doña Luisa welcomed Teresa warmly. The woman drew comfort from the nun's company and grew better daily. As a result, Doña Luisa became very fond of Teresa.

In the famous Moorish salon of the palace, Doña Luisa conversed with her relatives and friends who were of the highest nobility. Notwithstanding the solemnity of their names, the tone of the conversation was always familiar and un-rhetorical.

At Mass one day, Teresa felt an irresistible inspiration to pray for the priest who was saying Mass so he could become more perfect. Later she asked to talk to him and found he was García de Toledo, son of the Count of Orapesa. From then on, the priest felt drawn toward a complete break with worldly luxuries and strove steadily for perfection.

Meeting María de Salazar, a fourteen- or fifteen-year-old lady-in-waiting of the house, led to another historic episode. The girl possessed a keen intelligence, but was very fashion-minded. Her frequent encounters with Teresa made her see what splendid holiness Teresa had reached and from that time on the girl existed only for Mother Teresa's ideas. She later became an exemplary Discalced Carmelite. Speaking of Teresa's sojourn in Toledo she said, ''A different language would be needed to describe the change which her holy conversation and exercise of prayer and mortification wrought in all of us. Everyone began confessing to the Jesuits when before they did not go to holy Communion and did not practice charity. Seeing how much good our Mother exercised over everyone in the house, we greatly desired to see some of the favors God granted her. We would oftentimes look through the keyhole of her cell and we would see her enraptured. I, myself, saw her with my own eyes several times. She would always come out trying to conceal herself after her visions. Twice I assisted at her raptures in public, though these occurred after the foundations of Avila and Medina del Campo had been established, and we were at work on the Malagón Convent.[1]

Meanwhile, Teresa went over her plans mentally in order to make them become concrete. The most pressing problem of the foundation was its poverty—was it to be absolutely poor or would it have some sort of income? The meeting with María of Jesus[2] and a letter from Peter of Alcántara cleared the dilemma. The letter is eloquent in its support of absolute poverty. ''May the

---

1. From the trials quoted in Fr. Silverio, II, IV.

2. One day a woman of about forty asked to see Teresa at the De la Cerda home. She was María of Jesus, born in Granada. She had married early, only to be left a widow soon afterward. Ever since then she dedicated herself wholly to serving God. After having spent some months as a novice in the city's Carmelite convent, she left to found a convent where one could live according to the original rule. Strangely enough, Teresa began thinking of her reform during the very month and year María tried to satisfy her exacting spiritual needs.

María sold all she had and divided the money in two: one half to her friend and one half she sewed into her cape. She then put on a habit of

Holy Spirit be with you. Don Gonzalo de Orando gave me your letter and it certainly made me worry to see how you let the advice of the learned decide that which they are not capable of judging; if it were a case of law or conscience it would be wise to ask the advice of jurists or theologians, but when it is a matter of perfection in life, you must deal only with those who practice that way of life because no one generally knows that better. It is not the case to ask advice on evangelical matters if it is good to do this or that because that would be unfaithful. If you desire to follow the example of Christ who was of the greatest perfection in the matter of poverty, follow it. More was not given to men than was given to women, and He will see to it that all will go well as has been with all who have followed His example...."[3]

This letter influenced Teresa profoundly, making her all the more resolute in founding the convent on the principle of absolute poverty. Thus, her long inner debate on the economic form on which to base the future convent was resolved. At this time, the Provincial sent word whereby she was no longer bound by

---

sackcloth, and set off barefoot for Rome to acquire the papal brief for her foundation. Two Franciscan tertiaries accompanied her on this arduous 1561 trip. When she was admitted to an audience with the Pope, her feet left traces of blood where she stepped. When she described her inspiration to Pius IV he exclaimed: "Oh strong woman, let what you will be done!" Receiving the brief, she returned to Granada again on foot. There, she tried to found her first convent, but the obstacles were such that she was forced to desist. When she found out about Teresa, she went straight to meet her in Toledo.

María's sanctity deeply impressed Teresa, and for fifteen days they discussed the matter of their reforms. María of Jesus founded her Immaculate Conception Convent in Granada on September 11, 1562, eighteen days after the foundation of St. Joseph's in Avila.

3. Quoted by Fr. Silverio, II, 5, p. 92.

obedience to stay with Doña Luisa de la Cerda, but was free either to remain a little longer or to return immediately to the Incarnation Convent. The message was motivated by the fact that the Prioress was to be elected and Teresa should vote, too. In fact, several nuns were thinking of electing her, at which thought Teresa grew very uneasy.

CHAPTER TWENTY-FOUR

The Founding of St. Joseph's Convent in Avila

The very evening Teresa returned to Avila, dispatches addressed to Guiomár de Ulloa arrived from Rome containing the papal brief with authorization of the founding of St. Joseph's Convent.

Under the papal concession, the new convent was subject to the Bishop of Avila, Most Reverend Alvaro de Mendoza, an honest and virtuous man, prone to accept opportune innovations. Yet, just then he proved to be a new obstacle for Teresa. The projected poverty of the convent made him exclaim that there were already too many convents in Avila which were lacking in everything. "Prudence indeed imposes that others not be added."

Not even a letter and visit from Peter of Alcántara availed to change the Bishop's stand. However, he did consent to speak personally with Teresa and went to her accompanied by Alcántara.

When the nuns heard of the surprise visit, they were all excited over its meaning. Little did they realize that a conversation was going on in the parlor that was to decide the fate of a future grand religious organism.

The Bishop left, saying that God spoke through the mouth of that nun. He had tasted of the spiritual treasure which lay at the root of the reform project and now understood that the intention was entirely motivated by love, with no egotistic, vain, personal aims. The Carmelite Reform, full of love, now shone before the Bishop's eyes, and he, too, became attracted by the idea and resolved to welcome the new institute. From then on, he remained a firm and precious upholder of Teresa's work.

The first four postulants of the Carmelite Reform were Antonia de Henao, María de la Paz, Ursula de Revilla and María de Avila. They were all different in age, place of birth, upbringing and social position, but Teresa accepted them equally in the poor, small, three-story house she had prepared. On the ground floor, there was a miniature chapel where a double, heavily barred grate permitted the nuns to participate secluded at Mass. Over the two side doors of the chapel, Teresa placed pictures of the Madonna and of St. Joseph, just as she had been told during an ecstasy.

When Peter of Alcántara visited the house in August, 1562, as the finishing touches were being given, he was overjoyed by what he saw, exclaiming, "This is truly St. Joseph's home because I see the little portico of Bethlehem!" The space between the choir entrance and the tabernacle was not even ten feet. On a wall hung a small bell in lieu of a bell-tower as was prescribed in the papal brief. But all was harmonious from the bell to the rest of that tiny house. On August 24, 1562, a sudden tinkling sounded which surprised the inhabitants of Avila because they had never heard a church bell like that before.

The foundation was complete. Teresa with her four novices gathered in the little convent together with two first cousins of Teresa, Inés and Ana de Tapía, Juana de Ahumada and her husband, her faithful friends, Gaspar Daza, Gonzalo de Aranda, Julian de Avila, and Francisco de Salcedo. Daza had been delegated by the Bishop to give the first Discalced Nuns of St. Joseph their habits, to bring the Holy Eucharist into the chapel and to affix the papal vow of seclusion.

When the ceremony ended, the nuns retired into cloister to begin their new life. But Teresa's situation was difficult: even if the convent was subject to obedience to the Bishop of Avila, she was still personally subject to the Carmelite Provincial and belonged to the Incarnation Convent. Would she be able to remain in St. Joseph's long? But the moment was too grand to be spoiled by such thoughts. The first hours that followed were intense: a humble, yet sublime joy overcame her at first which she would not have exchanged for any other joy on earth, saying it was as though she were in a state of glory. Afterwards, a sudden psychic pessimistic prostration overcame her. She wondered if she had not perhaps acted wrongly, disobeying. Moreover, "would the nuns be happy to live so rigorously? Was it all not folly? Who made me do it? Did I not have my convent? I went before the Blessed Sacrament but was unable to pray. My anguish seemed agony. That was one of the most sorrowful moments of my life." This lasted until "I began to remember my great natural inclination to serve God and my desire to suffer for Him."[1] Tranquility returned after that strange uneasiness characteristic of elevated minds during moments of climax.

In the meantime, a group of neighbors had decided to go see why they had heard the bell ring. Stupefied, they had come upon a new convent! The news spread like wildfire, and someone who sensed what had

1. *Life,* XXXVI, 6.

happened went to notify the Prioress at the Incarnation Convent.

Recently elected, Mother María Cimbrón was beside herself when she heard the news; shocked and indignant, the nuns immediately began proposing penalties. Prudent and intelligent, Mother María was firm in her order to have Teresa return within the Incarnation walls in one hour's time.

When the order arrived, Teresa, after all the emotional impact, had just begun to rest. Though struck, the command did not surprise her. She was ready to fight, but she was bound by obedience. After crying with her new daughters over what their fate would be, she left. At that moment, at the Incarnation Convent, everyone was furiously whispering, "Prison, prison!"

CHAPTER TWENTY-FIVE

"Why Limit Love...?"

The convent Areopagus was not to be taken lightly; all the more because Teresa's humility made her feel that the nuns' judgment was based on justice. She had acted secretly and had really played a clever trick on them. Rapidly examining her conscience, however, she felt serene: the convent was founded; God's command had been fulfilled. But now she was to justify herself and seek pardon. She knew of the revelations and commands the Lord had placed in her soul, but in the eyes of the nuns to whom she could not reveal her inner splendors, she was at fault.

Once again the attitude she assumed was the correct one. The Prioress awaited her in the fault chapter hall alone. She wanted first to separate the truth from falsehood. This was why she began by accusing, not questioning. Teresa had prostrated herself before her, and then she stood waiting to be questioned. Mother María reprimanded her, citing articles of the code; she was reminding the wrongdoer of the dictates and reasons of monastic propriety which Teresa had not respected—why?

Teresa justified herself, exposing why she had acted in that manner. As she continued in her apology, María Cimbrón began to feel what the Bishop, Don Alvaro de Mendoza, had felt: that love was the only reality existing in Teresa—love of God and love of souls. Mother Cimbrón was too honest to oppose such a consoling discovery. Whenever Teresa treated spiritual matters, it always happened that the listener did not need to seek an interpretation or judgment because the angelic impression enveloped the listener directly. Mother Cimbrón felt the rays of that force of persuasion reach her, demolishing her resistance. Naturally, she could not surrender entirely, but she remained thoughtful, and all the accusations she had pronounced shortly before seemed to backfire. Why should she prevent that good work? And how was it possible to deny that the spirit of God reigned in it? Up to that moment, the horizon of her monastic duties had been clear and precise, with definite limits. But now her boundaries were brilliant with rays: why put a limit to God's love, to the thirst for penance, to the sacrificing of one's life? Why imprison those souls who had love and strength enough to suffer and offer themselves?

A new language opened before the Prioress, a language which she thought was only for heroes and saints. It had penetrated her, and even after Teresa left the room, the echo of her voice remained: "Why confine love?"

Teresa was definitely not to be imprisoned for this, but as Prioress Mother Cimbrón could not act according to her discretion alone. The best thing would be to entrust the matter to the hands of the Provincial who was in Avila.

A small group of "extremists," the most indignant and adverse toward Teresa, had waited to know what the decision was. But Mother María appeared dazed and did not speak of imprisonment. Instead, she ventured reflections and spoke of deferring the matter to a more competent and inspired authority.

Disapproving among themselves, the nuns would have been all the more indignant had they known Mother María had ordered a better meal than usual[1] to be served to Teresa who remained in her cell in order not to irritate the nuns.

Since the Prioress obviously had let herself be moved, the community of nuns was happy to have the affair pass into the hands of the Provincial. What happened there was similar to a session of monastic court. Seated about Fr. Angel de Salazar were the Prioress and the senior nuns of the convent. Instead of being overwhelmed, Teresa felt a great joy: "I saw that I could finally suffer a little for love of God because I truly did not feel I had committed any wrong either toward God or toward the Order. Indeed, I felt I had converged all my efforts for the betterment of the Order, and I was ready even to die for my cause. My only desire had been to follow my rule perfectly."[2]

There was no pride in her calmness, only love. "I remembered the slander Jesus had borne, and my trial seemed little indeed."

Prostrated before her superior, she waited for him to speak. He reprimanded her severely, but she had decided not to try to find excuses. Instead, Teresa justified herself by pleading guilty and asking pardon which was both intelligent and tactful on her part. It was natural and even necessary that she be reprimanded, and this act of humility and contrition disarmed those present.

Later on, she revealed some of her reasons, but was unable to relate all at that time. It was painful for her to

---

1. The incident was affirmed by Sr. María Bautista who was then in the convent.

2. *Life,* XXXVI, 12, also for the following.

speak of those things. Whenever she came to the most secret justification, the one that mattered most, she could not explain herself because it would have been imprudent to speak of supernatural phenomena after all the controversial talk on the subject. Yet, once again, the truth shone from within and gradually reached her listeners. When Teresa finished, a long silence ensued. Fr. Angel was grave; the nuns were struck still. They were all old, and most had entered the convent young, so their lives had been spent in serving God to the best of their abilities. Sincere, they still desired the glory of the God to whom they had sacrificed themselves. After so many years, they now felt a new and different reality before them. A voice heard only by the heart saying, "What do you want to do to this woman before you? Don't you see that she loves?" was perceived by them all. When Father Salazar pronounced his sentence, his tone had changed entirely, and he bore an expression of deep thought. He did not condemn Teresa, but spoke of the love of God and of its marvelous ramifications, of the innumerable aspects it assumed in the souls of those who lived this love sincerely. Here lay the beauty of Christian life and of the greatness of the Church—right in these multiple intentions which led to one goal. Consolation was proffered to the one who had been judged wrongly and to those who had not known how to judge well, having made a soul suffer in their intent to do good.

CHAPTER TWENTY-SIX

Opposition of an Entire City

A sense of peace did not reign in Avila concerning the new foundation. Both poor and rich alike opposed the institute's poverty. Two monasteries had been forced to close during the reign of the two Catholic kings while the others continued to be as poor as when they had been founded. This was the reason why another house committed to religious poverty did not seem possible.

The following day, August 25, the governor himself, García Suárez de Carvajal, went to the little convent. He told the four poor, frightened Discalced nuns that they were to leave the convent or gendarmes would break down the doors. After the nuns discussed the stand to take, one deferred, "We shall not depart unless she who let us enter orders it."

Since the governor's prestige was involved, he was about to order the guards to execute the threat when someone observed that the Holy Eucharist was near the door. That stopped him, and he was forced to remember that the convent was regularly founded and under obedience to Bishop de Mendoza. Reflecting that all was legal, they were forced to retreat to the City Hall.

On the guards' departure, the four nuns wept tears of gratitude, remembering that Mother Teresa had said that the Madonna would watch over one door, St. Joseph the other, and the Son in the middle, all three protecting the convent.

Meanwhile, Teresa remained in her cell at Incarnation Convent in a sort of moral siege, but friends kept her informed of the events.

Once the battle against the little convent had been contrived, the councilmen and governor studied how to make it most effective. Three meetings held the 25th, 26th, and 30th of August led to a plenary assembly which brought together all the city authorities: magistrates, members of the cathedral council, representatives from other monasteries and members of Avilian nobility. This all went on while Teresa prayed, closed in her cell, unable to do anything because the Prioress had forbidden her to look after the matter. The wave of adversity which swept over the city began to be felt even by the Carmelite superiors. "In the two days those meetings were held I was very worried, but the Lord said, 'Do you not know that I am almighty? What, then, do you fear?' He assured me that the convent would not be destroyed, and these words consoled me greatly."[1]

―――――――

In the meantime, the great assembly was united. There was not much to discuss because all were of the opinion that the little convent was a sort of calamity, a parasite which would dry the resources of the populace, leading the majority to vote for the immediate suppression of the convent. At this point, however, a

―――――――

1. *Life*, XXXVI, 16.

Dominican, Fr. Domingo Báñez, stood up alone in opposition to the rapid decision. He upheld that an institute bearing papal and episcopal sanction could not be repressed simply by a decision hastily taken by municipal authorities. A regular trial was necessary, and there really was no reason to hasten events. Furthermore, the Royal Council was the only court authorized to discuss such a matter.

These words cooled the burning spirits so that a prudent calmness set in. The adversaries then decided that if the Bishop would not resolve the matter, they would take it to the Royal Council of Madrid.

—————————

Legal procedure became increasingly elaborate and lengthy—the dispute slowly left Avila for Madrid where it assumed the seriousness of a state affair. But here the dying Peter of Alcántara's voice rose above the lawyers and public officials, speaking sublime words. Wasting away from his extraordinary sacrifices and suffering, the saint, consumed by a high fever, showed the end was near. During his last days of grave physical suffering he wrote a letter to Teresa encouraging her not to yield, but to continue her foundation in absolute poverty.

Upon receipt of this letter, Teresa spent many hours in prayer, and while at prayer that night she suddenly saw Peter's lean figure before her full of the brilliance of glorified bodies. This vision occurred to her on October 18, 1562—the saint had died just a few days earlier.

The trial lost intensity. Stretching to Madrid, it no longer had the eyes of Avila directly upon it and the early heat began to languish. After all, the four Discalced nuns were not the four knights of the Apocalypse.

CHAPTER TWENTY-SEVEN

Life in St. Joseph's Convent

In February or March, 1563, Teresa obtained permission from the Provincial and her convent superiors to transfer to St. Joseph's Convent together with four nuns of the Incarnation Convent. Before entering, the nuns stopped to pray to our Lady of Soterrana, and Teresa took off her stockings. She stepped over the threshold barefoot and prostrated herself before the Blessed Sacrament.

At that moment she was enraptured, and a heavenly vision appeared to her. "I saw Jesus Christ receiving me very lovingly, placing a crown on my head and thanking me for what I had done for His mother."[1]

With the little convent definitely settled, the Avilians slowly became accustomed to it and withdrew all opposition, enabling the nuns to carry on regular religious life.

From this point on, Teresa turned her thoughts to progressive construction, concerning herself with the growing and changing material necessities of the Car-

---

1. *Life*, XXXVI, 24.

melite Reform. From the spiritual world she passed to a bureaucratic one. Surprisingly enough, she was as adept at appraising land, buildings, and facing all kinds of economic situations as she was at forming souls. Always at the center of every new foundation, she formed and transformed everything with her faith and intellectual power.

The love which moved Teresa to propagate her work appeared in every aspect of her activity. It is certain that Teresa conceived the Reform and desired it to be an instrument of holy war against heresy. Protestantism was painful to her. The peoples of Europe appeared as lost children of Sion because formerly all were united in the universality of the Church. France, especially, troubled Teresa because she fully realized what an immense procession of the faithful to Christ there was in the Church from that country. Her Reform was offered as a sort of holocaust for this reason, too.

Above all, however, there was a more vast and general aspect of the Reform—the desire to combat sin which was spreading throughout humanity. As in all fervent souls, this intention became irrepressible. "My anguish then, and now still, lies in the fact that since the Lord has many enemies and few friends, at least let these few be good, ready to perform what little that can be done; that is, follow evangelical advice as perfectly as possible. The world is going up in flames; humanity wants to recondemn Christ, and a thousand witnesses are rising against Him. They want to tear down His Church. Shall we continue to waste our time in things for which, if God gave them to us, we would be lowered in heaven? No, my Sisters, this is not the time to ask God for unimportant things."[2] Anyone capable of believing and understanding cannot permit one minute

---

2. *The Way of Perfection*, I, also for the following.

to be lost in choosing the gigantic alternative of light or darkness.

Teresa's motto was "to suffer or to die." What means were there for women at that time to combat the world of sin? A woman could not preach or take an active part in the controversy, but she could suffer and offer. A grain of suffering could be infinitely multiplied by divine mercy and be exchanged for a shower of grace. There was not time for hesitation; just raise the cross and walk in Christ's footsteps. To prevent sin and make amends was what inspired her work and what flowered in the daughters of her reform.

In its basic themes, Teresa's spirit fit perfectly within the Catholic counter-reformation movement. She was at the beginning of a chain which would be held at the other end by Ignatius of Loyola. However, her ideas were still on the defensive, trying to put a stop to the crumbling of Catholicism in those countries where the Church was already established and seeking to liberate baptized souls from the shackles of sin. But her attitude was slowly to change from the defensive to the offensive and to conquering, after she had occasion to speak at length with Alonso Maldonado about the Indians in South America. "How many souls are lost there," he said, "because they do not know God!" That reflection created an irresistible call in Teresa; it awakened her childhood missionary dream to suffer martyrdom; it recalled a de Cepeda family tradition.

The Carmelite Reform thus acquired even the theme of conquest which is fundamental to the Church, drawing its origin from Christ's words: "Go forth and preach the Gospel everywhere." The first missionary auxiliary was undoubtedly Teresa of Jesus. In the Teresian Reform, prayer for the missions became the principal aim with innumerable mortifications offered for that intention.

In addition to the twofold purpose of the defense and expansion of the Church, a third embraced prayer for the clergy. Teresa was especially concerned about the "defenders" of the Church and often exhorted her daughters to "love the priests, preachers and defenders of the faith; pray for them so that they can fulfill their apostleship in spirit and in doctrine."[3]

These were some of the quietest years of Teresa's life. They were also constructive because between 1562 and 1567 she drew up the constitution which was later to extend itself, with slight modifications, to the whole Carmelite Reform.

According to the new rule, the days began at five in the summer, at six in the winter, and lasted until eleven at night. Seven hours of sleep were permitted in the winter and six in the summer, but an hour's rest period was conceded after lunch in summer. After washing (and Teresa emphasized personal hygiene), the nuns went to the choir to spend an hour in mental prayer. Afterwards, they recited the Divine Office, that is, the hours: first, third, sixth, and ninth. On Sundays and feast days, the singing of the Mass, vespers, and matins was obligatory. A light meal was consumed at ten; at two, vespers were sung and the spiritual reading lasted until three. At five or six, depending on the season, compline was recited. At eight, no matter the season, the bell rang for silence. After an hour of pious meditation, each nun retired to her respective cell to work, think, write and pray.

These were the precious, delicious hours of intimate life when the soul gathered benefit from the mental and vocal prayer of the day. Completely free from human bonds, it could seek the Lord more easily. Situated outside the city walls, the little convent was not disturbed by noises so that it was easy to feel near to

---

3. Fr. Silverio, *op. cit.*, II, 12.

God in the soul-saving mission. The intentions and invocations which had accumulated during the day could now be brought directly before God.

The nuns' whole existence pivoted about that lofty manner of prayer. Mortification was constant, dominating every recess of intellectual and physical life. Their dress was a habit "of the least quantity possible, yet considering the necessary ampleness." The sleeves were round, not at all comfortable, of the same width at both ends, without cuffs or pleats. The tunics were of worsted; their hemp bonnets were neither gathered nor pleated, but fitted to the head. For reasons of decency, as the constitution read, the feet were to be covered with hempen sandals and grayish stockings or stockings made of tow. In the cold hours of winter, the nuns, especially the sick ones, could cover themselves with capes or mantles of the same worsted material as their habits; elegant robes were not permitted. Naturally, there were no mirrors and the hair was to be cut "so as not to waste time combing it," as Mother Teresa would say.

There is an incident regarding going barefoot. Once a man who saw Teresa barefoot sarcastically remarked, "What pretty ankles you have, Mother!" Teresa replied, "It is the last time you will see them." When she reached her destination, she cut out stockings of coarse cloth, with no feet, to cover the ankles. They have been in use since that time.

The cells were tiny, containing a table and bed. The nuns could touch the ceiling when standing, and they were not permitted to have chairs, dressers or closets. The bed consisted of a straw mattress placed over some boards slightly raised from the floor. The sheets were made of hemp, and the covers were coarse. The pillowcases were also hemp except when for sick nuns they could be linen.

As for meals, fast was observed eight months of the year. During this time the nuns ate once a day; never did they eat meat. The food was to be sufficient in order to live and to work because the nuns had to work to help sustain their convent. It was not necessary that they did fine embroidery on rich materials, just so they spun and sewed. The only fancy embroidery the nuns of St. Joseph left was on the chapel hangings.

CHAPTER TWENTY-EIGHT

The "Way of Perfection"

Those were the visible directives of the Reform's external practices. But the spirit belonged to a new world molded on the basis of love. The formation of the Discalced religious took place simply in a homely, intimate atmosphere. Teresa educated her first daughters carefully through example, counsel and comprehension. Every sacrifice and joy was felt in unison, and as time passed, the solace derived became more lucid and more divine. Happiness reigned at St. Joseph's. Mother Teresa formed her novices by treating their inherent weaknesses at the roots. She had urged them to put away all personal pride before entering in order to treat each other as charitably as possible. Human and full of love were the contacts with human weaknesses. Humble and natural with her novices, Teresa had the distinct trait of always remaining understandable even in moments of divine revelation.

Her daughters felt this and had really banished discontent and ostentation from their relations. Since the intimate, practical side of the community was in order, peace was attained and grace was free to operate. Overcoming reciprocal animosities entailed practicing the sublime virtues of charity, humility, and patience. It was this peace that permitted Teresa to write during those five years.

Though she did not enjoy writing, she did it with love even if out of necessity because she wrote in obedience. At night she would hastily fill pages without interruption, never rereading anything. First she wrote her *Life,* setting down both treasures and shadows with extraordinary humility and sincerity. It must certainly have been difficult to reconstruct such complex, personal subjects, but her role was to put others into communication with the God she described.

Teresa's masterpiece is so great that alone it offers an argument for believing in God. What she did does not seem humanly possible. It indisputably savors of a first copy written off hurriedly as does *The Way of Perfection* written shortly afterwards. *The Way of Perfection* was also written out of obedience[1] (this time to Fr. Domingo Báñez), but with a different intention from her *Life.* This latter book was in part meant for her confessor, Fr. Pedro Ibañez, and in part directed to Fr. García de Toledo and a few other people of prayer. But *The Way of Perfection* was purposely written for her "daughters" and was to serve in their formation as a sort of monastic spiritual primer, which was really a paraphrase of the Reform's constitution. The book still serves that purpose today.

---

1. Teresa's "daughters" were greatly attracted by her manner of prayer and knew she had exposed her fullest moments in the book of her life; which Teresa, out of a feeling of humility, did not permit them to read. The nuns begged her confessor to order her to write a book for them, which Teresa did out of obedience. A study of the manuscript in the Escurial Library shows how rapidly she wrote; she never reread her writings, the whole reflecting absolute spontaneity and a firm hold of the matter dealt with. As the Reform grew, the nuns from the other convents also wanted *The Way of Perfection* so Teresa patiently copied it in 1568, modifying it somewhat, and this manuscript can be found in the Valladolid convent.

With a familiar and practical tone, its horizon is seemingly narrow. Teresa did not generalize, but spoke of particular problems which she had had to resolve and what personal intentions she had followed. Surprisingly enough, Teresa's personal application became vividly and universally efficacious. The little book which was designed to be a commentary on the Our Father, and was even called the "Our Father," contains universal doctrine. It is composed only of monastic rules and sound advice, but if we try to apply those pieces of advice to ourselves we see that they fit us perfectly. Proof of this is that the same can be done to it as is done to that inimitable and mysterious work of art which is *The Imitation of Christ;* no matter where we turn, the context corresponds to our soul's needs.

Immortal pages on love are contained in the first chapters. It is not seraphic love, but human love between creatures, and this is to teach her daughters to love one another. Teresa's method is plausible and psychological, full of intuition and experience. She studies the whole complex system of human affections, penetrating deep to reveal how they are or should be. It is a practical method based on reality, nonetheless succeeding in transporting love to the highest plane and attaching surprising applicability to it.

Two points are crucial in affections: the choice of the person, and the manner in which our love is reciprocated. All eventual delusion and bitterness can be traced to those two difficult points. If the person is unworthy, we are unhappy, just as if the person we love does not love us. Generous hearts do exist, content to give and never receive, but those are by far the minority. Normal affection needs restitution. Teresa applies her ascetic method to the analysis of these two aspects and the result is extraordinary.

The question is put: whom shall we love? A clear distinction is drawn between licit and illicit love.

"Heaven help me, for here I do not in any way allude to evil love which is hellish, and we should never tire of speaking against it because there are not enough words to explain only the least of the damages it causes. We must not even speak of such things, nor listen to stories of that kind, nor permit that it be spoken of jokingly or seriously in front of us.... Even to hear of it can be dangerous to us."[2]

These affirmations perfectly conform to the teachings of expert spiritual directors. Mentally to indulge in matters of illicit love without justification constitutes exposure to temptation. This concept was later to be coined magnificently by St. Alphonsus of Liguori: "Flee quickly, flee far away, flee always." Victory consists in keeping away from temptation; that apparent cowardice is, in reality, the highest manifestation of strength.

Having cleared this basic distinction, Teresa discusses what we should love in those dear to us. We should not attach ourselves to human qualities which are only superficial and temporary, but to the spiritual qualities of a person. Those who can do this know perfect love which is useful and devoid of delusions and terrestrial bitterness. "But you may say: on what do they base their love if they do not love what they see? I say that they love what they see and they become attached to what they feel, but they see only stable things. Their love does not stop at the surface of the body, but looks to the soul for something worthy of their love. Even if nothing is found but some beginnings of virtue or of a good disposition which seems to promise treasures within, they do all they can for its betterment because they know they could not continue

---

2. *The Way of Perfection,* VI and VII, here and for the following.

to love it if God's great love did not shine there. Not even if that person sacrificed himself for love of him could he be loved if God's love did not dwell there. Conscious of the worthlessness of worldly goods through experience, these people realize we are not meant to live together continuing in our love for each other; all will end with death, each to go in different directions if we have not all abided by the law of God in His charity."

The next point is: should we demand reciprocation of our love? Even honest love naturally desires its love returned, states St. Teresa. Setting aside this instinctive element, she analytically believes that "blindness leads us to desire to be loved unless it be a question of people who can help us to acquire true happiness. In fact, it is always in view of some interest or personal satisfaction that we want to be loved. Only when we have been reciprocated do we see that it was all but straw which the wind scatters. What is really left us after we have been loved greatly? For this reason perfect people don't bother about being loved or not."

To renounce being loved may sound unnatural, but it simply means not to go in search of love and not to be exacting. She does not say we should refuse the affection given us, but advises us not to worry about that point too much. Our aim should not be to be loved, but to love because it is holy to love. St. Augustine's axiom "let us love, but not to be loved" summarizes the concept well.

Such a victory is not easily gained, but it would signify a decided advantage for many and would be the only solution to the everlasting tragedy of the heart. Most of our human sadness arises from the fact that we do not feel loved enough, with a lack of comprehension which makes us sad and even malicious. Hence arises a most subtle temptation and sensitive wound. Teresa, instead, teaches freedom from bonds. Perfect people "remember this truth, laugh at themselves and at the pain they formerly felt when they worried about being loved or not." To give without receiving means overcoming our egoism; it is the most perfect love toward others because it seeks their happiness without care of personal recompense.

CHAPTER TWENTY-NINE

Continuing on the "Way of Perfection"

Thought fluctuation is the only order that seems to have been followed in the subject-treatment of *The Way of Perfection*. The themes of ascendence and mental prayer are interlaced, virtues and mystical impetus are flowers in the same bouquet. Teresa's spontaneity is at times disconcerting, so much so as to appear confusing, but this feeling disappears when she writes of her experimental mysticism, elevating it to theory, making all become perfectly planned and analyzed in her arduous spiritual flight.

Attentively reading even those parts which are not treated profoundly, we notice that the chapters follow a logical order. We rise higher without realizing it. After the discipline and perfection of affections, we pass to the various aspects of detachment. Here Teresa maternally frees her daughters of all bonds, including their family and their ego.

The positive search for depth and victory over the ego in order to offer oneself to God can be called the liberating ascetic climb since it frees the soul from its fetters. This striving is full of mortification. The part that deals with the concept of not defending oneself when one is unjustly accused reminds us of Therese of the Child Jesus. Her sanctity began from just such an act. When she had been blamed for the breaking of a fine vase, she accepted the blame without endeavoring to justify herself. Later, she confessed that her silence then had cost her immensely. It may well be that she was following the great Teresa's suggestions. *The Way of Perfection* depicts Christ unjustly accused and tortured: what better way is there to be like Him, to imitate Him, than to suffer unjust accusations? "I believe it is very important to become accustomed to this virtue, also, in order to obtain true humility from God which is basic to it. The truly humble soul desires to suffer disdain, persecution, and condemnation without cause. God's help alone is needed to succeed in imitating our Lord.

"My Sisters, I would like the goal of our studies and penances to be these virtues. As already mentioned, I shall attentively control the nature and number of penances because you could ruin your health if they are performed too copiously without discretion. But let your inner virtues become as great as they will, for they will never weaken you in practicing your religion, but will fortify your soul. Above all, accustom yourselves to overcoming little things, for by doing thus will you succeed when met by great ones."[1]

Here the book continues in a conquering tone. No longer a defense for liberating one from faults and weaknesses, it moves toward heroic acts. Inner heroism is given free reign; physical mortifications are limited, but spiritual deeds are infinitely encouraged. The daughters of the Carmelite Reform were to win thousands of victories over themselves to obtain the palm of

---

1. *The Way of Perfection*, XV, 2, 3.

secret triumph. Only after the soul's standing in relation to God and daily life is cleared up does Teresa start
speaking of prayer. Connecting it with its basic element, the will, she deals with one's direct relationship
to God.

Teresa treats three themes in connection with this:
vocal prayer, mental prayer and contemplation. First of
all, she insists that vocal prayer should not consist
merely of words, but should be joined to mental prayer.
Whereas the latter can do without the first, vocal
prayer needs mental prayer with it if it is to be efficient. This does not mean that imperfect, distracted
vocal prayer is useless or without merit, but the nuns
are definitely warned against negligence in this matter.
She further insists that one should not worry about
reaching contemplation because not everyone is suited
for it, and some attain it very late. But the truly humble
person is content to go wherever his Lord beckons.

A careful study of the different periods of spiritual
life follows, showing the basic characteristics of one's
internal and external moral life in relation to God and
neighbor. Prayer is then described as the dominating
element of Carmelite life with the subject treated following the sublime scheme of the Our Father. In this
way the early chapters on charity, humility, and detachment serve as preparation for the body of the book
which is a comment on the Lord's Prayer with which
Teresa intends to accompany her daughters on the "divine journey" of religious life.

"So I return to those who want to travel this road
without stopping until the true source is reached. Since
knowing how to begin is of utmost importance, you
must firmly and decisively resolve not to stop until that
source is found."[2]

---

2. *The Way of Perfection*, XXI, 2.

"Our Father who art in heaven!"

These words truly seem to open heaven to Teresa, causing her soul to become aglow. "How clear it is, my Lord, that You are the Father of such a Son, and that Your Son is the Son of such a Father! Blessed are You for all eternity! Let us leave the world, my daughters. It is not reasonable that after having known the excellence of such grace, we can still consider it so lowly as to wish to remain down here." [3]

The different states and manners of prayer which Teresa experienced are described next. By far the greatest writer of experimental mysticism, her revelations open unexpected horizons of seraphic tenderness. The tone of this book is very different from that of her *Life,* the latter written as it was for spiritual directors. Here the analysis of supernatural experiences is interwoven continuously with moral advice, warnings and exhortations, typical of a maternal attitude, whereas in the other, the tone seemed filial. A sense of reserve hovers over the whole book as if there were fear of revealing all lest the doves be shied away by the eagle's wings. But it is difficult to constrain genius or love, and both shine through the humble words. The admirable comment on the Our Father is interpreted in an original manner. The "heaven" where the Father dwells is the human soul, while the "kingdom of God" is the prayer of quiet and union; our "daily bread," the Holy Eucharist; "the evil" which Teresa prays to be freed from is the danger we run in life of offending God.

Lofty as the spiritual climate of the book may be, the wise reformer keeps her eye fixed on earth. Work is

---

3. *The Way of Perfection,* XXVII, 1.

still to be done, and her daughters are not yet angels. While she invites them to contemplate the divine, she regards them as human beings, watching their spirit of sacrifice. The book's continuous moral efficaciousness, in addition to its inimitable description of the states of prayer, keeps the work alive.

CHAPTER THIRTY

Father Rubeo

Teresa's 1563 "spiritual report" directed either to Fr. García de Toledo or to Fr. Báñez reveals her state of mind during the years spent in St. Joseph's Convent. "If until now I felt I needed others, counting much on help from the world, I now clearly realize that men are but dry rosemary twigs on which we cannot lean because they break at the slightest wind of contradiction or blame. Experience has taught me that the only way not to fall is to hold onto the cross and confide in Him who was nailed to it. He is my true Friend with whom I feel raised to such self-control that I feel I could resist anything as long as He is at my side.

"I greatly enjoyed being esteemed before this truth shone clearly in my mind, but now not only am I indifferent to praise, I even find it annoying, unless, of course, it is a question of having my esteem serve in dealing with those with whom I speak of my soul or whom I hope to help. Then I need it to be tolerated and believed when I tell them that all is vanity on earth.

"My Lord has favored me with much courage during the trials, contradictions and persecutions I have undergone in these past months: the greater the difficulty, the more I felt His help so I never tired of suffering. Not only was I not bothered by those who spoke against me, I even felt I loved them with renewed affection. Certainly this could only have been through a grace of God."[1]

Concerning joy and sorrow, she wrote, "I am so slightly touched by them that I feel totally incapable of feeling them, and I can live in this state for several days at a time."[2] She was subject also to a deep craving for penance. "Often I cannot even bear the necessity to eat, especially when at prayer. Indeed, at the present moment, it has become torturous. It must be serious because it makes me shed many tears and utter expressions of pain without my noticing that I do.

"There are days when St. Paul's saying is always in my mind. Even I feel, though not as he, that it is not I who live, speak, and desire, but another in me who directs me and gives me strength. It is as though I am beside myself because of the great pain life causes me. Yes, it is so painful for me to be away from God that the greatest sacrifice I can offer in His glory is to accept living for love of Him. I would like at least that my life be spent in the midst of continuous strife and persecution. Since I am no good for anything else, the least I can do is suffer."

This great superhuman exclamation sounds entirely plausible and natural from Teresa's lips.

It is 1567, and Teresa's Reform now begins to extend in a truly miraculous manner.

One day, a Franciscan, Alonso Maldonado, visited Teresa on his return from the West Indies and spoke to

1. *Spiritual Reports*, III, here and for the following.
2. Quoted by Fr. Silverio, III, V.

her of the many, many souls which were lost there on
account of the lack of priests and religious instruction.
That thought troubled the saint. Retiring to a small
hermitage which she had had built in the convent
garden, she knelt down and began to weep. Unknown
to her, she was being watched by Isabel of St. Dominic,
who in 1610 was to bear witness to what she had seen
and known during the beatification process. Teresa had
broken down in tears, praying to Jesus so He could
show her how to be useful in some way toward helping
those pagan souls. Her great missionary urge was forcefully flowering into one of the greatest moments of
burning missionary love in her life.

Then it was that Christ appeared to her, saying,
"Wait a while, and you shall see great things."

Not long afterwards the General of the Carmelite
Order, Giovanni Battista Rossi of Ravenna, called "Father Rubeo," went through Spain on a canonical visit.
In his sixty years of life he had been indefatigable, at
first in his studies and now in his active life as the
Carmelite General. His visit to the Spanish convents
has remained famous in the Order's annals. In May,
1566, the General left Genoa to disembark near Per-
pignan. On June 10, he was in Madrid where he was
received by Philip II. On June 16, he went to Toledo,
from whence he went into Andalusia. On September 20, he convoked the general chapter in Seville at
which time more than two hundred religious were in
attendance. At the end of the year he was in Lisbon.

But the Andalusian Carmelites did not appreciate certain measures of strictness and counsels by
Fr. Rubeo. In order to prevent the General's visit, they
decided to be placed under the jurisdiction of the bishops and obtained a papal bull granting this in April,
1567. However, the General did not know about these
doings and proceeded regularly on his trip through

Spain. He arrived in Avila on April 11, and called for a meeting of the provincial chapter.

When Teresa heard of the forthcoming visit she grew fearful and upset lest he forbid her to remain at St. Joseph's, ordering her instead to return to the Incarnation. But that did not happen. During the General's visit with Bishop de Mendoza, the latter spoke of a convent in which thirteen nuns lived in great fervor and austerity according to the primitive rule, and the General expressed his desire to see those solitary women in their convent.

The fearfully awaited visit took place. When he was told that Teresa belonged to the Incarnation Convent, he asked, "Then how is it you are here?"

A total explanation was necessary. With her usual sincerity, Teresa also spoke of the papal bull which she thought authorized her to change obedience, falling directly under the Bishop's jurisdiction.

"But that cannot be," Fr. Rubeo objected, "because no one has bothered questioning me about this passage of obedience and jurisdiction."

Teresa reflected that the General was right. As far as she was personally concerned, the papal bull did not authorize her to consider herself under a new obedience. She had truly thought so up until that moment, but now the General's response had suddenly illuminated her.

It was a question of coherence and humility, and Teresa mastered the situation, immediately recognizing herself as Fr. Rubeo's subject. This behavior confirmed Fr. Rubeo's judgment of her, and he remained with her at length discussing spiritual things. Teresa laid her whole life before him, then turned to matters of divine love.

Fr. Rubeo was edified. Skillful as he was at penetrating into ascetic and mystic minds, he admired that nun with the expressive face and easy manner. Sanctity breathed out from her words. During his nearly three weeks' stay in Avila, the General would go to speak to Teresa of spiritual things after his obligatory visits were paid. A year later, in a letter to the Mother Superior of Medina del Campo, he wrote: "I render infinite thanks to the Divine Majesty for having granted such a great honor to this Order through the diligence and bounty of our Reverend Teresa of Jesus. She is more beneficial to the Order than all the Carmelite Friars in Spain."

The practical consequences of their conversations were of unforeseen importance; the General left Mother Teresa with the necessary certificates to found other Discalced Convents in the province of Castile according to the unmitigated rule. One particular detail worthy of note was that he authorized her to take those nuns who wished to go into her foundations from the Incarnation Convent which still housed a hundred and fifty nuns. A few months later, he wrote specifying that the certificates were valid both for Old and New Castile.

From that moment, Teresa's horizon changed. Her superior blessed and approved her work, encouraging the extension of its sphere. It was now up to her to work toward this greater aim.

CHAPTER THIRTY-ONE

The Foundation in Medina del Campo

Medina del Campo was chosen for the first foundation because it was well populated and one of the most prosperous cities in Spain. Sixteen thousand inhabitants for a city in the sixteenth century was a considerable number. Prosperous and frequented by all Spanish mercantile companies and various European commercial houses, it was the site of famous fairs where nearly everything could be found. On the days preceding the great fairs, long lines of horses, mules and donkeys could be seen on the nearby hills carrying a variety of Iberic and colonial goods. They arrived at sundown, making a confusion of voices, all seeking lodgings and stalls. In the morning the merchandise shone brightly in the sun, arranged neatly about the square. There were a thousand two hundred and forty narrow streets and fifteen squares in the city, the Plaza Mayor being the largest and busiest square in Spain. Besides the two parishes, there was the collegiate church with two chapters of eighty priests. There were eighteen convents and nine hospitals.

Of particular encouragement to Teresa in founding a Discalced convent here was the fact that there were Jesuits in the city. She knew that wherever the Society of Jesus was, she could count on solid backing. By coincidence, Fr. Baltasar Alvarez, who had been her patient and devoted confessor, was living in Medina at the time.

Teresa went to the Bishop of Salamanca, to whose diocese Medina belonged, to inquire about the possibilities of appropriating funds for new convents. Firm in her decision to carry on in the principle of absolute poverty, she anxiously awaited the verdict which came in the form of assurance that the Discalced would easily find enough to live on in the town.

When the permits were obtained, Teresa decided to have the founding on August 15, Assumption Day. She imposed this date on herself and was thenceforth energetically attached to that day.

Now it was a question of finding the nuns. She gathered seven valorous ones: four from the Incarnation and three from St. Joseph's. Two of the Incarnation nuns, Isabel Arias and Teresa de Quesada, were old, while two, Inés de Tapía and Ana de Tapía were young. From St. Joseph's there were María Battista, Ana de los Angeles, and Ana Godinez. Again somewhat the same talk arose in Avila concerning this new foundation as had happened for St. Joseph's: criticism and disapproval of the undertaking. Even Teresa's best friends, Francisco de Salcedo included, hinted she should not commit such a mad thing. Everyone referred to her as "the crazy woman." But Teresa placidly organized things as best she could at St. Joseph's so that her absence would not cause a setback in anything.

Early on August 13, a strange caravan of three heavy mule-drawn carts left Avila. Fr. Julian de Avila led the way seated on a mule followed by the muleteers. The carts were loaded with nuns, sacred and secular objects, baggage and food. Before leaving, Teresa had prayed in the little hermitage dedicated to Christ scourged at the pillar, that she might find the convent the same upon her return.

Inside the carts, life was regulated monastically. The usual chorus and psalmody periods were respected. No matter the discomfort and the continuous jogging, a sense of retirement reigned with joy appearing during the moments of recreation. Mother Teresa was happiness personified and knew how to be comical at the opportune moment, but the joyfulness was candid, not at all disturbing to inner peace or the almost continual state of mental prayer.

Because the sun shone strongly and the beasts were tired, the caravan stopped at about eleven. The hottest hours were spent under the bridge of a dried-up stream. When they were about a mile away from Arévalo, a good friend of the saint's, Fr. Alonso Esteban, met them. He spoke at length with Fr. de Avila, handed him a letter, then turned back and accompanied the caravan. Fr. Esteban was acting as a messenger bearing sad news which the two priests wished they could conceal from Teresa. A certain Alonso Alvarez, who had agreed to rent his house for the imminent foundation, now wrote that it was impossible for him to keep his promise, notifying Teresa that he absolutely would not receive the nuns. Because of unforeseen circumstances, he really was in a difficult situation.

Both Fr. de Avila and Fr. Esteban felt at a loss. Here was a caravan on the road, eight cloistered nuns including the foundress, food, provisions, and all sorts of objects just thirty miles from their destination. Behind them was Avila in a dither with gossip and criticism. What now? It was impossible to go back, but a group of Carmelite nuns certainly couldn't live in the open or lodge in an inn. Moreover, with what money? Poor

Fr. de Avila scolded himself for not having come be-
forehand to make sure of everything instead of relying
on someone's word.

Courage to tell Mother Teresa came only after they
had reached Arévalo and were given shelter by a pious
woman of the town. Calling Teresa aside, the two
priests told her how things stood. Unruffled, she said
she trusted in God. Meanwhile, they learned that
Fr. Domingo Báñez, who had done so much for the
Reform, was in Arévalo. Teresa asked that he come to
her and together with the two other priests, they discussed what was to be done.

It was the evening of the 13th, and the foundation
was to take place on August 15. There was barely time
for Fr. Báñez to rush to Medina, using his prestige to
try to settle the difficulties and return to Arévalo for the
nuns and their baggage. Having decided upon this, the
four resolved to get some sleep. Meanwhile, the news
reached the other nuns and each imagined the return to
their respective convents under the ironic, triumphant
glares of the passers-by.

No one slept that night. In the morning another
surprise occurred. From Avila, Teresa had written
Fr. Antonio de Heredia to look for a house she could
buy in Medina, and by a strange coincidence, he arrived in Arévalo that morning announcing he had
found what she wanted. It was only a ramshackle
house, but there was no demand for immediate payment due to the generosity of the proprietress, Doña
María Suárez from Fuente del Sol. Fr. de Heredia had
learned of what happened to the house they were sup-
posed to go to, so he rushed to Arévalo to bring the
good news.

The mules were harnessed, and nuns with their
baggage got onto the carts. Due to the unexpected
difficulties, Teresa left four of the nuns, Isabel Arias,
Teresa de Quesada, and the two sisters, Inés of Jesus

and Ana of the Incarnation in a village near Arévalo called Villanueva del Aceral, where the brother of the two sisters, Don Vicente de Ahumada, was the parish priest. In Medina, the greatest difficulty was the house since no one had ever seen it, not even Fr. Antonio, who had made the arrangements quickly because of the desperate situation.

Now another problem faced the little group. It was not good that the caravan arrive in broad daylight or even in the evening. What would the people of Medina say seeing such a curious spectacle? No one would be expecting them, and they would risk being followed by snoopers, busybodies and children. It would be better to arrive when night had fallen and silently take possession of the house. In the morning, what a grand moment when the bell would ring out for the first time, surprising everyone as had been done at St. Joseph's!

So they decided to pass by Fuente del Sol to clarify and establish all the details of the house. Fr. Antonio went straight to Medina to notify the Carmelite Fathers who naturally were to take part in the foundation.

Doña María Suárez turned out to be a very good woman who gave Teresa a letter for her administrator in Medina to vacate the house immediately, turning it over to the nuns. Generous as well as courteous, she gifted the nuns with carpets and a beautiful blue spread.

Passing through Olmedo, the summer residence of Bishop de Mendoza of Avila, they went to visit him. The Bishop blessed them and then asked by what means they had traveled.

Mother Teresa pointed to the carts that could be seen outside, and the Bishop insisted that she accept a carriage for the rest of the trip, sending his personal chaplain, Fr. Muñoz, to accompany them for the remaining ten miles. The countryside was silent, and the nuns prayed and sang psalms, just as though they were in a convent.

Fr. de Avila went ahead on his mule to announce them. "In fact," he wrote, "at midnight I had to beat loudly at the door of St. Ann's Monastery to awaken the Carmelite Fathers who finally opened the door and let me in. When they heard why I had come and that Mother Teresa was already near, we thought of how to organize ourselves so that the convent could be founded in that house the next morning."[1]

The caravan arrived, but instead of finding Medina deep in sleep, it was wide awake with people as curious as at noon. Bulls for the following day's corrida were arriving to be placed behind their designated fences. Naturally, much of Medina was on the streets to observe, comment and predict victories. Some spoke impertinently. Upon seeing the nuns out in a carriage at that hour they said many insolent things, but the nuns did not listen and went straight to St. Ann's Monastery. There they met Fr. de Avila who had arranged things, and together with the friars they went on foot to Santiago Street, passing outside the city walls so they would not get mixed up in the crowd.

Continuing with Fr. de Avila's account: "Everyone walked loaded down, looking like gypsies who had sacked a church. If the police had met us, it would certainly have been their duty to put us in prison until they had verified where priests, friars, and nuns were going at that hour."

But now the majordomo had to be awakened to turn the keys over to them. The chief steward had not been notified of anything, and he was long in awakening. Hardly believing his eyes, he asked the Carmelite Fathers, whom he knew, what they wanted at that hour. Upon hearing that they wanted to found a con-

---

1. *Op. cit.*, II, VIII, also for the following. Cf. Fr. Silverio, Vol. III, VIII.

vent, he barked "After midnight?" Not until Teresa handed him his owner's letter, and he recognized Doña María's handwriting would he be convinced. It was after one in the morning when the group got to the house accompanied by the majordomo who now wanted to help, too.

An old door in poor condition was evident, as well as a corridor and a little court with stairs leading to the upper floor. The first thought was where to place the altar. Night had advanced and all remained to be done for the house that was to become a convent at the first cock's crow.

Unbelievable, the situation is strictly true, sworn to by all the protagonists later when they separately related the incident. Teresa of Jesus led everyone. Having chosen the best room on the ground floor, she set the example by taking hold of a broom and starting to sweep. The other nuns followed, taking up other brooms and pails of water to wash the floors. The friars and priests set to work with hammers and nails. In order to hide the bad spots on the door, Teresa hung Doña María's blue spread over it. In this manner, even a sort of hanging canopy found its way into the improvised church.

The altar appeared as if by magic. In the hallway, the bell was made ready for the great announcement.

Just before dawn the chapel was ready. No one had stopped a moment, but they were not tired. At the prescribed hour, the bell rang for holy Mass.

Teresa was transfigured with happiness. At the sound of the bell, the neighborhood awoke. As in Ávila, people ran to see what had happened. There, where at midnight had been a sort of abandoned shed, now stood a convent.

Looking about, the neighbors found that the nuns had already built a sort of cloister behind a grate, a small choir and a confessional. An old broken-down door full of crevices was made to serve the purposes of the grate behind which they retired as soon as their work was done to lead their life as Carmelites separated from the world.

The foundation was effected, observing canonical rules and, to avoid future probable disturbances, a notarial act authorized by the Bishop was drawn up. To do this, Fr. de Avila and the Carmelites were forced to perform another "serenata" (as Fr. de Avila wrote) at the home of the vicar general in order to authorize the notary to draw up the foundation. The act was signed by two Carmelites, Friars Lucas de León and Antonio Sedeño, and by Fr. Alfonso Muñoz who had accompanied the nuns from Olmedo.

CHAPTER THIRTY-TWO

"A Friar and a Half!"

The great surprise for the people of Medina turned out perfectly. Humbly, Teresa thanked God, full of exultation, love and hope. Yet she was again to fall prey to an inner crisis—just as she had done after St. Joseph's had been founded.

This time there was an external cause—the miserable condition of the abandoned house. Stucco fell everywhere, doors were missing, and the doors that were there were in the condition of the one in the chapel which served as a grate. The walls were insecure, and the roof, too, resembled a grate. Disregarding the fact that it was unfit for the nuns to live in, it did not seem fitting enough to house the Blessed Sacrament with such rickety walls and missing doors.[1]

The unacceptability of the house constituted a continuous torment to Teresa's conscience. A very serious point to consider was the fact that Medina, being a market and fair center, drew all sorts of people from everywhere. In 1567, religious strife was rampant, and

1. See Fr. Silverio, VII, VIII.

spiteful deeds to holy things were not uncommon. Teresa was troubled greatly by the thought of heretics breaking in to take away and profane the Holy Eucharist.

Prostrated before the Blessed Sacrament she wept, almost reproaching herself for having gone so far. True, on Assumption Day a new convent dedicated to holy Mary had blossomed in Medina, but what were the consequences to be? It was characteristic of Teresa of Jesus to fall back pessimistically on her own conscience after a great action had been completed, a trait due to her spirit being both highly contemplative and vigorously active. When these two elements were at variance, then Teresa's inner martyrdom took place, becoming a precious holocaust.

After she had suffered at length, calm returned with trust in God. Her concern was over three main problems: watching over the Holy Eucharist; restoring, or rather, reconstructing the house; and searching for another dwelling to stay in while the work was going on.

Night and day the nuns took turns standing guard in the chapel.

Work was begun on the house, on "calle de Santiago," thanks to two great benefactresses, Doña Elena and Doña Jerónima de Quiroga, a mother and daughter, who were later to present themselves at the convent to ask admission as postulants. Providence unexpectedly solved the third problem. A rich and pious merchant, Blas de Medina, offered the nuns the top floor of his splendid house situated in Plaza Major next to the Collegiate Church.

Other benefactors came to the rescue, making Teresa feel reassured enough to send for the four nuns who had remained at Villanueva. There was enough room in the apartment they had at their disposal to permit the group to be reunited. In October they returned to "calle Santiago" and the convent took on its regular aspect, even if not permanent.

———————

When all was in place, Teresa spoke with Fr. Antonio de Heredia, Prior of the Medina Carmelites, who had helped so much, asking who would be the spiritual director. "It would be behooving that priests existed of our own unmitigated rule to direct the nuns."

The idea of extending the Reform to the Carmelite Fathers had been with her for quite some time. Surprisingly enough, Fr. Antonio replied, "If you wish, Reverend Mother, I could become the first friar of the Reform!" Teresa took his reply as an exclamation of courtesy, but Fr. Antonio meant what he said. Later he spoke of another probable candidate to the Reform, a young friar who was studying at the University of Salamanca, but who was to arrive shortly in Medina to celebrate his first Mass.

Juan of St. Mathias was the student who went to see Teresa. When the short, thin, and fragile-looking friar left, the recreation bell was ringing, and the nuns went out to the garden. Joining them, Teresa joyously joked: "My sisters, help me thank God because we already have a friar and a half for our Reform!"

That "half friar" was to be none other than St. John of the Cross, a future doctor of the Church.

Diverse invitations came to Teresa, two of which were especially gratifying because they were requests for two foundations. One came from Don Bernardino and Doña María de Mendoza, a brother and sister of the Bishop of Avila, requesting that a new convent be founded in Valladolid. They possessed large farms in Ubeda near Valladolid and desired that the Discalced nuns go there, and Doña María would be amply beneficent.

Doña Luisa de la Cerda from Medinacoeli was the author of the other request. As soon as this great friend of Teresa's heard that she had permission to establish other convents, she wrote in the hopes that a convent would be founded in Malagón which belonged to her by feudal right. Numbering about a thousand inhabitants, it was rather the county seat of the surrounding vast rural possessions than a regular town. There was not the middle class needed to help a convent carry on, and most of the inhabitants were poor. Teresa certainly realized this, for we shall later see how she resolved this problem.

A third invitation was also of great importance in its own way. Sent by an intelligent, pious, and authoritative Portuguese woman, Doña Leonor de Mascarenhas, who had been the governess of Philip II and Charles, it meant going into the midst of that solemn, almost unreal court of Philip II composed of the most powerful men of the world.

All three invitations were answered. In mid-October, 1567, Teresa left for Avila after settling the foundation in Medina. On her way to Malagón she stopped in Avila to discuss the terms for a house in Valladolid with María and Bernardino de Mendoza. They asked her to continue her trip with them since they were going to go to Ubeda which was the center of their possessions. In one of the two heavy carriages was Teresa with two other nuns, Ana of the Angels and Antonia of the Holy Spirit, while the brother and sister traveled in the other. The trip seemed short because everyone was busy thinking of projects for the new house. There was always more to be accomplished, and this was how another dream opened up for realization: the first foundation for Discalced Carmelites at Río de Olmos.

María de Mendoza was full of enthusiasm. Her older brother, the Bishop of Avila, had spoken highly to her of Teresa, and what could be more beautiful than to help this new seeker for asceticism and prayer. During the stops, the passengers of the two carriages joyfully talked together. Each felt herself to be an instrument in the making of a masterpiece that was to rise to the glory of the Lord. Even though a man of the world, Don Bernardino also took part in the general enthusiasm, giving his opinion and advice, promising his contribution. In Madrid, the Mendozas went to the house of some relatives while the nuns went to the palace of Leonor de Mascarenhas.

Doña Leonor appears to have been an exceptional person. Perfectly at ease with the high aristocracy, she nevertheless kept up with and participated in the current thought of her times, and this was why she exercised such great influence over the King and court. Pious, austere, strong-willed, gifted with the tendency to favor asceticism and mystic prayer, she was the best person to understand Teresa. Born in 1503 of a prominent Portuguese family, she became a lady-in-waiting to Queen Mary of Portugal. When Princess Isabel married Charles V, Doña Leonor passed to the court of Spain where she vowed chastity. At twenty-four, she was assigned the difficult and honorable task of educating the future Philip II. The best praise he could give her was to place, in turn, his son Charles under her guidance later.

This was all long ago, for she was sixty-five now, still at court only because the King asked her to remain. "You are too useful to the world," he would say, "and your duty is not to leave it!" And she obeyed.

She would have wished to go into the religious life when her office as educator had ended, but she realized the King was right, and that her influence was needed at court. Humble as she was, she saw this clearly, but she longingly followed all the movements in the monastic life. She welcomed Teresa exuberantly, for Teresa was known in Madrid for her sanctity. Teresa's arrival had been made known so there were many ladies of the court watching for her arrival, curious to see and hear the saint. They had all heard of her visions and ecstasies and were impatient to see how she acted. Waiting in Doña Leonor's parlor to meet her, they expected to see something extraordinary, that the Carmelite's face would become illuminated and her body rise from the floor. Everyone desired to see a moment in which the divine joined the human.

When Doña Leonor entered with Teresa of Jesus, the women were waiting impatiently, chatting excitedly. They immediately gathered about, staring at Teresa. She walked calmly, naturally and nobly. She smiled and humbly greeted each one in a dignified manner, her pleasant, rather full face radiating warmth. Just as a woman of the world, she went around being introduced, courteous in a special manner to them all, demonstrating that self-assurance which naturally inspired respect.

When the introductions were through, Teresa became the center of the conversation. All present were expecting to hear unheard-of lofty things, for they knew that even theologians were enthralled by her speech. They waited for the sublime talk of a confiding nature.

Turning to the women near her, Teresa began to talk while they formed a circle around her. "Ah," she said, "what a beautiful city Madrid is! Such imposing streets and magnificent palaces!" And she continued describing what had struck her most, but the expected change of tone toward the sublime would not come. Where was that distance that separated her from the rest of humanity? Where was that superior concentration and continuous rapture? The conversation was pleasant, but nothing more. When the saint left, the usual polite forms of salutation were used. But the women remained bewildered: Was that all? Was that sanctity? One even went so far as to say: "But is this what she travels for?"

CHAPTER THIRTY-THREE

"Is This What
She Travels For?"

Teresa remained with Doña Leonor a fortnight, during which time she won the heart of the court. Her naturalness and distinctiveness, far from exhibitionism, showed the greatness of her personality. Having reflected a little, the women of the court understood the saint's manner perfectly. Philip II, his sister Juana, and others in the higher ranks saw how much distance separated this woman from all those pseudo-mystics, hysterics and frauds who infested Spain, for supernatural revelations had become the fashion. Side by side with the true saints, true poets of divine love, were numbers of imitators who lived prey to continuous real or simulated hallucinations. Intellectuals and religious, especially those of the Inquisition, kept on their guard against these visionaries in their attempt to eradicate those who publicly mocked the intimate and ineffable relations between Creator and creature. One such person, if invited to court, would undoubtedly have manifested some false transcendental show, but Teresa's sincerity and dignity were far from performing such demonstrations.

Smiling, humble, and dignified, she convinced the people at court, and they slowly understood how great she was. Behind those educated manners lay treasures witnessed by the most competent judges of souls. This simple manner proved to be the best lesson, destroying the mistaken devotional expectations, while calling attention to a serious moral-religious valuation. Humility and concealing discretion were what truly mattered.

One of the most interesting and instructive moments for Teresa was the visit to the "Royal Discalced" who lived in a Franciscan monastery following the very austere, primitive rule founded by Philip II's sister, Juana. Another Juana of royal blood, the sister of the ex-Duke of Gandia, Francis Borgia, was the mother Superior. Teresa could thus study the life of the Discalced and their rule which was of great benefit to her for her successive foundations. It also established a solid basis for spiritual fraternity with those nuns, some of whom were truly exceptional. Almost all of them were from very high social backgrounds, so their manners were polished, and their seriousness in monastic life was profound. Those nuns felt the vital air of love in the saint, and what they said of her was: "Blessed be God who has granted us to see a saint we can all imitate; she talks, sleeps and eats as we do, and is neither ceremonious in speech nor mellifluous in spirit."

Meanwhile, Doña Leonor explained to Teresa what delicate task she desired to assign to her. Here we must go back and remember María of Jesus of the Third Order who, in 1561, had gone to Rome barefoot to obtain the papal brief permitting her to found a convent of primitive Carmelite rule. On her return, she had gone to see Teresa who had been staying with Doña

Luisa de la Cerda. Views, inspirations, and projects were exchanged between the two Foundresses.

In 1562, with the help of Doña Leonor, María of Jesus had realized her dream of founding a convent in Alcalá which still exists. Donã Leonor was the institute's protectress and now turned to Teresa of Jesus to help order its internal situations because María of Jesus, Foundress, Prioress, and soul of the convent, had impressed her spirit of deep mortification into it. Since there was no concrete program of activities, the daughters of María of Jesus all ended up by imitating her seraphic life, but María could succeed in imposing continual penances upon herself. She was truly a person of great holiness; burning in her deep love for God, she found that terrestrial existence was but an incessant sacrifice. In the convent, however, sublime disorder and luminous intemperance rose from María's example. The poor nuns no longer slept nor ate, happy though they were, wanting nothing better, they could not hold up under the voluntary strain. María herself wanted to remedy the situation, but knew not what to do because for her it was so spontaneous and actually necessary to live in that way. Having notified her protectress about it, the latter called on Teresa because in her, seraphic love did not exclude balanced prudence. Teresa accepted the task of intervening, promising to stop at Alcalá on her way to Malagón, and upon leaving Madrid, she was in possession of the Archbishop's permission to change matters in the institute.

María of Jesus was overjoyed at seeing Teresa, openly accepting her outside help. Not at all hurt, she did not in the least feel humiliated by this intervention. The convent of the Pure Conception of the Image was established by her at a very high price. With true humility, she ceded her position of prioress to Teresa and helped to execute the latter's orders.

Teresa's method was very simple: she separated the beautiful but impossible aspirations from the possible ones. She taught the sickly, less resistant nuns to moderate themselves, satisfying their love with acts of virtue perhaps more meritorious in the eyes of the Sacred Heart. Above all, she drew up a well-studied program of life in the convent. Before leaving, she gave two copies of the constitutions of St. Joseph's in Avila for the nuns to follow experimentally and almost thirty years later it served as the basis for the formal rule of the convent.

María of Jesus was immensely grateful to Teresa because her work seemed both renewed and strengthened. After they affectionately embraced one another, Teresa took leave of Alcalá where she had been for two months and set out toward Malagón.

CHAPTER THIRTY-FOUR

Malagón, Río de Olmos; Durvelo and Mancera

In 1568, Teresa began two foundations of Discalced Carmelites, in Malagón and in Río de Olmos near Valladolid. For the first one she drew up a contract with Doña Luisa de la Cerda, donor of the convent, on May 30. The document was a model for the manner in which it resolved every possible problem; the convent was entrusted to the generosity of Doña Luisa by income assignment.[1]

But the nuns had already entered before this. "On Palm Sunday, 1568, they came for us in a procession.[2] So we went with our veils down over our faces and wearing our white mantles."[3]

The other convent at Río de Olmos was offered by María and Bernardino de Mendoza. A surprising drama took place within the framework of that good undertaking. Don Bernardino died suddenly, without confession,

---

1. From the De la Cerda mansion. *Foundations,* IX, 5.

2. *Foundations,* X, 2, 5, also for the following.

3. *Foundations,* XIII, 1, 2, 3, also for the following.

before the foundation was established. Shortly after, a revelation announced to Teresa that the donor was saved precisely by the grace of that charitable act, and that at the first Eucharistic Sacrifice celebrated in the convent, he would enter into glory.

With this celestial bond to spur her on, she could not stop. "Though I wished to go to Toledo, I could no longer, but dedicated myself wholly to making the foundation at Valladolid a reality."

On August 15, the nuns entered into the donated house in Río de Olmos, but on February 3, 1569, they transferred into their definite residence in Valladolid donated by María de Mendoza. While attending the first Mass celebrated in the chapel in Río de Olmos when the building was still being remodeled, at Communion she saw Don Bernardino's soul radiant with joy, ascending to heaven.

"May the Lord be blessed forever," she wrote, "because He recompenses such trifling actions as ours with eternal life and glory, making our worthless acts become great."

A problem more complex than in the past now came up for Teresa to solve. The Discalced possessed a distinctive spirituality which was austere and profound, not easily maintained in its early integrity. The Foundress observed this fact and thoughtfully considered what was to be carried out to assure primitive fervor in the spirit of the Reform as time went on. This problem of guaranteeing an integral spiritual heredity to several generations of nuns came to her when she realized what great possibilities for expansion there were in the movement she started.

Certainly the basis of a strong spiritual direction was necessary to achieve this, but what would happen when she was no more? Besides, she couldn't travel

continuously. This serious difficulty could only be resolved with creating a Reform for Carmelite Discalced
Friars, based on the same spirit and rule—which would
provide the convent's natural spiritual directors—acting
as depository of the original spirit of Teresian Reform.
But if her first tiny convent for nuns had cost so much
effort and anguish, what would be needed to create one
for friars?[4] Teresa had begun working on this in 1567,
when Fr. Rubeo had given her the authority to extend
her reform for nuns. She had spoken to him of her
problem then and had obtained authority to found
monasteries also for friars.

As we have seen, she had two friars[5] in Medina
with whom to begin: Fr. Antonio, Prior at St. Ann's
Monastery, and young John of St. Mathias.[6] Friar John
was most enthusiastic about the idea, and Mother Teresa saw that his soul overflowed with love for God.

"I was very satisfied with my two friars," she
wrote, "but since I could not find a house for them, I
could only supplicate the Lord.

"At that time a certain man, Rafael Meja Velásquez
of Avila, whom I had never met, learned that we
wanted to found a monastery for Discalced Friars. He
came and offered me a house he owned in a little
village of hardly twenty families." The village was Durvelo, situated about twenty miles from Avila, and the
house was rented to a farmer who worked for the
proprietor. Teresa understood what type of house it
probably was, but she praised God and thanked the
gentleman warmly. On her way from Avila to Medina,
she went to see the place.

---

4. *Foundations,* XIV, 6, 7, 8, here and for the following.

5. Two, because elections were being held and both the new and old
Provincial were to be consulted.

6. John of St. Mathias chose a new name upon entering the Reform.

"Not knowing the way, we took the wrong road and could find no one to put us on the right track, for the village was not well known. We walked all day under the burning sun; whenever we thought we were near, there was always just that much more to walk. I shall always remember the fatigue and all the turning we did on that trip." That was no exaggeration because they had left Avila at dawn on June 30, and arrived at their destination at sundown. "We found the house so dirty and full of workers that we did not deem it wise to remain for the night. The building for our monastery was nothing but a small portico, one room divided in two, an attic and a small kitchen! I thought the church could be constructed below the portico, the choir in the attic, and the dormitory in the room. But my companion, who is much better than I and a great lover of penances, could not resign herself to the fact that I thought of making a monastery there. 'No spirit, Mother,' she said, 'no matter how good, could bear to live here. Renounce it definitely.'

"The priest who accompanied us was of the same opinion, but when I exposed my plans to him he did not oppose them. So we went to spend the night in church; we were so tired that we certainly did not wish to stay up all night."

They set off for Medina the next morning, and there Teresa went to speak to Fr. Antonio, describing the house and village to him.

"But if you will have the courage to remain there for some time," she persuaded, "God will surely put things right quickly; what is important is to begin." As she spoke, she mentally saw other houses, places and religious, making her feel sure that other new foundations would be erected. Continuing in her arguments to convince Fr. Antonio, she said, "If we were to begin our reform for friars in a well-constructed, comfortable, and important-looking house, the two provincials who must approve would be poorly impressed and perhaps would grow suspicious. If we start in a broken-down house, they can put forth no obstacle."

She had put to practice her gift of converting people in persuading the future Discalced Friar, but his reply made her realize her words had been superfluous because he seemed to have more courage than she.

"Reverend Mother, not only am I disposed to go into that house, but I would even go into a pigsty!"

Friar John felt the same way, so the three set about obtaining the permits which were acquired with relative ease.

From then on, the history of the first Carmelite Reform for Friars became poetry. To Teresa those unforgettable days were the visual result of her prayers and aspirations. "When authorization from the two provincials was obtained, I felt nothing else was lacking, so we decided Fr. John of the Cross would go to the house and fix it in such a way as to become habitable. I wanted to finish quickly because I feared unexpected difficulties.

"Fr. Antonio had already collected several necessary articles. We did all we could to help him, but that was not much. He came to Valladolid to see me, joyously showing me the list of what he had gathered. There was little; all he had was an abundance of hour glasses—five of them, which made me laugh. But he said that it was a good idea to have several on hand if the hours of the day were to be well-regulated. But he most likely had not found anything on which to sleep.

"The house was ready shortly. There was not enough money to finish things as they would have liked. When the work was done, Fr. Antonio generously renounced his priorship, promising to observe the primitive rule. He had been counseled to give it a try first, but he would not consent to that and marched off toward the hovel feeling deeply happy. Friar John was already there.

"When in sight of the village, Fr. Antonio told me later, he felt an extraordinary joy in his soul, sure he was through with the world, leaving everything to bury himself in that solitude. The house did not seem uncomfortable to them at all; indeed, they felt they were in a magnificent place."

That was November 17, 1568. The countryside about was bleak, and the days were short. At night the house was cold and a great sense of solitude swept over the village. Yet, those two were happy! They had built a chapel in the little portico which Mother Teresa called the portico of Bethlehem "because I don't think it must be any better than that one." Naturally, the choir was necessary, so they built it toward the middle of the attic where the roof was highest; since the attic sloped toward the chapel, it was the perfect place to have it. They recited the Hours there and assisted at Mass. If they inadvertently stood up without remembering to bend, their heads bumped against a joist.

Their first Mass had been celebrated in the beginning of Advent, and from then on the Blessed Sacrament had always been with them. What mattered the dark and the cold? When there was oil for the lamp they would remain after choir hours, reading and praying, but the sanctuary lamp was always lit, flickering at the wind that entered everywhere. From the beginning, two other friars joined them: another Carmelite in his woolen habit which he did not change because he was too old and rather sickly, and a young friar who called himself Joseph of Christ. Four were enough to form a community. Mother Teresa visited them during Lent, 1569, on her way to Toledo to open another foundation.

"I arrived in the morning while Friar Anthony of Jesus was sweeping the doorway of the church with his usual smiling countenance. 'What is this?' I said. 'Where then is your honor?'

"'Cursed be the time such a thing mattered!' he answered, showing me he was truly happy.

"Upon entering the church, I became filled with admiration. The spirit of fervor which the Lord had spread there enraptured not only me, but the two Medina merchant-friends of mine also; they simply wept all the time we were there."

Mother Teresa was struck especially by certain details which became delightful poetry in her hands: "I shall always remember a small wooden cross placed over the holy water font on which they had pasted a paper image of Christ crucified which inspired more devotion than if it had been made of gold. In the two corners near the chapel, two tiny hermitages had been placed in which they could either prostrate themselves or be seated, and then their heads almost touched the ceiling. Here there was straw because it was very cold. The altar could be seen through the tiny window in each hermitage, and two stones served as cushions. I learned that after matins, instead of retiring to their cells, they remained there until prime, praying so intently that at times when they got up they would find their clothes snow-laden without having noticed the snow fall."

But their life was not all contemplative. The first Discalced began immediately to preach with good results. "They preached in many nearby villages whose inhabitants were without religious instruction. That was one of the reasons I joyfully accepted that they become established there because I had been told that no monastery existed in the surroundings, and the poor people had no means of being instructed, which grieved me. Their esteem for the friars was so great that they were conquered quickly, and this filled me with joy.

"I was saying then that they would go five and six miles out to preach, absolutely barefoot because the 'alpargatas' cord sandals which they did not wear were ordered later. Even when it was cold, and there was much snow, they went this way. After having heard confessions and preached, they would return to the monastery very late to eat, but the joy they felt made everything easy for them."

In this manner, a breath of sanctity spread over the countryside. Astonished, the farmers could only reflect that their own poverty was nothing next to that voluntarily imposed poverty of the friars. To see learned men who could certainly have lived comfortably was, of course, the best example possible. The monastery never lacked food because families all about kept the friars well-supplied with eggs and vegetables. Many had brought chickens and meat in the beginning and had marveled when the friars gently refused them, but even the farmers gradually learned the rules and brought the prescribed food at the right times.

The poor were not the only ones to frequent the monastery; even rich proprietors began to go to Our Lady of Carmel and feel the superhuman air about the place. Its chapel, hermitages, the friars, all served as an examination of conscience to them. They began hesitantly, but then some special attraction won them over—either the fascination of renunciation, of truth, or of holiness. "Lords of those parts went to confession there and would immediately offer more comfortable houses on their own land." The Discalced were firm in not accepting, but one did succeed in persuading them. His name was Luis, Lord of Cinco Villas, that is, five towns, Galmoral, Naharros, San Miguel, Montalvo and Gallegos. In the church he built in honor of the Madonna to whom he was very devoted, was a picture of Mary which had a strange story behind it.

Of early sixteenth-century Flemish origin, it depicted a slim, pale Virgin with a blue cape. Luis' father had decided to send it to his mother from Flanders and had entrusted it to a Spanish merchant who was returning to Spain, but the merchant became so attached to the picture that he kept it for himself and only on his deathbed did he order that it be delivered to its legitimate owner.

Thus, the picture entered into the Cinco Villas family, and now Don Luis placed it in a church built expressly to house it in Mancera. "To this day I have never seen anything more beautiful," St. Teresa wrote, "and many other people say the same thing."

Fr. Antonio was invited by Don Luis to see the picture. When he saw it he became so taken by it that he immediately assented to transfer the monastery there even if there was no water well about, nor did it seem probable to find any. Don Luis "built them a small monastery conformable to their wants, providing decorous holy furnishings." The transfer took place June 11, 1570, with the provincial, Fr. Gonzales, celebrating the first Mass in the new house at Mancera. By that time, there were seventeen friars, all from mitigated orders. The first to come from the world was Fr. John the Baptist of Avila who professed his vows in October, 1570.

Even water was found at the new monastery. One evening after supper, Fr. Antonio, who was the Prior, was discussing the need for water with the other religious. All at once he got up, picked up his walking-stick and made a sign with it at a certain place in the monastery. "Now dig here!" he said. They dug a little and so much water came out that "now when they want to clean the well it is difficult to empty it." And this was how the first Discalced foundation for friars became situated less isolated from the world.

But how much maternal worry had that foundation cost Teresa? "Since I am weak and imperfect, I insistently begged them to moderate somewhat their austerity which was excessive. It had cost me so much prayer and sighing to obtain the right persons with whom to begin that when I saw things had begun well, I feared lest the devil try to finish those friars before my hopes could be realized. Imperfect and of little faith as I was, I did not stop to think that it was the work of God, and that His Lordship would have watched over it. But those friars possessed that virtue which I lacked; they simply continued on their way paying little attention to my words. I left them overjoyed, far from rendering proper thanks to God for such a great favor. May the Lord in His bounty grant me to serve Him in some way for all I owe Him."

These lines were written by Mother Teresa many years later when there were already ten Discalced monasteries: Durvelo, Pastrana, Mancera, Alcalá de Henares, Altomira, la Roda, Granada, la Peñuela, Seville, Almodovar del Campo.

CHAPTER THIRTY-FIVE

The Foundation in Toledo

We already know what place Toledo held in Teresa's heart: her family's cradle, a city of dear and holy personal memories, the most loved city of Spain. To every Spaniard, Toledo inspired patriotic love. To be able to found a convent there would be the realization of a splendid dream.

In 1569, the offer came. On his deathbed, a rich merchant, Martín Ramírez, had decided to leave his vast fortune to religious beneficence. An honest business man, alert and prudent, he had made use of his riches to help others. By his personal savings and because he was not married, he had put aside his earnings and income so his patrimony automatically became greater. The larger part of it was distributed later to the poor. About to die, Don Martín wished to give the finishing touches to his good works, designating his money to Masses for the dead, to establishing stipends, to good works of both spiritual and temporal nature.

Someone had spoken to him of the Teresian Reform underlining the fact that a Discalced convent in Toledo would be of great merit to him and useful to the city.

Those nuns knew how to spread the light of Christ and to draw blessings. Why did he not leave them the various bequests which he had in mind to do? Yes, that was probably the best thing, but he was so ill he could no longer write. Having called his brother, Alonso Alvarez, he clearly explained that he wished to leave all to the Carmelite Reform, and that together with his son-in-law, Diego Ortiz, he was to act as executor of his will with full liberty of decision. Diego was learned in canon law and theology, so much so that he was often called "the theologian."

When Don Martín died, the two executors wrote to Mother Teresa inviting her to come settle matters. Busy as she was with her new foundations, it was March 24, 1569, before she could get to Toledo together with two other nuns and Julian de Avila. Here they were guests of Doña Luisa de la Cerda.

Negotiations began immediately, but they were not easy. Strange to say, Diego Ortiz was the one who complicated matters. "Though he was quite a good man and had studied theology," Mother Teresa wrote, "he was more tenacious than Alonso Alvarez and would not give in easily, not even if he was wrong."[1] Then, too, the problems multiplied, branching out into questions of patronage and special family rights so that nothing was finally settled. To avoid a double loss of time while negotiations were being carried on, Teresa and the testament executors looked about to find a house for rent. Though many persons canvassed for a house, none was to be found for the nuns.

These were not all the difficulties Teresa had to face. What afflicted her more than Ortiz's obstinacy and not having a house was a consequence of the dramatic imprisonment of the Archbishop of Toledo,

---

1. *Foundations*, XV, 4, 5, 6, 8, 9, 10, 12, 13, 14, here and for the following.

Bartolomeo Carranza, a Dominican accused of heresy. Not defending himself sufficiently, he was kept in the Valladolid prison, only to be transferred to Rome to die. Don Gómez Tello Girón was the apostolic administrator substituting for the Archbishop, and the one who caused Teresa grief.

He had perhaps been warned against the Carmelite from Avila and her Reform, and he would not grant permits, so Teresa asked two of her influential friends, Doña Luisa de la Cerda and Don Pedro Manrique, the cathedral pastor, to intercede for her. Both were zealous supporters of the Reform and were much respected in Toledo. The choice of her intercessors was sure to bring positive results. Instead, they had tearfully to report the failure of their mission; the diocesan administrator was courteous, but would not grant the least concession.

The joy of a foundation in Toledo was going up in smoke, and, what mattered most, the Reform was losing a magnificent base. "I did not know what to do because we had come expressly for the foundation, knowing well that if we left without having concluded anything, we could have given rise to unpleasant interpretations." But the license was not to be had.

After two months, she decided it was useless to have recourse to intermediaries; she would go herself to talk to the administrator. Entering a church near his house, she sent word asking that he deign to grant her an interview. It was her duty to break down his resistance as quickly as possible. "When I was before him, with God's fearlessness bolstering me, I said, 'It is very strange that those who spend their life in the midst of luxury dare to cross the desire of some poor women who wish to live in great austerity, perfection and seclusion as a sacrifice to the Lord.'"

The cutting blow could not have been better calculated. She continued on different subjects which produced an obviously profound effect because he changed his mind, and she left with complete permission! Teresa took the positive outcome as an important sign. "I went out feeling very happy, and even though I had nothing, I felt all was ready. My wealth consisted in three or four ducats with which I bought two pictures to place on the altar (because I had none), two straw mats, and one blanket." It was characteristic of Teresa to supply herself with pictures for the chapel when there was no house in view. To make matters worse, negotiations with Alvarez and Ortiz ended in nothing. "Moreover, there was no hope for a house because I had already broken with Alvarez."

A benevolent merchant who was an expert at curing the most difficult souls in prisons provided some hope. Alfonso de Avila was from Teresa's hometown and offered to find her a house, but he unexpectedly fell ill, causing all hopes of a house to fade away.

It so happened that Friar Martin of the Cross passed through Toledo just then and heard of Teresa's difficulties. As a cure-all, the old man sent Teresa a young man by the name of Andrada who was neither a religious nor a man with possessions. Indeed, he looked as though he could just as well be looking for his own bread instead of helping the nuns set up a monastery for which he had no experience.

Obediently he presented himself in the church where Teresa was assisting at Mass. He explained that a Franciscan friar had sent him there to do all he could for them. Teresa thanked him kindly, but inwardly wondered how strange of Friar Martin to send that sort of help. When he left, Teresa said, "We could not keep from smiling among ourselves at the help that saint had sent us.

"Even with the permit in hand, we had no one to help us, and I knew not what to do or how to find a house for rent." Desperate, she decided to make use of

Andrada while the other nuns laughed at her idea. But Teresa insisted that "if that great servant of God sent him to us, there must be some mystery behind it." Calling him, she told him a house had to be found. When Andrada asked how much money was available, Teresa, having none, answered as a lady of class would have: "For the rental I would have given as surety my good friend Alfonso de Avila, the merchant who fell ill."

On this chimerical pledge executed in grave terms, the two parted amid the stifled hilarity of the other two nuns.

———————

Andrada returned the next morning reporting that the house was ready. At first all the nuns looked at him in an almost menacing manner, but their expressions soon turned to wonder, and Teresa exclaimed, "What do you mean, ready?"

Andrada simply pulled out some keys from his pocket, saying, "Here are the keys. It is nearby."

It was all so miraculous, but the house really existed, seemed to be in good condition and was even well-situated in Barrio Nuevo Square, near the church of Our Lady of Transit. "When thinking of this foundation," Teresa wrote later, "I often become filled with amazement, considering the ways of God. For almost three months influential people had hunted for a house unsuccessfully; then along came this poor young man, and the Lord let him find one immediately."

From then on, everything went easily. It seemed as though the thread of the skein was found, the rest unfolding itself without effort. Mother Teresa thought it best to take immediate possession of the house to avoid any probable inconvenience, entrusting Andrada with the arrangements. On his return, he announced that on the next day the house would be at their disposition, adding, with emphasis, that the nuns could start taking their household implements there.

Mother Teresa candidly objected that there would be little to carry because they owned only two straw mats and a blanket.

When Andrada left, her companions said it would have perhaps been better not to speak to him so openly, for it could be dangerous to be thought so poor. What if he should become discouraged? Teresa became aware of this, confessing: "I had not thought of that, but fortunately Andrada was not discouraged. He who had given him the will to help us made him remain helpful to the end. He became so zealous in finding workmen and putting the house in order that his attentions were no fewer than ours.

"At dusk, after we had borrowed all that was necessary to have Mass celebrated, we went to the new house with a workman, taking along one of those bells that are rung at the elevation for want of something better to ring out possession. We worked all night while I feared someone would discover how we had arranged things. The only place that seemed suitable for the chapel was a room with no outside door; to get to it one had to pass through the house next to it. We had rented that house, too, but there were several women still in it for the time being.

"Everything was ready and day was breaking. No one had yet dared to speak to those women for fear the news would spread.

"In order to create an entrance to the chapel, we decided to open a door which was filled in with bricks and which led to a small court. These women were still in bed, but at the sound of those blows, they woke up frightened, and we certainly had our 'to-do' to calm them down. It was time for Mass, and it was celebrated immediately so even if they had wished to continue bothering us, they could no longer do any harm. But the Lord calmed them when they learned what was going on.''

Fr. Gutiérrez, Toledo's Carmelite Prior, offered the first Mass with Doña Luisa de la Cerda and several members of her family present.

But their difficulties did not end there. Later in the day the proprietress of the house arrived; since her husband had the right of primogeniture, the house was to remain in the same state it was. Only her husband could be responsible for it before the law and before the others who had interests in the property. You can imagine her face when she saw the wall torn down and everything changed in the twinkling of an eye. The house she had given the nuns the night before was altogether different from this one, and to believe her eyes, she was forced to touch different articles to keep level-headed. Nevertheless, she began to grow excited. Her husband was responsible before the law, and she was responsible before her husband for having rented a house without establishing precise agreements. What would her husband do or say to these women? Furious, the woman felt that the nuns were in turn responsible before her. Her logic exploded in this connection, condemning the nuns. ''Finally she realized that if she satisfied us we could have repaid her well, so she calmed down.''

When the woman left, the nuns looked at each other as though to say ''and what now?'' The ecclesiastical council was not long in breaking in upon the nuns. The members of this council had sided with Msgr. Tello Girón in the governing of the large diocese and had already turned down Teresa's petition to open a convent in Toledo. This council was also one of the reasons why the administrator had persistently said no to Teresa for two months. Though he had given in by dint of Teresa's discourse, he had been called away without having had the time to inform the council that he had become favorable to the Discalced convent.

Those who formed the council were all strict ecclesiastics or laymen who were ignorant of the true identity of Teresa. To see a house almost miraculously transformed into a prohibited convent, ringing its little bell of existence, was surely another trick played by that indomitable nun, establishing herself in Toledo complete with bell, followers and a few rags. Unable to protest to the administrator because he was out of town, they went to a cathedral priest, Don Pedro Manrique, to plan a counter-program. But Don Pedro was the very one Mother Teresa had kept informed of everything. Before his indignant colleagues, however, he simulated surprise, saying only that since Teresa of Jesus had already established foundations elsewhere, she must certainly be experienced at it and would not have acted unreasonably; she must certainly have the necessary permit.

His words, however, proved of no avail in calming them down. In fact, a few days later, still in the absence of the administrator, the council members sent an injunction to the nuns forbidding Mass to be celebrated any longer in the convent under penalty of excommunication until a regulation permit was obtained.

Showing great humility, Teresa answered that she would do what they imposed though she was not obligated to do so. "We succeeded in calming them because the thing was already done; otherwise, who knows how much trouble they would have caused us!"

After that storm passed, there remained the problem of living in the new convent and becoming settled, so to speak. "We spent several days with only our mats and one blanket, lacking all else. The first day we did not even have a piece of wood to roast a sardine. But the Lord moved someone to leave a small bundle of firewood in church, so we got by." One night when the cold seemed unbearable, the saint called her "daughters." Shivering, in the name of charity, she asked that they cover her a bit more. But those two joyfully replied that all the covers of the convent were on her already; that is, their two mantles. "Our mantles certainly do us a lot of good!" commented the saint.

That extraordinary poverty proved to be a great attraction to the three Discalced nuns and they felt happy. They had nothing, therefore they could feel themselves privileged, like queens or empresses. It was a great poetic contentment with poverty. "Such great penury was most advantageous to us because we derived so much joy and inner consolation from it that when I think of it I can only admire what God encloses in that virtue. That complete destitution seemed to keep us in a state of tender contemplation."

But alas, that secret world of joy was quickly discovered, and Toledo's heartstrings loosened. An hidalgan city at heart, Toledo felt it was her duty to help three poor, half-frozen, and half-starved servants of God. Alvarez, the executor of the will of his brother, Martín Ramírez, was the first to help. An honest man, he realized that the conditions in which the nuns were depended on the rigidity with which he and his son-in-law, Ortiz, conducted the affairs of the will. His conscience awakened, leading him to pick up negotiation with Mother Teresa.

Unbelievable as it may seem to us of little faith, the danger of suddenly becoming rich through Ramírez' inheritance severely frightened the nuns. "I was extremely saddened; it was as though someone had taken away my abundant gold jewelry, leaving me in misery. I greatly grieved at seeing poverty disappear, and my companions felt the same way. When I asked why they looked so sad, they answered, 'The reason, Mother? We no longer feel poor.' Even my desire to be poor grew, and I felt so elevated as to disdain all tangible good things, for when these are lacking, interior joys grow, filling the soul with peace."

Thence, back to the burdensome negotiations, Doña Francisca Ramírez, the wife of Diego Ortiz, obtained patronage of the greater chapel provided the nuns furnish it, the altar, and the holy vestments within ten years, and provided they agree that the body of Martín Ramírez be transferred there. Five thousand three hundred forty ducats were paid them by the Alvarezes, and in addition, they established eight stipends for the convent.

In the following year, 1571, the nuns negotiated for the purchase of a house adaptable to the institute's growth and development. The sum of twelve thousand ducats to pay for the new building was reached by adding two important dowries belonging to wealthy novices and other recent beneficence to the money received from the Alvarez family.

Teresa was human enough to prefer to remain in the little house on the Square with her pious garden of delights (her country-house, as she called it), but she was also saintly enough to yield the constitution's aims of glorifying God rather than to think of her own personal holy joys. It was her duty to think of all the nuns who would come into the Carmelite Reform, of which there were six for the time being.

═══════════

And what happened to Andrada? We don't know much about him. In his *History of the Reform,* Fr. Francis of St. Mary says that God did not leave him unrewarded. He led a comfortable life cheered by a healthy, loving family; the descendants contemporary to the historian attributed the favors the Andrada family received to the intercession of St. Teresa.

CHAPTER THIRTY-SIX

A Princess and the Foundation in Pastrana

"The first fifteen days following the foundation in Toledo, where we remained a year, were generally spent in putting up grates and organizing. There had been work enough, and I was very tired, having spent all that time with the workmen. Finally, on the day before Pentecost (May 28, 1569) all was ready.

"That morning while at lunch, the thought that all was finished, and that on that feast day I could spend some moments with our Lord, filled me with such great joy I could hardly eat."[1]

At that moment, the outside bell of the convent rang, followed by the message of the lay sister that a messenger sent by the Princess of Eboli was at the door. To know the Spain of Philip II necessitates meeting the Princess of Eboli, Ana de Mendoza y la Cerda, related to the most important families of the kingdom, including Spain's great Cardinal, Don Pedro Gonzales de Mendoza. Diego Hurtado de Mendoza was her fa-

---

1. *Foundations*, XVII, 1, 2, 3, 11, for all quotations in this chapter.

ther, and Doña Ana de la Cerda, Luisa's sister, was her mother. Her family tree was full of great names and influential people.

A girl of remarkable beauty and strange temperament had been the fruit of such illustrious alliances. At sixteen, Ana married Ruy Gómez, a Portuguese lord who had come to Spain's court as a child. After marriage, the Princess' natural inclinations became accentuated, revealing her as a complex woman: generous, authoritative, intelligent, sensitive and easily susceptible to anxiety.

In addition to being a courtier, Ruy Gómez was also a statesman. As a page he had followed Isabel of Portugal to Toledo and Madrid when she married Charles V and had grown up as the future Philip II's playmate. Along with Doña Leonor de Mascarenhas, who was a relative, and Doña Isabel de Brances, he belonged to that select small Portuguese group which had borne such a good influence on Spain's court in the sixteenth century. Intelligent, thoughtful, prudent, and kind, he exercised considerable influence over Philip II and over those near him. An esteemed friend and expert adviser, he was no ordinary courtesan adulator; and the King was generous in rewarding him. Even if his Portuguese birth prevented him from possessing ancestral Spanish titles, he abounded in princedoms and dukedoms. In 1559, Gómez became Prince of Eboli, Duke of Estremera in 1568, Duke of Pastrana and Financial Minister in 1572. Pastrana was a town of about a thousand inhabitants, belonging to the Ebolis by virtue of grandmother Ana de la Cerda de Mendoza's inheritance.

Returning to the Princess, we can fit her into Schiller's opera "Don Carlos" in the midst of that austere group of leading men in Madrid. Though beautiful, she suffered inwardly as the result of her whimsical nature which was in turn due to her upbringing. In a famous portrait by Sánchez Coello she is shown with a thick opaque glass over one eye. It is uncertain whether this was due to mere whimsy or if it constituted a defense to vanity, hiding a cross-eye. The latter seems probable because at eighteen we know she fell, injuring an eye. This incident may perhaps have contributed to the Princess' susceptible temperament, for the thought of such an uncomely defect might well have become unbearable.

In the formation of the Princess' character it is important to remember that she was very privileged from birth onward. No one had ever opposed her, neither her doting parents, nor her even-tempered husband who was always perfectly courteous. All the members of Court ended by trembling before her. To be appeased in everything had become a necessity to her; woe if at any time a wish of hers was not carried out. Ana was really generous at heart, easily moved and ready to help the needy, but her generosity often turned into a caprice if any obstacle presented itself. In her desire to help others, she found herself satisfying her own ego to the point of exasperation. She would suffer and become excited. Her eyebrows would arch imperiously, and her voice would acquire a bronze-like hardness. It was in those moments that her command was inflexible.

On the whole, the Princess of Eboli serves as a lesson in life. Gifted as she was by both nature and society in the requisites for happiness, she created unhappiness for herself and distress to others because she could not moderate her faults. However, she always bore true affection for her husband.

Let us now see how the Princess of Eboli and Teresa of Jesus, two immensely different personalities, met and acted.

When Fr. Rubeo passed through Madrid in 1567, he spoke with admiration of Mother Teresa of Jesus, and from that day on Ana desired to see the reformer. In

Madrid the following year, Princess Ana spoke to Teresa of a possible foundation in Pastrana.

Pastrana did not become a duchy until 1572, but it was the princely pair's favorite possession. A large Renaissance palace crowned the village spread over the sunny slope below, enclosing beautiful formal gardens within its high walls. Governed by these new lords, the village had taken on a different aspect: a hospital, dignified buildings and the collegiate church which was richly endowed with holy vessels and vestments, hangings and precious objects. Many a city cathedral could not have rivaled it. There was no cloistered convent so the Reformed Carmelite Order could well fill this gap.

This is why Ana's page came to Teresa just as she was preparing for deeper contemplation. "But I could not enjoy meditation for long because I was interrupted by the announcement of the Princess' servant. When I spoke to him he said the Princess of Eboli had sent for me to found the convent at Pastrana of which we had spoken long ago." Ana had kindly sent her courier with a beautiful carriage.

But the news struck as lightning in a clear sky. "I became troubled because aside from not having thought the thing was to be accomplished so soon, I did not feel it was wise to leave a convent which had been founded so recently and in the midst of so much contradiction." What could she do but courteously reply that she could not go. She saw the messenger's face become tinged with fright, and when she had finished, he looked at her so fixedly that his eyes seemed to say: "But don't you know who the Princess of Eboli is? Think well before saying no."

Teresa felt and understood that look. Yes, she knew who the Princess of Eboli was, but, sorry as she was, she could not go. Then the messenger spoke: "This is not possible because Her Excellency is already in Pastrana awaiting Your Reverence to start the foundation. Everyone knows that she has come for this purpose; just think what an affront it would be not to fulfill her wish." This further explanation had the effect of a second bolt of lightning. The situation was more serious than Teresa had at first imagined. She needed to act prudently, so she told the servant to have something to eat while she wrote a letter to the Princess explaining her point.

Tormented, "I went before the Blessed Sacrament to ask for the grace to write to the Princess in a way which would not displease her." Yet, the thought that she was as a general moving her pawns according to a strategic plan ran through Teresa's mind. One of these pawns was the Discalced Reform begun at Durvelo. It was a much more difficult undertaking than founding convents for nuns, and someone to stand for it before the King would probably be necessary. Was not Ruy Gómez the most influential man? To refuse now signified not only alienating a powerful protector, but would perhaps create an overwhelming enemy. Teresa did not know the Prince well enough to realize he was not overly sensitive, but she knew the Princess was very much so. Those thoughts moved in and out of her prayer.

Suddenly her inner conflict became resolved by the echo of a voice which left no doubts. "While I was with these thoughts, the Lord told me not to forbear going because I would be going for something more important than a foundation of nuns, and that I should take along the Rule and Constitutions. No matter what serious reasons seemed to oppose my departure at first, after those words all I could do was submit myself to the decision of my confessor." As she was wont to do, she said nothing of what she had heard while praying to avoid influencing him, and again her inner voice was confirmed by the decisions of her spiritual director: she was to leave.

This occurred on Pentecost, May 20, 1569. On May 30th, Teresa was traveling toward Madrid on her way to Pastrana with two nuns accompanying her. Now was the time that stupendous coincidences took place. They stopped in Madrid at the Franciscan Monastery founded by Doña Leonor de Mascarenhas, which was a vast assembly place for religious, mystics and founders. During her visits to the capital, Teresa was always an illustrious, welcome guest.

Doña Leonor lived in her monastery leading a cloistered life when she could. Upon Teresa's arrival the woman said, "Ah, my dear Mother, you are just in time. There is a hermit here who wishes to see you. He and his companions seem to have much in common with the rule of your Reform." Thinking of her two friars in Durvelo who were trying to live as a community, she agreed to speak to the hermit immediately.

It was Mariano de Azaro, an Italian from Bitonto near Bari, who had a whirlwind past. A doctor of both law and theology, he had taken part in the Council of Trent, had been assigned to important posts in northern Europe, and had made a name for himself. Then the Queen of Poland wished to entrust him with the office of majordomo of her household. In need of an honest man, the Queen had turned to de Azaro who was known for this quality. After a while he gave up this position because he felt imprisoned there and went into the army. In 1553, he was in Philip II's ranks at the battle of San Quentin, a great victory for the Spaniards who entered the city. The usual plundering and immoral behavior of the soldiers forced Mariano to prove his good faith by defending two girls who were being threatened. Mariano saved their innocence with his sword. Later, he was falsely accused of homicide by two perjured witnesses who claimed that he had led them to the scene of crime. For this he remained in prison two years and would not defend himself until his innocence was recognized. He was freed and entrusted with high offices. Knowing de Azaro excelled in geometry and hydraulics, Philip II assigned him to make the Guadalquivir navigable from Cordova to Seville.

Obviously de Azaro led a strange, fast-moving life, and he applied himself earnestly in each different category of work. Easy as it was for him to change any number of times, he could never fully live the life he was leading. While in Seville attending a course on St. Ignatius' spiritual exercises, he resolved to leave the world. He went to an isolated place called Tardón in the Morena Sierra which was conducive to reliving the times of ancient Thebaid. A group of hermits lived there in a midst of continuous severe mortifications. Since the region was full of thistle, it was called "Cardón" after its Spanish name and then changed to "Tardón." Here Mariano spent eight years.

In 1568, he was obliged to leave Tardón because Philip II called him to Aranjuez to direct the construction of a great canal which was to improve the land and permit irrigation. Upon execution of his task, Mariano went to Madrid where he was given hospitality at Doña Leonor Mascarenhas' palace. He felt that to meet Teresa there was most significant. The next morning he reported that he was determined to enter the Reform. He well realized what good he could do the Carmelite Order through his renewed life, intelligence, and energy, Teresa knew how important it was that such an idealist who could never definitely decide on his state should suddenly be there, resolved to pledge the Carmelite Reform forever.

There was something more. Prince Ruy Gómez had spoken to him promising a hermitage in Pastrana for him and the other hermits, especially since Pope Pius V had recently required the Tardón ascetics to enter regularly constituted orders. This was certainly a strange coincidence. Here was Teresa of Jesus traveling toward Pastrana to found a convent when on the way she found a candidate for her Reform who had also been invited to live in a hermitage in Pastrana! Would not the result be still more glorious if the two undertakings and concessions were fused?

Moreover, Mariano was not alone. Another hermit, also Italian, and a roving ideal-seeker was with him. John Narducci was of a poor Abruzzi farm family. He had worn the habit of the Friars Minor in Italy, but had not reached profession. Now he was traveling the world, full of devotion, on a pilgrimage to St. James of Compostella. When he heard that Mariano de Azaro was in Tardón, he decided to contact him, feeling great esteem for the man he had served in Italy. But he did not feel that shared isolation was a true hermitage, and retired to a still more rigorous solitude in an uninhabited region near Jaén. One day Mariano de Azaro came after him saying he had been called to build a canal and needed a trusted man. Narducci followed, serving de Azaro humbly. On their return he, too, lodged in Doña Leonor's palace.

Teresa rightly recognized another recluse of a strong spiritual sentiment in John Narducci. The name he chose reveals his wandering yet humble spirit: Brother John of Misery. But we must not forget that John was an artist, in love with color, with an overwhelming desire drawing him to his palette and brushes. At Aranjuez his happiness reached heights because the King's sister, Juana, found a way for him to study under the famous painter, Alfonso Sánchez Coello. There John could pour himself out onto the maestro's unfinished paintings. His passion was alive, but he could not transfer it into his brushstrokes; his style was flat. Yet, his candid pictures showed an attentive and conscientious look at nature. To him, nature, which was the work of God, seemed too beautiful to warrant a man's changing it, even if done ingeniously.

Greco's genial hallucinations would have appalled him, and Vasari's phrase, art being an imitation of the truth, would have become his artistic credo. Friar John's pictorial vocation proved to be fortunate because he was the only one to paint a portrait of Teresa during her lifetime. He painted the saint in 1576, when she was sixty years old.

John Narducci was ready to enter the Reform, and Mariano de Azaro was bent on using the Pastrana concessions to found a Discalced monastery. "I was very grateful to him and thanked God very much because our General had given me permission to found two monasteries, and only one had been established so far."

Mother Teresa immediately wrote to Fr. Gonzales and to Fr. Salazar, the late and newly-elected provincials who both replied favorably; the permits were to arrive soon. At this point, Teresa left the two future friars in Madrid to await the permits, while she went to Pastrana with a joyous heart.

───────────────

After her warm welcome, Teresa was amazed to find that the house destined for the convent was still to be systematized. Consequently, the nuns were given an apartment in the grandiose palace and were provided with a small choir in the chapel. The future convent was below, just at the west entrance to the town.

Princess Ana personally directed the activities while Teresa accompanied her. Their conversations underlined the paradox of their situations. On the one hand, there was the greatest friend of poverty: rival to none other than St. Francis of Assisi. In her enthusiasm and joy of poverty, she had battled against a whole city to found her convent on absolute poverty in Avila. On the other hand, we have the most lavish woman of Spain, a person of great elegance who loved to be surrounded by beautiful things, drawing triumph from power and wealth.

What were these two women—Mother Teresa and the Princess—saying to each other as they almost daily crossed the town to superintend work on the building? At variance concerning the new convent, it was the Princess who wished the foundation to be in absolute poverty, while the saint upheld that a steady income should be provided.

The Princess obstinately retained her romantic, aesthetic idea, while Teresa once again demonstrated she had a practical head on her shoulders. Malagón Pastrana was a feudal, rural village with no well-to-do families on whom to rely to sustain the nuns. Little as the Discalced might consume, some sort of food was needed. If they were to rely wholly on what the cupboard offered daily, they would be often compelled to skip meals. Since they belonged to a cloister, Teresa did not want them to go about begging from door to door. Furthermore, those hundred families would end up by being annoyed with the nuns if daily they were to see a messenger of famine.

This was Teresa's sound opinion, but the Princess preferred the grand gesture of founding in poverty. There was certainly no thought of any financial saving prompting her in this, for she had a generous heart. We need only consider what she was spending to transform the house into a convent—all but the outer walls were torn down—to realize that she was easily moved to donating huge sums of money. Avarice, then, was not the reason why she wanted poor nuns. It was only a matter of obstinacy now, for she had formed a concept of the Reform and no one was going to change it. Probably impressed by the talk of how the Discalced heroically venture into their monastic future devoid of all, Doña Ana did not want "her" nuns of Pastrana to be considered less than the others.

Teresa went slowly in opposing the Princess. First of all, Ana was a great benefactress to whom one should have been grateful; then her temperament was known to all. "Unable to agree, I had already decided to leave without having founded the convent." Ruy Gómez intervened fortunately and things smoothed out, thanks to Princess Ana's absolute confidence in her husband's judgment. In principle the question was settled, leaving now the amount to be set. Knowing the Princess to be generous, Teresa no longer worried about the convent being without future income.

Another controversy arose over the prospective admission of Sr. Catalina Machuca of the Humility Convent. Though protected by Princess Ana, Teresa opposed the nun's admission because she did not want to develop the practice of admitting nuns from congregations she was not thoroughly acquainted with. Again the Princess insisted, but Teresa held firm, and to everyone's amazement, the Princess gave in.

No matter how small and pious they were, two defeats were not so easily inflicted on the Princess of Eboli with impunity. Unaware as she was of her vindictiveness, she was nevertheless an imperious woman. This caused a certain disposition to form in her subconscious mind which was to surface in a forthcoming incident.

CHAPTER THIRTY-SEVEN

The Discalced Friars in Pastrana

It seems the very nun who had been refused entrance by Teresa first spoke to Ana of the saint's *Life* which was circulating in the most cultured monasteries of Spain. What she knew was that those few who had read it spoke with great enthusiasm of the mystic marvels described in it. Certainly Sr. Catalina did not imagine the consequences that bit of news was to foster. Princess Ana insisted that she be permitted to read the book. Was it possible that something precious and unique, a masterpiece that was reserved for privileged persons, could be found right here in Pastrana, and she, Ana de Mendoza, not be permitted to read it?

Well, she knew there was little to do when that smiling, humble Carmelite nun opposed something, but she was intently determined not to lose another battle. As much as Teresa did not want to appear discourteous, she nevertheless continued to say "no" with her heart in her throat. She knew just where the Princess' comprehension could reach and feared setting all her soul's secrets before such a person. Princess Ana turned to her husband for help, and he in turn, could not see why his wife should not be permitted to read the book. Teresa was forced to break down and let the Princess read it.

The book, however, was read through the prejudiced eyes of a woman who had been thwarted twice in her vanity—perhaps for the first times in her life. She began reading the book most attentively and anxiously, only to turn progressively amazed, diffident and incredulous. As the supernatural element in the book became more strongly affirmed, so did the Princess' mind steadily retract, as though offended. Unable to grasp the supernatural light therein, she was vexed. What she had accumulated in her subconscious mind slowly sprang to work, her secret hostility coloring things in its own light. Finally, her diffidence turned into positive denial, while her stupor became indignation.

Sarcastically criticizing the book, the Princess set the manuscript down, only to hand it to a maid who happened to pass by, telling her to read it since Mother Teresa had written it. Pleased, the maid delved wholeheartedly into the book, for she, too, was full of curiosity concerning Teresa of Jesus. Not very literate, she asked another servant to help decipher Teresa's running, uneven handwriting. A page joined the two, and comments started. Again, just as the supernatural became more apparent, their reaction became more stupefied, giving vent to witticisms and giggles.

Teresa learned of her great secret circulating from servant to servant, causing merriment, and became most pained to think they were directed against God's favors.

The story even got to Madrid, where the witty remarks pronounced by the Princess circulated in high aristocratic circles, amusing some, while others deplored the incident. However, since no one had read the book, the incident could not be deplored enough.

Looking at the matter from this distance, it seems very strange that Princess Ana could not have felt the mystic light, personally experienced, penetrate her.

Saddened as Teresa was at being the target of so much discussion, she completed the foundations.

On July 13, a procession for the first Discalced Friars left from the outskirts of town to the new monastery. It stopped before the Discalced Carmelite Convent where for four days the nuns had been praying in their newly-acquired isolation. The priests of Pastrana, including the collegiate church canons in magnificent vestments, princes, members of court, the whole servant-body of the palace, people of Pastrana and neighboring villages, all took part in the event.

There was quite a climb to reach the monastery which emphasized the spirit of superiority and unreality of the institute. A chapel dedicated to St. Peter had long existed at the top of the hill, and it was the custom to go there yearly on a pilgrimage. Halfway up was a delightful, peaceful house which seemed to have been prepared especially for the Carmelite Reform and was opportunely called the "dovecot" because a great number of pigeons lived there.

Founded by St. Teresa with St. John of the Cross as its first spiritual director, this monastery was to become one of the most glorious in the history of the Reform. An excellent example of the new rule to the whole of Europe, it was held as a model of perfection to the other Discalced monasteries, and formed founders of many European communities.

Though conditions of the house were no better than those which had been found in Medina del Campo and Durvelo, these new friars did not lag behind their founders. The roof resembled a grate; there was no plaster on the walls, but an abundance of holes! The land about was as hard as stone, and Friar Mariano wondered why the earth was so arid.

But after the remodeling that Ruy Gómez had ordered, the house definitely looked different. Singing the Psalms, the procession went up past the "dovecot" to the top of the hill where the Blessed Sacrament was exposed amid the mountains and valleys.

———

When the friars were established, they looked around, and again Friar Mariano, who was an expert in hydraulics, wondered why the earth should be so compact and siliceous. He borrowed a sort of hoe and dug a little; below the stone-like crust was good earth, and he sighed at the thought of not having water. He had resolved great hydraulic problems, and finding water would render the community independent. We know not how, but he found water. Overjoyed, he called his companions together and began planning what could be done. "We must open a conduit here," Friar Mariano said, "and construct a tunnel." The two friars looked at each other thinking, a tunnel? With three of us in all, and no instruments?

But Friar Mariano continued: "This tunnel must widen at the right point because there the water will be at such an inclination as to branch out, fertilizing the land. While we build this aqueduct, others must shape the land into terraces, held up by stone walls, because only then can the land be cultivated."

His two companions remained silent so his enthusiasm cooled while looking at the stone earth and the dovecot convent housing three inhabitants. That night all three pondered how to solve the problem, but the solution came the next day. Ruy Gómez passed by, and Friar Mariano spoke to him of his dream, to which Gómez simply answered, "How right you are. This shall be done without delay." When he set about to employ the workmen, an amazing thing happened. The people of Pastrana wanted to contribute work for the monastery, each family promising a week or two of manual labor.

So it was that the steep hill was transformed into a series of terraces, and the aqueduct was built from the spring to the inside of the house. Upon accomplishment of the project, the Friars were left to their own resources.

Friar Mariano had earlier discussed the matter of manual labor with Teresa and found that she, too, was favorable to its use in the Discalced lifestyle. So the terraces began to take on life, just as though a squalid, solitary piece of earth had been brought to sing the praises of the Lord.

CHAPTER THIRTY-EIGHT

Foundations in Alcalá de Henares and in Salamanca

Shortly after the establishment of the monastery, the Reform swept to a famous university town, Alcalá de Henares, and its founding bore a special important characteristic to the movement. Not only were the ordinary problems of monastic contemplation, income and continuation of hermitage life decided, but a new motif entered the picture.

In the Church's great strife against its enemies, sanctity and strokes of the pen defended Catholicism, demonstrating how much the intellect and culture could serve God, as had been shown at the Council of Trent. If it is true that each historical period must perform a special mission for God, the sixteenth-century Catholic was to defend the intellectual field, for the adversary was strongest in philosophical circles. European universities served as battleground where the counter-Reform could freely turn humanistic culture into criticism of its opposers.

No Catholic thought could estrange itself from this fact, and so it was that the Discalced Carmelite Friars were faced with the dilemma whether to maintain their hermitic tone, excluding active intellectual life, or combine contemplation to action, and if so, in what proportion? This was no problem for the nuns because women could not have performed any outside activity effectively in those times. St. Teresa and St. John of the Cross felt the problem deeply. They were responsible to God for the two movements, and God's trust destined them to choose the "better way." But just how much were the friars to seclude themselves while strife was all around them? Even though recent religious movements tended to direct action (St. Ignatius had founded the perfect militia for modern times), how could the Discalced Carmelites shut themselves up in their ivory tower of prayer looking at the war from afar?

The first Reform's college of Alcalá[1] concretely stated that the Discalced would attend universities, participating in outside life in a restricted manner. Teresa of Jesus and John of the Cross were of the same opinion concerning the mixed vocation, but the proportion in which to divide contemplation and studies was still to be decided. Contemplation was given the vantage. The active life was to be a grafted branch in the main trunk of prayer, which was never to harm the primary growth in any way.

It was a difficult union, and the task was assigned to Alcalá's spiritual director, John of the Cross, whose method was based on the ascetic motif: preach by example more than with words. John of the Cross taught that the Church already had many learned men. New orders were not needed to preach eloquent sermons. The novices of the Reform were called to preach through their good example where actions speak louder than words. They were to consider themselves already

---

1. *Foundations*, XVIII, 3.

orators in this type of eloquence because they could edify the faithful through their mortifications and modesty. The Discalced Carmelites were true descendants and heirs of those marvelous preachers of virtue who in ancient times lived in solitude and rose to such heights of holiness that they were venerated by all. They chose to imitate those saints, bearing in mind that the virtues learned as novices are far more useful than all the knowledge gathered in schools.

The innovation was profound. University work was secondary to the study of daily virtues. To practice the good was the most important subject. The focus of every studious Discalced Carmelite was humility, mortification and prayer. These were basic to their lives, but did not hinder research for truth, which is the expression of science. Ascetic endeavor would sustain intellectual thought. The life of prayer would dissipate all residues of passion, pride and mental inertia in the conquest of genuine knowledge. In this way, science would be considered in its pure state, stripped of all human pride.

The group of Discalced students astonished the people of Alcalá who gathered in groups to watch those tonsured, poorly-dressed, thoughtful-looking young men walking in step. For months people gathered to observe those exceptional youths as they passed in a group.

Francis of St. Mary and Fr. Alonso of the Mother of God, both of whom had had personal contact with the college, used seraphic terms to define the spirit and life existing within. It is therefore no wonder that its graduates became leading figures in the Reformed Order.

═══════════════

On the very same day that the Friars entered Alcalá, Teresa of Jesus founded a convent in Salamanca. Alcalá and Salamanca were the leading university towns of Spain, Salamanca bearing the nickname of "little Rome." But Teresa found that the city was poor. There was no industry. It was not surrounded by fertile ground, nor was it an agricultural center. There were no great markets or international fairs as there were in Medina del Campo. An austere center for advanced studies, the attention and ambition of the inhabitants focused on school activities. The city could be said to live off the students' allowances, which caused everything to be organized with this in mind.

For this reason, Teresa hesitated. She preferred to found the convent with an income, but the request for the foundation had come from Fr. Martín Gutiérrez, a Jesuit, who knew Teresa and represented so much authority, she could never have refused. Since he was the rector of the Jesuit College in Salamanca, the foundation had strong support. Moreover, Teresa rejoiced at the prospect of the advantage her daughters would gain by settling near that famous university.

Before leaving Martín Gutiérrez, let us glance into the future and see his dramatic death. On his way to Rome three years later in 1573, he fell into the hands of the Huguenots who chained him, and after only eight days in their prison, he died praising God and accepting the suffering that had been his lot.

Returning to Teresa, it was All Saints' Eve when she arrived in Salamanca accompanied only by María Suárez and Fr. Julian de Avila "after having traveled most of the night before in freezing weather." The cold had aroused Teresa's circulatory and digestive disturbances, causing the travelers to stop overnight in a village, and it was noon on October 31, before they reached Salamanca. Another Gutiérrez, Nicolás, a trusty man, was to have seen to the vacating of the house that had been rented. Nicolás was a sort of Job who had known the bitterness of financial ruin and had seen his opulent patrimony slowly slip away; however, he was better-humored since he had become poor. Six of his daughters were nuns at the Incarnation Convent and were later to join the Teresian Reform.

Nicolás Gutiérrez' task turned out to be arduous, unpleasant, and even dangerous, for the house he was to have vacated was inhabited by students. Moreover, it was not yet time for the end of the lease which was calculated according to the school semesters. Poor Nicolás went to the hotel where Teresa was staying to announce that he had not succeeded in sending the students away. Teresa grew fearful for a moment. "If the news of my arrival gets around, they will no longer give us the house!" The owner of the house was the only possible source to press so Gutiérrez went to him. The latter was moved to compassion and tried to persuade the students to leave, but they would not listen. Finally, they grumbled that they needed another place to go. Gutiérrez and the owner found them another house and they left angrily.

Teresa listened to the dramatic account of the rage shown by the departing group, and all but María Suárez laughed heartily over the incident. María, however, grew fearful at the account and whispered to Teresa her distrust of the students.

The house was a sight. "Apparently students don't cultivate cleanliness because the house was in such horrible condition it took all night to put it in order." Two young friars had been sent by Fr. Gutiérrez to help prepare the chapel. While waiting at the hotel, Teresa had eyed two oil paintings, one of the "Ecce Homo" and the other of the deposition from the cross. Her funds consisted of the leftovers of the trip, fourteen reali, which she offered in exchange for the pictures, and was overjoyed when the offer was accepted. So now the two pictures were put up for veneration.

On All Saints' Day the first Mass was said. Except for the nuns, the foundation was complete. There were to be three from Medina del Campo and three from Avila, so Fr. Julian de Avila was sent to inform the nuns to begin the trip.

At this point, a most amusing incident took place. On the night of November 1, Teresa and María slept alone in the rented house. The rooms were large with broken-down walls, the ceilings black and fear-inspiring. After a rough, hard journey, and physically run down from the hard manual labor, the two women were left alone in the large house.

María was fear personified, and Teresa, too, felt squeamish, so they thought it would be wise to make a tour of the house with a lantern in hand to see if anyone was hidden there. María insisted that some student was bound to take revenge on them. They ended up, however, by deciding it was more prudent not to look in every room, but to close themselves in one where they had gathered some straw and two blankets. María bolted the door, trying time and time again to make sure it was secure. Somewhat relieved, she nonetheless continued to glance about the room, so Teresa could not help asking, "But what are you looking for? Do you think someone can still enter?" María's most unexpected reply was, "What would you do, Mother, alone as you are, if I were to die?"

It was the night before All Saint's Day so that the church bells rang out intermittently their cadenced lament. Mother Teresa's sense of humor did not leave her however. In answer to Sr. María's question, she retorted, "I'll think of what I'll do when what you said happens, Sister, but for the time being, let me sleep...." "If this had happened," she wrote later, "I would certainly have been at a loss. The thought horrified me because though I have no fear of the dead, my heart weakens even when not alone. Furthermore, the tolling of the bells increased my apprehensions. Having hardly slept for two nights, our fear soon dissipated in sleep,

and when the other nuns arrived the next day, we no
longer thought of it."

———————

So it was that the Reform entered the two cities of
knowledge on the same day, All Saint's Day in 1570.
Though the college in Alcalá was already a center of
Carmelite study, the convent in Salamanca was but a
stepping-stone because the nuns acted as announcers
for one of the most noteworthy colleges of Teresian
Reform that was later to be established there.

CHAPTER THIRTY-NINE

Francisco and Teresa Velásquez

About fifteen miles from Salamanca lies Alba de Tormes, the ducal seat of one of the most renowned families of Spain. The city and fief were immortalized by Fernández Alvarez de Toledo who was the Duke of Alba. Any European peasant in the second half of the sixteenth century would have heard of this famous general, for the eyes of all the nations were on him and his undertakings.

Alba was a small town thrown together on the slope of a high hill. It ended abruptly at a jut overlooking the vast Tormes Valley and the river's course. On the projection's brink, as though a continuation, was the castle which served as palace and fortress, built reflecting the austere grandeur of the family. Beyond the Tormes Valley the last Spurs of the Guadarrama can be glimpsed, those that are seen resplendent from Avila.

Who could have foreseen that Teresa's tomb would one day be in that village? The Carmelite of Caen was to write: "It seems that Avila and Alba, the places where our saint came into the world and left it, were designated by the divine hand to reflect the austere, beautiful, yet simple image of her soul."[1]

Teresa was not called to Alba by the ducal family, but by an elderly couple, Francisco Velásquez and Teresa de Layz. The woman was of pure noble blood, but was not too warmly accepted in the family, being the fifth girl when her parents ardently desired a male heir to their name and patrimony. She was often left uncared for. On her baptismal day she was alone for hours until a woman picked her up saying, "Poor girl, aren't you Christian, too?" She responded, "Yes, I am," and surprised everyone.

This served as a warning to her parents who embraced her and raised her in an atmosphere of faith, and the child grew up greatly inclined to things of the spirit. When it was time for her parents to consider suitors for her, she was most reluctant to think of marriage. Only when they mentioned the name of Francisco Velásquez did she accept, though she had never met him. The happy couple settled in Salamanca where Francisco's qualities were appreciated. He was nominated to a high administrative office at the university.

His wife shared his difficulties and tasks, but their happiness was not complete because they had no children. For many years, Teresa de Layz prayed to the Lord and asked the intercession of the saints, especially St. Andrew. Only after many prayers and many tears did an internal voice make her understand that God did not wish her to become a mother, for a different maternity was asked of her. In her sleep one night, Teresa heard the following words, "Do not desire children because it would be your damnation." What could such strange and fearful words mean? And how could they be accepted as supernatural? Dismayed and uncertain

---

1. *Histoire de Sainte Thérèse,* par une Carmelite de Caen, I, XX.

as she was, she gradually convinced herself she was not obligated to believe them and again took up desiring a child. But one day a fascinating vision of certain supernatural source appeared to her, showing a house surrounded by a meadow where white and blue corollas bloomed, representing small gifts of paradise with a meaning. A well could be seen below the porch, and a man whom she recognized appeared beside it; certainly that was St. Andrew, and he spoke to her: "Here are other children, different from the ones you desire." He pointed to the floral constellations, but Teresa understood he was not inviting her to terrestrial gardening. The symbolism was not new, but efficacious. The corollas represented virginal souls and the house a convent. From that moment on, Teresa de Layz knew she would become a foundress.

Far from opposing his wife, Velásquez went so far as to accept what had been addressed to his wife for himself, too, and prepared to share ordeals, expenses, and merits. While the great project was forming in their hearts, the Duchess of Alba unexpectedly called for them.

Engaged in a war in Flanders, the General had long been absent, and the vast patrimony was difficult to control. A firm hand and a clear conscience were needed to direct things so Velásquez was asked to assume control of the administration, necessitating his moving to Alba with his wife. Teresa de Layz was most unhappy about leaving Salamanca, but followed her husband shortly. He had already bought a house and was settled when she arrived. Dissatisfied with it, she felt all the more miserable. The next morning Teresa went to visit the house and garden where the sight of the well there greatly startled her. It was the very one she had seen in her dream with St. Andrew standing beside it! That was enough to change her completely. She returned to her husband in serenity, announcing she would be happy to remain in that house where her foundation would be established.

Neighboring buildings were purchased and amalgamated while the couple looked around for a satisfactory order to inhabit it. This was when Teresa of Jesus met them. The couple had heard of her elevated state and Reform. Correspondence began between them through the intercession of Juana de Ahumada, the saint's sister. Teresa requested income according to her established method since Alba de Tormes was a small, feudal town, and the Velásquez' increased their offer to assure the Discalced Nuns independence.

After a year of negotiations, the Holy Eucharist was solemnly brought into the new convent's chapel on January 25, 1571. The couple gave up their now comfortable house to their adopted daughters and moved into an uncomfortable modest one. Five nuns and Teresa opened the foundation.

Teresa quickly became the center of interest in Alba. Her sister, Juana, was constantly at her side reminiscing over past adventures concerning the foundation in Avila, and the evening the preacher had openly criticized Teresa. At the time, Juana had asked to return to Alba out of fright and admitted it to anyone who would listen. But in the ten years since then, ten convents had been established and everyone desired to meet the Foundress. Even the Duchess of Alba, Doña María Enríquez, had long prepared what she would say to the Carmelite when she should chance her way. Now that she could feel the direct fascination of the saint's sweet and penetrating eyes, she unfolded her innermost doubts and hopes to the nun who understood and cured. Teresa de Layz and Francisco also sought her balsam, coming away healed of the haunting sore they had borne for so many years. The Duchess of Alba's sister, Juana de Toledo, was another great woman who sought consolation from Teresa, for she had been ailing almost all her life. So it turned out that the humble Carmelite who had no money, wore a mended habit and loved poverty, had friends that represented the most influential people of Spain: the King's sister, Princess Juana, Doña Luisa de la Cerda, the Duchess of Escalona, the Princess of Eboli, the Marquise of Velada, Countess Monterey, and the Duchess of Alba, wife of one of the country's most powerful men.

But Teresa remained impassive in her modesty. Greatness worried her and honors embarrassed her; demonstrations of esteem only pained her. Only during persecutions did she feel secure, for then did her thirst for love become satisfied, "the soul becoming sovereign and all worldly things were below her feet."

———

Delightful as her sojourn was, Teresa bemoaned so much sweetness, thinking of her daughters in Salamanca who had nothing. She started off again to settle things better there. Just before returning to the convent she stopped for a short interval as the house guest of the Count and Countess of Monterey, where she was instrumental in the performance of two miracles.

When Teresa arrived, one of the household's most faithful maids was seriously ill with scarlet fever, so much so that the doctors had given up her case. But just as the centurion who had interceded for his sick servant, so did the Countess of Monterey beseech Teresa to see the sick woman. Drowsy and wan, the woman's livid complexion was covered with rose-colored spots. Laying her hands on the woman's forehead, just as though feeling how much she burned, Teresa kept them there some moments while the Countess pleaded with her eyes because she was particularly fond of the maid she had permitted her children's tutor to marry. Nothing but the woman's heavy breathing could be heard. All at once the maid looked around startled and exclaimed, "Who touched me? How well I feel!" Teresa retreated at that expression of a supernatural occurrence, muttering, "Poor thing, it's the delirium which makes her speak like that." But the maid had risen from her bed energetically and had prostrated herself before the saint with conviction. It was definitely evident that a miracle had been performed.

But what follows is even more marvelous. Perhaps through contagion, one of the Monterey daughters caught the disease and it, too, seemed mortal. Her prostration worried everyone, for her pale, lifeless body appeared to be in agony, awaiting only death. The Count and Countess invoked Teresa to intercede with God for them again.

Teresa agreed to see the sick daughter and was sincerely and deeply moved by pity at the sight of the dying girl. She knelt at the girl's side and prayed long. No miracle took place. And yet, from a human point of view, the Monterey girl was worth more to the happiness of a whole family than the maid. María herself would have preferred to forfeit her gift of life and give it to the girl.

But a saint can pray only in submission to God's will. While praying alone in her room, Teresa was unexpectedly confronted with a new type of vision: a vision of saints. St. Dominic and St. Catherine, the two pioneers of the Dominican Order, appeared to her, saying that the girl would be healed. In recompense the girl was to wear the Dominican habit for one year. When the figures clad in white disappeared, Teresa was alone with her joy. All she had to do now was to obtain the sick girl's promise to do what the saints desired. But here lay the difficulty: to ask this would entail explanations and talk of supernatural visions. Teresa believed in her visions within the limits of obedience to the Church and her spiritual director, but she was reluctant to speak of them out of humility.

However, the Gospel says "simple as doves and prudent as serpents." Teresa was shrewd, and her very desire for concealment made her even more clever. She related all to Fr. Domingo Bañez in whom she had often confided, and he took the task upon himself, talking to the Montereys with few explanations, asking a spiritual kindness of the girl: to become associated to the Dominican Order for one year, donning the white symbol. The Montereys regarded this as an honor, and hope began to shine in their eyes. Indeed, the girl got better and was ultimately healed. But everyone understood who had been the instrument of Providence in renewing the girl's gift of life, no matter how Teresa sought to conceal the power of her prayer.

From that moment, the Montereys felt a bond of gratitude toward the saint which took the form of protection. Teresa needed that protection all the more since the miserable house right next to the Monterey palace where the Salamanca foundation had been established was cold, damp, and unsuitable. Not yet known in the city, the Discalced Nuns did not receive sufficient outside help. But the advantage of living next to that famous palace was soon felt. [2]

Before continuing, however, let us consider the figure of a man well-known all over Europe in the seventeenth century. He was the "Count-Duke" Francisco Olivarez, the son of the Monterey girl for whom Teresa had interceded with God. During the anguish and dangers of the Thirty Year's War, he had been Spain's Plenipotentiary Minister. During the great political, national and military duel against Richelieu's France, he

---

2. There is a detailed description of the palace in G. C. Graham's *Saint Teresa of Avila.*

constantly invoked St. Teresa, his mother's savior, as "Spain's patron."

Returning to 1571, it is certainly evident that the bond of gratitude produced its effects. Teresa returned to her coveted convent, and the Countess of Monterey tried to improve the building, but probably it would have been wiser to have torn it down completely and then reconstructed it. Teresa was happy to share the blessings of those discomforts, for her stay there was particularly intense in mystic prayer, and many "celestial favors" occurred. In February that year, when Teresa was still at Alba de Tormes, the Lord had said to her: "You are always desiring to suffer, but then you refuse misfortunes. I dispose of things not according to your sensibility and weakness, but according to the desires I see in you. You see I am helping you; take courage then. I have wished you to earn this crown. Living, you shall see the Virgin's Order blossom copiously."[3] These words undoubtedly referred to the tribulations the Salamanca foundation was causing Teresa in addition to the concern over her newly opened foundation in Alba.

April in Salamanca marked a sublime period in Teresa's mystic life. Whenever she was in that special state called the "night of the spirit," when the soul felt arid and far from the Lord, then would the luminous streaks of God's faithfulness shine through.

In such a state of tormenting longing for God during Holy Week, 1571, Teresa wrote, "Yesterday I felt profoundly alone, excepting the moment when I received Communion, and it's being Easter mattered nothing to me." At recreation with her daughters, she asked that they sing for her since she enjoyed hearing them so much.

---

3. *Spiritual Reports*, XIV, XV, here and for the following.

"Let my eyes see You,
Sweet, good Jesus,
Let my eyes see You
And then let me die."

The sad words of the slow, almost colorless song corresponded to Teresa's inner conflict. Turning pale and clasping her hands, she slowly became stiff and beside herself from the great pain she felt. Stifled moans were heard just as from one in agony. The misery of feeling far from God had never before caused her to lose her senses, but that day the grief was so penetrating and acute that it reached bottom. "But now it is so overbearing as to be called a wound so I can better understand what the Madonna suffered."

Teresa's definition for the wound was the "ecstasy of pain." To her confessor she wrote, "I became so broken in body, and my hands so dislocated and sore that even now I can barely write. You will probably ask if this ecstasy of pain be possible, if I am feeling things as they actually are or if I am not perhaps deceiving myself. The pain lasted until this morning when, at prayer, I was overtaken by a great rapture when I thought I saw our Lord bringing my soul to God the Father, saying, 'I am returning whom You gave me before,' and it seemed as though the Father drew me to Him.

"This did not happen through the means of images, but by a very great certainty, accompanied by such intense spiritual delicacy that I cannot explain it. The Father spoke words I no longer remember, some referring to the graces He would bestow upon me. Speaking thus He kept me near Him for a little while."

To underline the splendor of this episode is superfluous. The simplicity with which such a lofty flight is explained can belong only to truth. The emotion of mystic concentration can facilitate our following such an extraordinary rapture.

But that was not the only favor received at that time. "After having received Holy Communion once, it seemed most clear to me that our Lord sat next to me, consoling me with many proofs of goodness, saying, among other things, 'Here I am, daughter, it is I. Show your hands.' And it seemed as though he took them, and bringing them to his side, added, 'Look at my wounds! You are not without me. Life passes rapidly.'"

For us who observed those favors, the loftiest thus far for her, and knowing the events that were to follow, we can consider that sojourn in Salamanca as a preparation for the ensuing serious struggles.

CHAPTER FORTY

Nomination to Prioress of the "Incarnation"

From her mystical elevations in Salamanca, the saint was summoned to Medina del Campo to undergo a series of moral trials. A delicate question was to be resolved with the Carmelite Provincial there. Isabel Ruiz, who as a religious became Isabel of Jesus, was at the center of the controversy because of her immense wealth. An orphan, her relatives sought to exercise more authority than was lawful both by human and divine laws. Wishing to follow her vocation, Isabel wanted to offer her riches as alms to the Reform. A part of it was to be used to erect a chapel which the convent so sorely needed. At this point her relatives intervened, saying, "If our cousin's decision is inflexible, then let us at least have the title of patronage to the works which will be constructed."

The request, however, was not a purely honorary one because a patronage in the sixteenth century entailed the right of veto or of council, the complications of interference which could cause trouble to the Order. Inés of Jesus, the Prioress of the convent in Medina, was still reticent about the request when Isabel herself settled the matter by simply saying she could freely dispose of what was hers alone.

Unmoved, the relatives appealed to the Carmelite Provincial, Fr. Angel de Salazar, and argued so convincingly that Fr. Angel became favorable to the patronage. Poor Prioress Ana refused to go further and sent for Mother Teresa.

Upon arrival, Teresa went to speak to the Provincial, but did not succeed in persuading him. Perplexed, she did not see how it could be proper to accept the patronage and oppose Isabel. All she could think of doing was to transfer the novice to Salamanca out of Fr. Salazar's jurisdiction. By resolving the matter in this way, Teresa showed she was defending the freedom of action due the Reform when dealing with its own members and served to recall that, after all, the religious houses of the Reform depended directly on the General of the Order. That just and energetic manner, however, was not appreciated by the Provincial, who, as a consequence, treated Teresa severely.

As it happened, Inés of Jesus had just completed her third year as Prioress in the Medina convent so that new elections were due. Inés had been present that famous night when María de Ocampo had offered her dowry to start the Carmelite Reform.

Having revealed great competence at spiritual government, she was re-elected by her fellow sisters. Just as Teresa, Inés was still bound to the Mitigated Order since her profession had been made at the Incarnation Convent. Fr. Angel de Salazar grasped this opportunity to put things in order. Probably frightened by the loss caused by Teresa's clever move, he clearly saw that the Reform could become an important branch of the Order. He therefore felt it was his duty to send Teresa and Inés back to St. Joseph's in Avila, while the new Prioress in Medina would be one sent from the Incarnation, Teresa de Quesada.

To accept such a decision was certain to cause a radical revolution. Difficult as it was to accept the change, the two nuns obeying promptly, were forced to leave a house built on tears and hard work. Teresa was suffering from a paralysis at the time, but the two left anyway at eventide. Unable to find a carriage or cart, they set off on foot, preceded by a water-bearer and his two mules carrying their possessions—clothes, documents and books. Late at night they stopped, only to start out again at dawn.

No high mountains were to be crossed, but the road seemed long before they could see the grandiose profile of the bastions of Avila and pass through its gate. Apprehensive, many memories filled their minds as they walked through the narrow streets. They led the water-bearer to St. Joseph's convent where cries of surprise and tears of joy intermingled.

Life was starting anew for Teresa at St. Joseph's, only this time she was in a sort of confinement. She suffered, but was grateful to be able to do so. The soul weakened in the midst of satisfactions and honors, whereas it truly lived during persecution. Glorious days were spent in the silence of the convent. Just after Ascension Day in 1571, on May 20, Teresa had received Communion distractedly, and while praying, bemoaned how miserable human nature was. Just then her soul became inflamed, and a splendid vision appeared. It was an intellectual vision which permitted her to see clearly the Holy Trinity within herself. "I saw it represented as an image of truth enabling my cloddish mind to understand how God is Three in One. It seemed as though the Three Persons were distinctly represented in my soul, speaking to me in unison, saying that, from then on I would improve myself in three things, thanks to the help granted by each One: in charity, in suffering joyfully, and in feeling the ardor of love within me. Seeing the Holy Trinity within me, I understood that passage where our Lord says that the Three Persons inhabit the soul in grace."[1]

In thanksgiving, Teresa spoke to the Lord, overflowing with affection. "But if You are truly to grant me so many graces, O Lord, why do You not uphold me with Your hand until You preserve me from all the miseries for which I have repented and anguished continually, considering my sins?"[2] Further on she comments: "The image of the Three Persons in one God became so impressed in my soul that I felt I could remain inwardly withdrawn with such divine company forever."

Teresa's life at St. Joseph's was full of mortifications, impetuous love and visions. Even before this last memorable grace she had seen a sort of dove flap its wings loudly just as she was about to receive Communion. So surprised and moved was she that she had to gather all her strength to receive the Host.

Francisco de Salcedo, who had become a priest after the death of his wife, was the one administering the Eucharist.

While Teresa was fulfilling her mandate of obedience, the apostolic visitor, Fr. Pedro Fernández of the Order of St. Dominic, a person who was to cause a great change in Teresa's life, was nearing Castile. How was it that a Dominican was entrusted with the delicate and honorable mission of visiting both mitigated and reformed Carmelite convents and monasteries? Pius V, himself a Dominican, was trying to effect a drastic reform in all religious orders, and he knew he could count on the well-chosen man of his Order whom he

---

1. *Spiritual Reports,* XVI, XVII, here and for the following.

2. Testimony of Mary of St. Francis and cited in Fr. Silverio's book, vol. VI, ch. 1.

knew well. Fr. Fernández was one in whom the Pope's slogan of kindness and energy could produce the best results. Being Spanish and a Provincial of his Order, he had often heard of Mother Teresa, and Fr. Domingo Báñez had given him further details concerning her.

Before reaching Avila, he stopped in Pastrana for a few days at the Discalced monastery. There he witnessed much silent praise for the Foundress, and the visitor marveled at the austerity, mutual charity and spirit of self-sacrifice that prevailed within the small community. It is told that a novice asked permission of the apostolic visitor to enter the most mortified and austere Order. The reply it is said he gave was, "Believe me, my son, that as much as I have seen or read, there is no Order in the Church possessing greater austerity and perfection than this!"

Fr. Fernández' stay in Pastrana confirmed all the more firmly the visitor's favorable impression of Teresa's Reform. He desired to meet the "little woman" who was sure to be someone extraordinary if she was able to give life to such elevated communities. Fr. Fernández' meeting with Teresa in the convent surpassed all his expectations, for he immediately recognized the exceptional gifts of nature vivified by grace.

While the two were enrapt in spiritual conversations, in Medina the newly nominated Prioress resigned, expressing a firm desire to return to the Incarnation. It was to be expected because the pious nun who was holy corresponded to the vocation of a Mitigated Carmelite, and could not live up to the obligations of the Reform. She must not be considered lacking in virtue for this because she had long inhaled the spiritual atmosphere of the Mitigated Order which contains the seed of evangelical perfection. She was the other Teresa with whom Teresa de Ahumada joked, around the year 1545, at the Incarnation. "There is the prophecy," St. Teresa had said happily, "that a saint

called Teresa will one day leave this convent. Pray God
it be one of us, and that it be I!''

"Pray God it be I!'' was Teresa de Quesada's energetic reply.

The two Teresas had truly walked the ways of
perfection, but now the one was renouncing Medina.
New elections were necessary, and these were to take
place under the auspices of the apostolic visitor. Tact
was needed in order that the nuns did not again vote
for Inés of Jesus, the one they had voted for before, that
they not appear disrespectful to the Provincial. But
Fr. Fernández suggested they vote for Teresa of Jesus,
thus loosing all the knots of misunderstanding in Medina. The nuns could never have hoped for so much.
The recompense for Teresa de Quesada's good, but
unsuitable direction, was far too great.

Unanimously elected, Teresa was off again toward
Medina which meant another separation and another
trip. Notwithstanding all the difficulties, Teresa calmly,
but steadfastly, led the small group in serenity and
prayer. It was while working at this task that something
which would greatly surprise all those acquainted with
the situation and Teresa herself, was about to ripen. It
was being silently prepared by Fr. Fernández in con-
formity with the Provincial, Fr. de Salazar. The first
was probably being led by an ascetic motive, full of
faith and admiration as he was for Teresa; the second
was no doubt acting from a practical standpoint. Without a doubt, the result was most unexpected to all.
Teresa was nominated Prioress of the Incarnation by
authority!

Shortly before, a nun of the Mitigated Carmelites
had been called by authority to govern a Reformed
convent, causing the humiliating exclusion of Inés of
Jesus. Now the Foundress of the Discalced Reform was
being called to govern one of the most important convents of the Mitigated Order where she had tasted all

degrees of bitterness and felt acute disapproval. That proof of faith was a source of torment for Teresa, but the visitor's order was precise and Teresa could only exclaim, "Lord God of my body and soul, behold me. I am Yours. The flesh aches because it is weak, but my soul is ready. *Fiat voluntas Tua.* ("Be it done to me according to Your will.")

Thus resigned, she left for Avila to bear the heavy burden placed upon her.

CHAPTER FORTY-ONE

An Exciting Installation Ceremony

Fr. Salazar had been the one to suggest to the apostolic visitor such an astonishing nomination. To Fr. Fernández this represented a greater good to the nuns of that institute, for he had noticed the tepidity that had filtered into certain aspects of their lives, and no one better than Teresa could remedy the situation with her language of love. But was the betterment of the convent the sole reason for Fr. Salazar's sending Teresa there? Above personal pride, he truly did want the convent to become better. However, he was thinking also of the bewildering progress of the Reform. That nun was capable of having convents spring up anywhere she stopped, and this disturbed him.

What better way of imprisoning her than by her own merits and prestige? To place her at the head of the important and famous Incarnation Convent was the best solution. That "wanderer" of the Lord had been a postulant there and was now returning as prioress—an office that would serve to "chain" her. This could be considered neither vengeance nor punishment, only a simple brake dictated by higher necessities of the Order. Above all, the two branches of the tree would be kept united and interpenetrated, this being the principal aim.

Teresa saw only that she would be leaving her marvelous cultivation of new Carmelite flowers. Moreover, how long would she have to suffer before the nuns would accept her as the new Mother Superior, for she did not overlook this side of the situation. In fact, nuns at the Incarnation were upset because, according to their way of reasoning, Teresa had offended them with her foundations which amounted to the same as branding them as monastically unsatisfactory. Now she was to be the one to govern them! What exaggerations would she demand, and what sacrifices would be imposed on them?

At recreation time in the convent the long corridors were full of excited whispering nuns all talking either for or against Teresa. A hundred and thirty nuns were presently at the Incarnation—more than all the nuns of the Reform convents founded by Teresa so far, put together.

From St. Joseph's, Teresa sent an important message to the Incarnation. She could not accept the post of prioress until all of the laywomen, who were installed there through long abuse of the law, left. Most of the nuns had anxiously followed Teresa on her trip from Medina to Avila feeling a sort of nemesis coming upon them, while others exulted over the approaching arrival. Now that Teresa had really come, and her first action revealed how indomitable her will was, the convent was undecided whether to obey or rebel. At first, the convent sent away its abusive guests in a gesture of obedience. Naturally, the operation did not go smoothly. For example, there was the pitiful case of María Jimenez who lived in the convent with her aunt, a professed nun. An orphan, María had nowhere to go.

Feeling sorry for the child, her aunt asked permission to keep her at the convent. Teresa granted it.

As the day that Teresa would take office drew nearer, all the more did the nuns feel slighted because their right to vote had been suspended by authority, submitting them to this punishment. Their complaints did not bother the Provincial or apostolic visitor because they had the right to nominate in certain cases, and Teresa's entrance was fixed for October 6.

Avila, meanwhile, had become acquainted with the situation in the convent, every family having some relative or friend at the Incarnation. The parlors were crowded, and all the news spread quickly. In those times in Spain the separation between family life and convent life was not strict. A small, believing town, Avila was immensely interested in ecclesiastical questions and jealous of all that happened within its walls. This explains why a considerable crowd awaited Teresa's entrance to take "possession" of the convent.

The Prioress arrived solemnly, escorted by the Provincial, Fr. Salazar, Fr. Ledesma, representing the apostolic visitor, Julian de Avila, Francisco de Salcedo and other officials, as well as citizens who were to maintain order. A certain presentiment vibrated in the air, and emotions became tense as the group approached. At the sound of the bell the gate swung open onto the outer court before the cloister entrance. After announcing their arrival, the Provincial went toward the door, but there he found a surprise. A barrier of nuns on the other side pushed against the door so it could not be opened. Though expecting some resistance, the priests and public officials were taken aback. From behind, women's voices could be heard reclaiming the right to vote, protesting against Teresa as their prioress.

Fr. Salazar was definitely perplexed. What could be done to combat all that shouting? Remembering that there was a side door to the convent through the church, he silently made signs to the others to follow him out and into the church.

Teresa did not follow, but serenely seated herself on the well's edge, completely hidden in her white mantle. This was narrated at the beatification process in 1610 by an eyewitness. When the nuns realized what was being done, they gave a cry and ran to the choir door, but it was too late. Fr. Salazar and the others were already inside. The Provincial then calmly explained to them how, according to the superiors, the measure taken was for the good of the convent. Nonetheless, when he had finished, the protests again arose. Fr. Salazar reminded them of the right the superiors had of nominating a convent prioress, and that the manner in which the community was behaving demonstrated how much they lacked discipline.

Meanwhile, an important thing was happening. Those who rejected Teresa were not the majority, but only an active minority. It so happened that the majority, disturbed by this sort of struggle, hurried to the choir. Seeing so many approaching, Fr. Salazar felt the situation beyond control and gruffly declared he was ready to withdraw the nomination. But just then Catalina de Castro, one of the many who venerated Teresa, cried out above the others, ''We want her, and we love her!'' She then started singing the *Te Deum,* which is the ritual hymn in thanksgiving after the election of aprioress. A hundred voices chimed in, and the opposition was forced to realize how few they were in number.

The battle won, several nuns went to welcome Teresa, accompanying her to the choir. Here Teresa proved she was worthy of the post. Upon entering, she neared a wooden image of the Madonna and placed it on the chair where she should have sat, placing the keys of the convent on the Madonna's hands. Then, putting a statue of St. Joseph in the Superior's chair, she seated herself at the feet of the Madonna. The effect was tremendous, for the idea was clear that the Virgin would be Prioress and Teresa only a humble servant. Excitement ebbed, permitting a calm sense of reality to fill everyone. Feeling that resistance had been excessive, the guilty nuns began to become uncomfortable. Teresa's gentle and luminous eyes full of love looked out over them all.

Various witnesses have left a summary of the speech she then gave. What she did to calm the fiery ones was to expose her program. In substance, this is what she said:

"Through obedience, our Lord has sent me here to fill an office to which I was both adverse and undeserving. This election has caused me great pain because it has placed on me a responsibility which I do not know how to fulfill, and because a prioress has been assigned you against your will and not to your taste. But I come only to serve you and to be of what help I may be to you; I hope the Lord will greatly help me in this, and I shall be most grateful to any of you who will teach me and correct me. Therefore, look for what I can do for each one of you. Even if I were to shed my blood I would do it willingly.

"A daughter of this house, I am one of your sisters. I know the necessities of the greater part of you so do not be afraid of one who feels she is one of you. Do not fear my government for even if I have governed Discalced Carmelites, I also know how the others should be ruled. My desire is that we all serve God agreeably, and that we do what little our rules and constitutions command us to do for the love of the Lord to whom we owe so much. Great is our weakness, but there where our deeds cannot reach, let us be with our desire, for

God is so merciful that He will slowly make our deeds equal to our intentions and desires."[1]

More suitable words could not have been found, nor a more opportune tone. A feeling of calm pervaded even the most excited. They had feared the frown of an offended Prioress who had succeeded in triumphing all the same, but they now saw her eyes smile with love for them all.

So it was that Teresa's priorship was definitely established. The next morning the fact that Teresa had calmly received Communion had topped everything. The rebellious nuns were still emotionally upset, and they knew that in the tumult of the preceding day Teresa had not gone to confession. Had she not felt any rage whatever against them? How could she have remained so impassive within! But just one look at Teresa's celestial face receiving the Eucharist was enough to convince anyone that she bore no one a grudge.

---

1. Fr. Silverio, IV, 1.

CHAPTER FORTY-TWO

The Foundations of Altomira and La Roda

While Teresa was starting her priorship, the Reform was facing new problems. By this time the branch of Discalced Friars was no less important than that of the nuns. It was, however, more difficult to treat.

Pastrana was its stronghold. Even with the university-toned college in Alcalá, the true life of the novice from whence so many champions of the new Order arose, was in Pastrana. Youth there became an ascetic flame. The method used by St. John of the Cross, the greatest Carmelite teacher of perfection, can be summarized thus: "To let go and detach oneself from every created thing in order to praise the Creator is the goal to be gradually attained, each step being closely studied and prudently applied to each novice. Prayer must be adapted according to the habits of each, so in each case advantage can be drawn from it, the senses purified and the powers of the soul explored—all done delicately and purely as only that great master of souls could do."

A book written by St. John of the Cross in 1591 entitled *Instructions to Discalced Carmelite Novices* contains such thoughts as these: "First, and above all, as our Mother Teresa says, endeavor to teach your inner self, for from there arises the splendor which makes outer actions illustrious, just as in the transfiguration of the Lord when the light emanated from the soul's inner glory to the body and from thence to His clothing. This must be done in order that the virtue the novices possess may not be superficial, but will be stable and long-lasting since its foundation is in the innermost part."[1]

Meanwhile, two picturesque monasteries arose, one in Altomira and the other in La Roda. The Altomira monastery stood at the top of a rocky mountain about 3,700 feet high, isolated at the limits of the Cuenca and Madrid provinces. Mazarulleque, numbering perhaps a thousand five hundred inhabitants, was the only town nearby. Why had a monastery been founded there? The story goes that during the time of the Moors some Christians climbed up there to save a holy picture of the Madonna from profanation. In the mid-sixteenth century the picture still existed and was venerated by all in the nearby valley and hills. Fr. Diego del Castillo finally decided to take it upon himself to construct a small hermitage where he celebrated Mass before the holy picture. But to live up there was impossible. The winds lashed implacably no matter what the season. No one but a group of Discalced Friars could exist up there. With this idea in mind, he went to Pastrana where he spoke to Fr. Baltasar of Jesus who was the acting Provincial Vicar of all Discalced houses. The undertaking he proposed was so pious and extraordinary that Fr. Baltasar was fascinated by it. After obtaining Fr. Rubeo's permission for the new foundation, he

---

1. Both excerpts taken from Fr. Silverio, *op. cit.*, IV, II, III, also for the following.

asked the Bishop of Cuenco for possession of the hermitage in order to establish a small community there. This unbelievable proposition became a reality on November 24, 1571, when a great crowd, gathered from all around, accompanied six Discalced Friars to the top of the mountain, everyone singing exultantly.

Those friars' names went down in the Reform's annals: Francisco of the Conception, still a novice, and who was to die in Mancera seven years later; Brocardo of St. Lawrence, who later was to fill high offices for thirty years; Alberto of St. Francis, a great servant of God; Miguel of the Conception, the future prior of Marzañares. Two lay brothers completed the fearless group of the Virgin of Altomira.

Winter began for the Friars as the sound of the singing faded away. First the hermitage was to be enlarged; small huts were poorly walled about the grotto Don Diego had built. Snow quickly filled in all the holes which those self-made masons left.[2] It was so cold that to say Mass the water and wine vessels had to be heated over a small fire-pan in order to melt the liquids. No trees grew on the top part of the mountain, forcing the friars to go a mile and a half down for wood. Water had to be carried from Salceda. Each morning the band of friars could be seen on the mountain's crest, each carrying his own jar. Because of the strong wind, it was necessary to thaw their frostbitten hands by the warmth of the lantern on their return.

Most of their food consisted of herbs in the beginning. Yet despite the environment, the small community did not in the least transgress its rules. Up at midnight for matins, the same hours of silence and adoration were kept as though they were in Pastrana. On certain nights, the winds roared so loudly that they could not even hear themselves sing. Then they would

---

2. *Foundations,* XXVIII.

interrupt choir-singing and take refuge in mental prayer. These conditions were borne for fifteen years, that is, until 1586. During this time those who venerated the image of the Madonna of Perpetual Help grew in number and fervor.

To speak of the La Roda monastery entails first a picture of Doña Catalina de Cardona who played an important role in Spain from 1565–1575. The natural daughter of a valiant general faithful to the Spanish monarchy, Don Raimundo de Cardona, some say she was born in Naples in 1519, while others say she was born in Barcelona and brought to Naples as a child, where her father was engaged in battle against the French on behalf of Francis I. She never knew her mother, but the Cardonas were of a noble family related to the Aragón dynasty. Having safely deposited his daughter in the Capuchin Convent in Naples, Don Raimundo continued his roving, warring life.

The charming little girl grew up, dreaming of her glorious homeland where the most powerful king of the world resided, and where the well-to-do lived with royal custom. She married a Neapolitan, however, which naturally confined her all the more to Italy. But Catalina had always felt another call when she gazed on the crucifix and the Madonna. Living an intensely religious life, even her husband followed in her steps. He put down his arms and gala dress and turned to deeds of beneficence. Ill as he was, this did not happen early enough to permit him to do good for very long. In her widowhood, Catalina regained her solitude and a chosen life.

In 1557, she accompanied the Princess of Salerno on a trip to Spain. It was a pompous journey which brought them in personal contact with the most significant people of Spain—Philip II, the royal princes and feared ministers of the government. Everyone marveled at the grandeur which surrounded the princess. The closest lady-in-waiting to the Princess, Catalina met everyone and was acknowledged by all. The Princess died in Toledo honored and famous. Before dying, she recommended her dear Catalina to the Princess of Eboli, and without delay, Ruy Gómez named her the one to distribute alms in his palace, an honorary office which demonstrated his great trust in the woman. Catalina was most appreciative of the gesture, for doing good was what her heart desired. She set about her task in such an efficient manner that her qualities were noticed, and it was a short step from the Eboli palace to the royal palace. In fact, Philip II saw she would be ideal as a governess for his brother, Juan of Austria, and for his son Don Carlos, thus placing her in the heart of court. Juan became so attached to her that he always continued to call her "mother"; in fact, this is how he addressed her in a letter, and Catalina, on her part, called her pupil "son," in the only letter written by her which has remained.

But Catalina's true vocation was yet to begin. Her time was now divided between court and the Eboli palace, but deep within she felt daily a strong ascetic call, not for the convent but for the desert. Confiding her feelings to Peter of Alcántara and Francisco de Torres, she asked if they thought she should follow her inclination. They both agreed it was the voice of God and that she should follow it. But Philip II and Ruy Gómez would never consent to such a thing. Ruy Gómez openly repeated that Doña Catalina was too valuable in his own household to complete the beneficence given by the Princess of Eboli with justice and clearheadedness.

Her inner voice, however, persisted all the more until circumstances tempted her so much that she planned an escape. While touring in Olcarria with the Ebolis who wished to buy land, she met an extraordinary man, Fr. Piña who lived as a hermit in the Vera

Cruz grotto. When she revealed her overbearing desire, he encouraged her so that she ended by begging him to prepare suitable shelter for her and to help in the escape she was planning.

Don Martín Alonso, the Ebolis' chaplain, was also drawn into the plot. On a certain day, Catalina was to meet them to be accompanied in her search for some suitable hermitage. To pass for a man, dressed in the fashion of Fr. Piña, was indispensable for the project to succeed.

So it was that some time later in 1562 a silent figure slipped out of the Eboli palace just before dawn, hurrying down the street that leads to Alcalá. No one paid any attention to that little thin man who walked with a cane, thinking him a beggar or a hermit. Catalina had cut her hair and her face showed the signs of penitence and privation. Her yellow face resembled tree roots just as Peter of Alcántara's face had seemed to Teresa.

Before leaving, Catalina had written letters for the King and Prince and Princess of Eboli. "I beseech you not to have me followed because I am resolute in my decision to spend the last years of my life in solitude." She also begged that her excuses be made to the royal princes, especially Juan of Austria, whom she left most sorrowfully. Ruy Gómez, his wife, and Philip II were all saddened by the news, but they obeyed Catalina's wishes.

Meanwhile, Catalina had met the other two accomplices of her plot at the appointed place. They started out from there into the vast countryside looking for a refuge. Near Jucar, which lies at the far end of the Del Rey Valley, they spied a small grotto, and she announced she would stay there. Her companions wished her to go farther out, but she decided to begin her solitary life there. This confirmed, Fr. Piña took leave, returning to his far-off hermitage, and Fr. Martín

Alonso returned to the Eboli palace relating the unbelievable truth.

Catalina was then forty-three years old. For the next eight years she ate wild herbs and raw roots. Whenever shepherds gave her some bread, large rats always took part in the meal. She scourged her body long and fiercely. Feast days were celebrated by the eating of a patty made of flour and vinegar.

St. Teresa wrote concerning her, "I have heard many things about the bitter life she leads. These things are known by us in small part because she must certainly have maltreated her body horribly during those years she spent in solitude with such great desire for penance. She never drank wine as far as I know. Disciplines consisted of scourgings lasting up to two hours. And her hair shirts were so harsh that a woman on a pilgrimage who had slept in her grotto reported to have seen her take off the hair shirts to clean them, and they dripped blood."

She slept very little, spending most of her time in prayer, both mental and vocal. Enchanting scenes took place about her: partridges and hares were familiar with her, running to her for safety when rapacious animals were after them. Scenes of horror also occurred: demons appeared in various forms. Fr. Silverio says that something similar to the torment she felt can only be found in the man of Hus. But Catalina would remain serenely prostrated before Christ, unmoved.

Even the inhabitants of the region became accustomed to seeing that mysterious hermit, and they were struck by "his" voice whenever they chanced to hear it. Though Catalina's voice did not betray her because it had become colorless, void of every feminine grace, the great reserve and a certain fear in her eyes impressed all to whom she spoke. Taking her for a man, everyone marveled at the hermit's great haste to conclude a conversation in order to return to the grotto.

What could be the meaning of those frightened eyes, and what could "he" be concealing so anxiously? Moreover, the few shepherds who had spoken to "him" noticed that, even though poorly dressed, "he" was very different from them. There was always something noble and dignified which distinguished the hermit's gestures and looks.

Speaking of the strange hermit, the inhabitants of the hills would respectfully lower their voices and conjecture on "his" past. Their curiosity grew so great that some followed Catalina at a distance, spying on her penances from nearby hills. Finally, some priests from close by went so far as to enter the grotto in her absence. Little as it was, there was a sort of cell at the far end into which Catalina's body could barely fit. Instruments of penance lay among a few letters and books. Searching the letters they were struck by the word "mother" in one of them, which, wonder of wonders, was signed by Don Juan of Austria, the King's son!

What mystery lay here? A friar who knew Philip II decided to visit the hermit for himself. While closely examining the rare objects that were in the grotto, he found the following written on the first page of a Book of Hours: "This Book of Hours was given to Doña Catalina de Cardona by the Princess of Eboli." The friar had heard the story of the royal princes' governess, who having abandoned the world, disappeared. And he had heard also that no one knew where she was since her protectors would not reveal her hiding place. Now it was clear that the hermit was none other than Catalina de Cardona!

With wings on his feet, the friar left the grotto bursting to spread the news. That woman was probably a saint! Her heroism was certainly legendary, and there were the hair shirts, iron chains and the impossible cave to prove it. The years of a sublime and intense existence of renunciation were all synthesized there.

This knowledge produced admiration for the solitary woman in all, and devotional respect for her grew. The word spread and flocks of people came to her grotto imploring her intercession in special petitions. If that "good woman" could not obtain the particular grace, who then could?

Catalina wondered at this sudden interest in her, but thought it was sporadic curiosity and welcomed everyone with her customary exquisite courtesy. But her visitors increased daily, and she began to grow wary. What was happening, and how was she to behave? Charity would not permit that she refuse to see them. And it was natural for her to leave a good word full of understanding. This only caused her success to become even greater. The slope where her grotto was became filled with carts and carriages in line, the passengers waiting their turn to speak to the "good woman," asking her intercession for them with God. Catalina listened, comforted and promised to pray for them all. Whenever someone left, she would naturally lift her hand and bestow a sort of blessing on her visitor. This particular gesture became a habit, and gradually people came asking for the "saint's" blessing. Catalina felt as though she could mother everyone who suffered, battled and believed, so she willingly imparted her blessing just as children ask blessings of their parents. She did not in any way consider herself great, firmly believing only in the unlimited mercy of God. She exhorted everyone to be devoted to Mary. "For through our Mother shall we reach Paradise."

But her fame troubled her to the point where she felt she should leave that hermitage for one farther out in the desert. Before she could change dwellings, however, she fell ill and it was during this period that the idea of founding a monastery came to her. Then she chanced upon some workers returning from Pastrana who spoke to her of the monastery founded there by the Prince and Princess of Eboli. She was overjoyed at this bit of news. Separated from the world for eight years, she had not even heard of Teresa's Reform. The fact that the Ebolis had concerned themselves with such pious deeds greatly pleased her. What she heard of the Reformed Friars' fervor impressed her to such an extent that she decided to write to Ruy Gómez about the matter.

Naturally, the letter proved to be a most pleasant surprise. What luminous ideas from the dear, voluntarily exiled fugitive! Gómez and the Princess immediately went to the monastery prior, Fr. Baltasar, to discuss the matter.

The next day, Fr. Ambrosio Mariano set out for Doña Catalina's hermitage to invite her to come to Pastrana to settle many questions which could be resolved better through direct conversation. Catalina's arrival was hailed festively. The castle was full of guests, and everyone wanted to meet this strange hermit. Those who had known her could not believe their eyes. How that once gracious woman had changed! Several even cried to see her so disfigured, deep wrinkles crossing her ghastly pale face. Wearing a poor man's coverall, her whole aspect did indeed inspire pity.

Her old friends surrounded her tenderly while the populace felt veneration for her. Crowds came to Pastrana to see her pass by on her visit to the two Discalced monasteries, in the hopes of touching her clothing. How great was the contrast between the small formless hermit and the elegant Princess of Eboli who accompanied her, walking side by side. But the people admired the small woman who had renounced even her feminine appearance. Everywhere parents held out their children to her, shedding tears of affection for her.

She answered them with a small sign of the hand which was a slight gesture of benediction that had become habitual to her.

When asked to don the habit of the Discalced nuns, she replied, "I am not worthy!" But the real meaning of her words was that, entering a convent, she would no longer be permitted to carry out her type of penances. Returning to the state of "womanhood," she would have to comply with the confessor's concern for her health. To be deprived of her world of renouncement and voluntary suffering terrorized her. A superhuman strength long sustained her in that coveted calvary, and she did not wish to lose her mysterious privilege. All she would accept would be a monk's habit.

Surprisingly enough, everyone thought this to be quite natural on Catalina's part. And the incredible investiture ceremony was held in that picturesque pigeon-house convent. The same procedure was held as for a Discalced Carmelite Friar. Throughout the whole ceremony tears were seen on the faces of all those assisting while her boyish saintly voice asked admittance into the Order.

It was established that Catalina would found a monastery for Discalced Friars near her hermitage in La Roda. Though she would not live within its walls she would receive the Sacrament of Reconciliation from them and accept food from them. But just as she was about to leave, an unexpected invitation complicated matters. Juana of Austria, who was Philip II's sister and the mother of Portugal's King Sebastian, had heard of Catalina's return to the world and wanted to see her. Not feeling she could refuse to comply with the wishes of such an illustrious person, Catalina set off for Madrid, accompanied by Ambrosio Mariano in a beautiful court carriage.

In Madrid, Catalina again found that inimitable environment which surrounded Philip II of Spain. He who lived in the largest palace of that century, but who, out of a spirit of mortification, chose a dark room where only an inner window allowed light to pass for his private room, could well understand Catalina's type of heroism. For eight days Philip, Juana and Catalina lived closely together, vastly different each from the other, yet each comprehending the other.

Meanwhile, all Madrid was anxious to see the "good woman." Thus it was that Philip ordered her portrait painted so that the people could see how she was. Copied many times, that picture still exists, showing the strange, thin, figure of Catalina with her tattered habit and prominent hood which cast a shadow over her wax-like face.

Whenever Catalina was forced to leave the palace, the passing of her carriage was never unannounced, and crowds would gather to hail her, beseeching a prayer for their children and for the sick. From inside the carriage, Catalina would smile and give her customary sign of a blessing. It was indeed strange to see that small "friar" between two women of court. Those who did not know of Catalina were truly puzzled by that spectacle. In fact, one zealous man reported the incident to the King's Papal Nuncio: a small wrinkled Carmelite was riding through the streets of Madrid accompanied by solemn, elegant ladies and blessing crowds as though he were a bishop! When the Nuncio heard the friar was of Teresa of Jesus' Reform, he thought the Reform was becoming a bit excessive. Called to explain matters, Fr. Ambrosio Mariano happily told the surprising story of Catalina de Cardona. But when the Nuncio heard it was a woman dressed as a friar who blessed the crowds, he was even more scandalized than before and ordered her to be brought before him.

Shrewd as the Nuncio was in detecting sanctity, Catalina's extreme simplicity, shriveled body, and friar's garb made him critical of her. To top it all, Catalina ingenuously raised her hand tracing that slight sign of a blessing which she was wont to do, and Nuncio Ormaneto was taken aback. The idea, a woman dressed as a friar blessing His Holiness' Nuncio! This was too much!

Fortunately, though, he asked her a few questions which caused her to rise in his esteem. So profoundly religious were her words that the priest slowly glimpsed the true nature of that supremely candid soul. Upon her departure, he could utter no restriction about the way she was spending her life.

After that it was a simple matter to get all the permits necessary to found her monastery. On her return to Pastrana and La Roda, accompanied by Fr. Ambrosio, crowds acclaimed her all along the route, for through her adventures she had gained steadily growing fame.

The monastery grew up near Catalina's grotto, and unawares, she became a sort of spiritual director for the small community. Notwithstanding the friars' reserve, silence and life apart, she reached them through setting her example. Even if they lived apart, it was impossible to ignore her, and the friars felt a sort of obligation not to let themselves be surpassed in virtue and penance.

Teresa's Reform thus acquired another monastery and another "half-friar," and what a gift of God for the good of the Order. Catalina de Cardona maintained her life of virtue and penance up to the time of her death which was admirable indeed. Extremely ill, she remained in deep absorption during the Holy Week of 1577. On Easter Day the procession reached as far as her grotto to console her. Shortly afterwards she was moved to the servants' quarters of the monastery, in order to be assisted by two good women. The friars visited her daily, reading a few pages of the *Flos Sanctorum*. She continued, sustained solely by her daily Communion until May 11, when after speaking tender words about heaven, she died.

Two glorious titles were immediately bestowed upon her by learned religious and the people alike: "prodigy of penance" and "marvel of the centuries."

CHAPTER FORTY-THREE

Prioress of the "Incarnation"

When the Altomira and La Roda monasteries were being established, Teresa was busy at the Incarnation convent with her difficult task of sowing seeds of perfection in that institute. Though the Rule remained mitigated, love was the basis of everything. To teach her one hundred and thirty subjects to love with greater perfection was her aim. They were to love God with faith, and their neighbor with charity. Basically good in a common, average way, the nuns needed injections of spiritual fervor.

Three main points were immediately set down to be followed: a more exact observance of their Rule, fewer visits outside the cloister, and restricted meetings in the parlor. By reordering external acts, Teresa meant to gain a greater sense of withdrawal into an environment more apt to promote intimate life with the Lord. It was necessary for them to feel more dedicated if they were to love better. Distractions were disastrous for mental prayer, Teresa having felt it herself in her early days. The "homey" air about the parlors was to be removed, and in this the nuns were ready to obey. The

visitors, however, did not enjoy having their easy ac-
cess to the nuns denied them. Many had family ties
with the nuns, and everyone enjoyed speaking with
them because conversation with the nuns was more
elevated than normal layman to layman talk, and they
could gain spiritually from such meetings.

But Teresa was energetic in carrying out her program.[1] During Lent, 1572, visits were forbidden, even
from parents. A certain man of nobility, however, insisted he be permitted to visit a relative of his. Seeing
that Teresa persistently refused permission, he went to
see the Prioress personally, protesting loudly against
such tyrannical restrictions, threatening to refer the
matter to higher authorities. It was clear that his "point
of honor" had been touched and that he would not
retreat with the eyes of the city upon him.

Not at all alarmed, Teresa firmly replied to his
admonitions, ending by stating that if he continued to
be annoying she would have recourse to the king.
Overcome, he could only give a cross look and walk
out. Though he never returned to the convent again, he
did not bear Teresa a grudge. Instead, he would often
say that you couldn't joke with Teresa, to the delight of
everyone who saw he had been pulled down a peg.

Observance of the Rule was rigidly imposed only
on the healthy members of the community, while the
sick were cared for as never before. Teresa even appealed to the city for gifts to alleviate their suffering. So
it was that the healthy were fed frugal meals while the

---

1. On November 7, 1571, Teresa had already written the following to
Doña Luisa de la Cerda: "Oh, after having been in our calm convents, I
don't know how one can live in this agitated one. At any rate, we must
suffer. Nevertheless, glory be to God, peace reigns and that is important.
The nuns are slowly giving up their conversations and liberties, but notwithstanding the goodness and great virtue in this institute, they say that the
change of habits is death for them. They bear the burden well and are
respectful toward me, but you can understand what care is needed to put
things to order in a house with a hundred and thirty nuns."

ill nuns ate chicken and peacock. Once someone donated sixty-two hens all at one time. The news spread,
and a game of trying to outdo the other started so that
the nuns not only no longer suffered from hunger, but
reasons to go to the outside world were reduced to a
minimum. Formerly, the nuns were forced to beg material help from their families and friends, but this undig-
nified way of leading convent life was abolished under
Teresa's priorship.

This exterior program served only as the frame
around Teresa's prodigious personal work on every single soul there. Her example was the most effective
argument. Accustomed as she was to mortification, it
was easy to be the most frugal both in food and sleep.
She was always the first at choir and the last to leave.
No nun could doubt she was very virtuous. But love
was the weapon she could handle most dexterously,
capable of penetrating even the most reluctant and
rebellious of souls. Her method was simple: to identify
herself completely with the other person, feel her difficulties, and suffer with her.

All this Teresa did while afflicted with continual
maladies. On March 2, 1572, she wrote to María de
Mendoza, "As for me, this earth has taxed me as
though I truly do not belong to it. I think there was
about a month and a half at the beginning of my work
when my health was good, for the Lord knows I could
not have succeeded in doing anything otherwise. Now
the Lord does everything, and I can only rest. For three
weeks now I have been suffering from a piercing pain
on one side and spinal arthritis in addition to my quartan fever. Only one of these maladies would be sufficient to kill me if God wished it, but it seems that he
does not for the time being. I am a little better after
three bloodlettings, for the quartan attacks have left
me, but the high fever persists, for which I will take a
purge tomorrow. I know this will depress me so that I

shall remain in some corner unless to assist at Mass, nor will it be possible to do otherwise. A facial neuritis also has distressed me greatly for a month and a half now. I tell you all these things in order to excuse myself for not having written until today."

In the midst of all these physical sufferings, Teresa effected an important and delicate spiritual restoration. She changed confessors for the convent. Until then the mitigated Carmelite fathers in Avila came regularly to hear the nuns' confessions, but Teresa realized what impulse a truly exceptional director could give the convent. She, therefore, begged Fr. Fernández, the apostolic visitor, to order John of the Cross to come to Avila as convent confessor.

No priest in Spain at that time could offer as much as he. Thirty years old, he already possessed spiritual maturity. Using discretion, he proceeded with the nuns by degrees so they would not be frightened by too much asceticism. A mitigated Carmelite friar took turns with Friar John of the Cross at the convent confessional, and it is said that at first the nuns would ask, "Father are you Calced or Discalced?" and John, covering his feet with his habit would reply, "Calced." But the nuns soon grew fond of their new director and sought him more and more. Upon request and acceptance of another Discalced Friar, the whole direction of the convent was in the hands of the Reform.

Teresa had a small house built at the far end of the convent garden for the two confessors. John of the Cross had arrived in September, 1572, and on February 13, 1573, Mother Teresa could already write of him to Father Gaspar de Salazar: "The Lord has favored this house with many graces for I can tell you that I no longer have reason to grieve because of resistance or lack of obedience or concentration, just as if I were among the nuns of St. Joseph."

That was the highest praise she could give the Carmelites of the Incarnation. Continuing, she said, "It seems that the Lord grants grace to these souls so rapidly that I am astounded, just as the visitor who came last month marveled that there was nothing to correct. Please thank the Lord for this, that one of the Discalced Friars here is very holy and has brought such good influence."[2]

There is an interesting document which demonstrates the renewed fervor that swept the convent. A spiritual challenge chart was sent the nuns by the friars of Pastrana. In their proposed contest of fervor, the stakes would be penances and mortifications. Teresa liked the idea and replied with perfect wit: "Upon reading the challenge chart, we do not feel strong enough to compete with such expert and valiant knights as you. Your certain victory over us would serve only to discourage us from doing the little we can do, and it is for this reason that no one wishes to enter the contest, least of all Teresa of Jesus, this being the unadulterated truth.

"However, we have decided to test our strength by trying our hand at these favors in the hope of signing a chart some day soon if helped and favored by the valorous knights who will take part in the tournament.

"But this only on condition that the defenders not escape the battleground by retiring into hidden caves. They must come out onto the field of the world where we are. Perhaps with the realization of constant war without respite to change arms, and unable to be off guard in order to rest, your confidence will be lower because there is much difference between one and the other, just as between speaking and doing, and this we know by experience.

---

2. Quoted by Fr. Silverio, IV, VI, as are the following.

"Come out, then, from your cozy life and take care not to be thrown to the ground so you will need help to get up. It is a terrible thing to be continuously in danger, loaded down with arms and with no nourishment. You defenders must then send us provisions which you have in abundance because if you win us by hunger, small glory or vantage it would be indeed."

In details the challenge read:

"Those knights of the Virgin who will daily pray for Sr. Beatriz Juárez to be preserved in grace so that she may reflect before speaking, seeking the glory of God in everything, will receive two years of merit earned while caring for troublesome patients.

"Sr. Ana de Vergas declares that if said knights and friars will beg the Lord to free her from a contradiction and give her humility, she will reward them with the merit that will come as a result of their prayers.

"Sub-prioress Mother Isabel of the Cross declares that if she be delivered of her self-will, two years of her merits will be the reward.

"Sr. Sebastiana Gómez declares that to him who will gaze at the crucifix and meditate on the three hours our Lord spent hanging there, permitting her to overcome a strong passion which torments her soul, she will donate the merit she may gain from having conquered it.

"Mother María de Tamayo declares that to him who will daily recite an Our Father and Hail Mary so that she may become submissive and patient in the endurance of her sickness, she will give a third of the merits she will gain every day. Her illness is grave—for it is a year now that she has been unable to speak."

And so on, with each combatant adding her stake, Teresa finished with this underlining note: "We do not feel equal to competing in penances and disciplines, but we accept and desire to vie in acts of virtue and perfection."[3] These words served as an admonition not to forget that the most difficult and most beautiful disciplines were those of inner striving and not the voluntary torments of the flesh. This type of spiritual challenge still remains in the Carmelite Reform with the sending of holy charts from one monastery or convent to another.

═══════════

What filled Teresa's inner life in this period of intense activity? Strangely enough, those were the years of the greatest graces the saint had ever received, which is saying a great deal considering those which had already been allowed her. The first which occurred on January 19, 1572, is related by Teresa: "On St. Sebastian's eve of the first year as prioress of the Incarnation, just as I was about to start singing the Salve Regina in choir, I saw the Blessed Virgin descend from heaven amidst a great multitude of angels. She placed herself in the prioress' seat, there where a statue of her rests. The statue seemed to disappear before my eyes to make room for this honored Lady who somewhat resembled the picture donated by the countess.[4] I was barely able to observe her closely because of my immediate enrapture. Angels seemed to fill the backs and arms of the choir stalls, not in bodily form because the vision was intellectual. Our Lady remained there for the duration of the Salve and said, 'You have done well to place me here. I shall be present at the praises directed to my Son and will present them to Him.'

"After that my soul entered mental prayer in company with the Holy Trinity, and it seemed that the Father drew me to Him, speaking kindly to me. Among

---

3. *Spiritual Reports,* XXV-XXXV, from here to the end of the chapter.

4. Doña María de Velasco y Aragón, the Countess of Osorno. The picture is still venerated in St. Joseph's in Avila.

other things, He showed me how much He loved me. 'I have given you my Son, the Holy Spirit and the Virgin. And what can you give me in return?'"

The early weeks were full of anguish since certain nuns persisted in their opposition. Already in March, however, Teresa wrote of an advancement in those nuns. On Palm Sunday at Communion she was extraordinarily favored with the vision of Christ's Blood. This happened after having spent three arid days apparently distant from the Lord, when the anguish had been so strong she felt she could no longer bear it.

In recompense, the favor was special and precious. She did not see the wounds bleeding, but the Blood of Redemption appeared in great abundance signifying divine purification. Fifty years later in France, another great mystic, Marie Martin Guyard, called Marie of the Incarnation, was also to witness a similar vision. She saw herself immersed in the Savior's Blood, thus washed of all her sins. Teresa described the Blood contemplated as "felt" by means of the Holy Eucharist, for she found herself enraptured as soon as she had received the Host, unable to swallow it. Reviving a little, but still holding the Host in her mouth, it seemed that the Blood was just then shed, enfolding her, penetrating within. While enjoying this state of supreme felicity, the Lord said to her, "My daughter, I want you to benefit from my Blood. I shed it in bitter pain, and you derive indescribable delights from it. You see then how well I reward you for the banquet you prepare for me today."

"This referred to the fact that on Palm Sunday for thirty years," Teresa wrote, "I had always tried to receive Communion with my soul prepared as well as possible to house the Lord, for I felt the crowds had been cruel in welcoming Him triumphantly and then permitting that he go afar for dinner; I sought to keep Him with me, offering a miserable lodging." Remembering that Jesus went to Bethany for the night after his triumphal entrance into Jerusalem, she would mentally accompany Him on that day, not eating until three in the afternoon. For even greater practical adherence, she would invite a poor person to the meal meaning to refresh the divine Abandoned One in this manner.

Teresa had long lived closely the Passion of Christ, but she did so even more during her priorship at the Incarnation. With so many afflictions, she sought to live nearer to the Lord. In May, she heard these words of friendship and chiding: "What worries you, poor sinner? Am I not your God? Do you not see how that offends me? And if you love me, why do you not pity me?"

Later she was to hear a marvelous locution, full of revelation concerning the state of grace. "My daughter, the light is very different from the darkness. I am faithful, and no one will be lost without knowing it. He is deceived who feels secure because of the spiritual consolations he receives. True security lies in the evidence of a clean conscience. No one can think of staying in the light through his own strength, just as night cannot be held off, because this grace depends on me alone. The best way to keep in the light is to persuade oneself that the soul can do nothing alone because everything originates from me; if the soul is in the light, night falls as soon as I move away. True humility lies in the recognition of what man can do and what I can do."

It was in this period that Teresa sought to penetrate the problem of union with God in two aspects: mystical union and simple union of grace. She had heard these words spoken by our Lord: "Daughter, do not believe that union consists in being very close to me because those also who offend me are near even if they do not wish to be so. Neither does it consist in the delights and joys of prayer, even if these come from me and are lofty. Really, this is often a means of attracting those souls which are not in the state of grace."

While those words were being spoken, Teresa's spirit was "in high elevation."

"The Lord," she wrote, "let me understand what the spirit is, what the state of my soul was then, and how we should interpret the words of the Magnificat 'my spirit rejoices.' But now I could not explain it. I think I understood the spirit to be the superior part of the will."

Meditating on the intimate values of union with God, the great mystic continued, "Returning to the union, I understood that it consists in a state of the spirit which is pure and free from every terrestrial thing, that not only offers no opposition to God's will, but forms a single spirit and single will with God, detached from everything, and so taken with Him as to exclude every shadow of love for itself and for any other creature.

"If this is what union is, I then thought, a soul which remains determined could be said to be continuously in the prayer of union, yet we know that this prayer can perforce be brief.

"I then thought that it must be in reference to walking righteously, in progressing and acquiring merits, and not meaning that the soul is united to God in contemplation. In fact, though not explained in words, I understood that our misery, the defects, and obstacles we meet are so numerous, rendering it impossible for the spirit to remain as pure as when united with God because this state is out of human bounds. If union consists in making our will and spirit one with the will and spirit of God, I believe this can be possible only in the state of grace, no matter what has been said to me in this matter. And since we cannot know whether we are in the state of grace, it seems to me that it must be indeed difficult to be able to recognize if it is union without light from God."

The series of stupendous visions and illuminations culminated in a "spiritual marriage" which took place on November 18, 1572, in the form of both an intellectual and imaginary vision. "On the Octave of St. Martin's Day in the second year of my priorship at the Incarnation, Fr. John of the Cross was about to give me Holy Communion when he divided the Sacred Particle in order to give half to another nun. I immediately thought he did this, not for lack of Hosts, but to mortify me because he knew of my fondness for large Hosts even though I well knew the Lord is whole in a particle of one. Wanting me to understand this was of no importance, the Lord said: 'Do not fear, daughter! No one can separate you from me!' Then He showed Himself to me in the innermost part of my soul by means of imaginable vision, gave me His right hand, as He has done at other times, and said, 'Behold this nail; it is a sign that from today you shall be my spouse. You had not merited this grace until now, but henceforth you shall care for my honor not only because I am your God, your King, and Creator, but also because you are my true spouse. My honor is yours, and yours mine.'

"I was so impressed that I was beside myself and went into a sort of delirium during which I begged the Lord to deign either transform my misery or not grant me so many favors because I felt I could not bear them. I remained absorbed the whole day. I later felt great advantage from it, but greater confusion and sorrow in realizing I could never deserve such favors."

Thus we see how special graces abounded during Teresa's sojourn at the Incarnation Convent. Notwithstanding severe, troublesome illnesses, she directed the nuns confidently, thinking, battling, suffering, and praying. With the limpid eyes of her spirit, human figures and circumstances were clearly seen in their correct dimensions. Her judgments were sure and easily classified according to values. Everyone who came in contact with Teresa marveled at her wisdom and immediate, sure penetration into matters, leading them to believe such intelligence to be supernaturally illuminated.

CHAPTER FORTY-FOUR

Journey to Salamanca and the Segovia Foundation

Teresa was called away from Avila several times to settle difficulties arising in her reformed convents during those three years of priorship. After two trips to Alba, she went to Salamanca in 1573 because the community there was being transferred into a better habitat. The trip to that city was an epic one.

One evening in early August, Mother Teresa with a nun, a maid, and Fathers Antonio of Jesus and Julian de Avila, set out on muleback at dusk, because Teresa felt the heat too much during the day. Things started happening from the very beginning; in fact, not far from Avila, Fr. Antonio fell off his mule, miraculously escaping injury. Shortly afterwards, (Fr. Julian later wrote of the whole trip) the maid fell, striking her head against a rock. "I thought she was dead," he wrote. Instead, strangely enough, the woman felt better than before, and the group moved happily on. About ten-thirty, however, the most important mule of the band slid off the narrow path in the black, moonless night. Those behind heard it disappear from ahead, unable as they were to see. General alarm followed because it was the mule which was carrying a load of packages, one containing five hundred ducats—that is, all the money Mother Teresa had been able to get together for the first indispensable repairs of the convent. It consisted of the whole dowry of a novice.

Needless to say, everyone continued disconsolately, and toward midnight they reached a sort of resting station. In the morning, a boy was sent to look for the mule, and he found it waiting exactly where it had fallen on a mountain landslide. And what counted most, its cargo was intact. Overjoyed, the group took off that evening.

During that second night another loss occurred, still more important than the first. This is how Fr. Julian related the incident: "Since we were traveling by night, and it was very dark, we formed two groups. The guide who was to help Mother Teresa, whose name I shall not mention to save his honor, left her with Sr. Quiteria on a village side street while he returned to the main road to await the others. When the latter appeared, he went back to get the two women, but could no longer find where he had left them. Going around in circles in the blackness, he never did find them. Thinking they were ahead with the first group, we went quite far before we had caught up with the others. Simultaneously, we asked each other if Mother Teresa was present. Finding she was not, we felt two darknesses—the night, and, what was worse, the loss of our Mother."[1]

Confusion resulted. What was to be done? Go ahead or go back? Compromising, they did both by dividing into two groups. No one replied to the calls until after much fright and suffering, Teresa and the other nun arrived. They had waited so long they had decided to wake up a farmer and offer him pay if he

---

1. Quoted by Fr. Silverio, *op. cit.,* IV, VI, also for the following.

would accompany them. That was how they had reached the group. They again continued together until they reached an inn for travelers which was so over-crowded there was no room for them.

All this was endured just to go to Salamanca. But the worst was yet to come! Moving the nuns to a better house brought a host of difficulties, too many to list separately. Nevertheless, the transfer took place sol-emnly on St. Michael's Day, 1573. The evening before, rain poured down. Everything was prepared for the ceremony which included a procession. Worried about the consequences the rain would cause if it continued for another day, Prioress Ana of Jesus went to Teresa who was in the chapel observing the effects of the rain there together with Fathers Julian and Nieto. With a decisive tone, Prioress Ana said to Teresa, "Seeing that it is still raining hard and tomorrow we are expecting so many people, could you not ask God the grace to have it stop raining?"

Teresa scolded her. After some time it did stop raining, however, and the sky cleared. Ana of Jesus then turned to Teresa saying, "Couldn't you have asked God for this grace before? Now let me go and set the chapel in order." Laughing, Teresa went to her cell. And the next day the ceremony took place with the sun shining brightly.

Another convent was about to spring up in Segovia. Francisco Barros de Bracamonte's widow, Doña Ana de Jimina, insisted that a convent be established there, and she had already rented a house for the community.

Misfortunes were in store for this foundation, too, because of a serious misunderstanding with the dioce-san Vicar General who was irritated because he had not been consulted about the new foundations; he had learned of the event by chance. Though verbally autho-rized by the Bishop, Teresa possessed no written docu-ments, and the Bishop was away.

In his natural good-humored manner, Fr. Julian recounts the following episode. "Upon entering the chapel, the Vicar General looked for the one who had placed the Blessed Sacrament there. The nuns were already cloistered, and I, sensing trouble ahead, climbed a ladder near the door and hid. Thus he bumped into Friar John of the Cross who had come with us.

" 'Who did this?' he asked. I don't remember what Friar John replied, but the Vicar continued. 'Remove everything immediately, for I am about to put you all in jail.'

"I do believe the only reason he did not was that John was a friar, but if he had run into me, I certainly would have ended up behind bars. That would have been a good one on me who has closed up behind bars so many nuns, but they get shut up of their own accord, whereas that would not have been the case with me.'

Leaving a guard at the door with orders to permit no priest to enter to celebrate Mass, the Vicar General summoned the nuns to present the documents by which they claimed the right to found the convent. Considering the Bishop's absence, the situation was difficult indeed, but Teresa and her collaborators resorted to an affidavit drawn up before a notary public with witnesses showing that the verbal authorization granted by the Bishop was fully valid. With that, the Vicar acquiesced.

CHAPTER FORTY-FIVE

Consequences Wrought by the Death of Ruy Gómez

After the annoying events of Segovia and Salamanca, still greater trouble loomed in Pastrana. As we
know, there were two Carmelite Reformed foundations
there, one for friars and the other for nuns, both under
the patronage of the Prince and Princess of Eboli. Until
July 29, 1573, when Ruy Gómez died, the two institutes had flourished. But the loss of the Prince's just,
calm, yet firm hand guiding affairs caused a radical
change in the communities. Generous at heart, the
Princess was unfortunately extremely sensitive. Her
husband's death caused her unbearable grief, and
many of those who went to pay homage to the Prince's
corpse could see by his wife's face that something
serious was maturing within her.

Indeed, Princess Ana sought comfort in a complete
change of life. No doubt the idea had lain latent in her
mind during the long months of her husband's illness
whenever she foresaw her widowed future. This secret
preparation explains her conduct immediately following the Prince's death when she asked for the Carmel-

ite habit. Accompanying her husband's hearse to Pastrana for burial, she requested admission into the Carmelite Order, thus retiring from the world.

Evidently she was capable of strong feelings and great resolutions, though her contemporaries were awe-struck by the suddenness of her ascetic endeavors. Indeed, in sign of sudden poverty and mortification, Princess Ana followed the hearse in a cart all the way to Pastrana which must have added a picturesque note to the funeral train: Princess Ana in a Carmelite habit, her mother Countess de Mendoza y la Cerda, Fr. Ambrosio Mariano, several ladies-in-waiting deeply fond of the Princess, and officials of the Eboli household, all in characteristic vehicles.

Mother Isabel of St. Dominic, Prioress of the Pastrana convent, knew nothing of the decision that so closely concerned her convent. Notwithstanding her great sorrow, Princess Ana told Fr. Mariano to go on ahead to announce her arrival to the Discalced Carmelite nuns. A surprising but significant conversation resulted on Fr. Mariano's arrival. Not believing her ears, Mother Isabel made him repeat the news. Another less intelligent prioress would have been happy perhaps to hear that a princess would become a nun in her convent in consideration of the glory the convent would gain in the eyes of the whole country. But Mother Isabel, not at all elated, sighed prophetically, "The Princess a nun? Our convent is ruined!"

Shortly afterwards, Princess Ana arrived, starting life anew as a Carmelite. The Countess de Mendoza, her mother, also remained to comfort her.

Full of fervor and surprises, the Princess proved to be an extraordinary novice, serious in every way. She refused to have the Prioress prepare less austere meals for her to be served in her cell. Instead, she went to the refectory along with the others where she would not accept the others' invitations to be seated near the Prioress, invariably insisting on the humblest seat.

Yet no matter how much will power she put into being humble, certain lacunas in the practice of that virtue were bound to appear sooner or later, and they did. It was all very laudable to seat herself at the lowest place with all the smiling nuns inviting her to the place of honor, but how would she stand up to renouncing her own affairs?

The funeral rites were impressive. An immense crowd paid homage to Ruy Gómez in gratitude for his protection and help. Afterwards, the Bishop of Segorbe, the governor, and other officials went to the convent to pay their respects to the widow. Mother Isabel politely invited them to wait at the grille and sent for Princess Ana who arrived ordering that the cloister be opened to let her visitors in. Though more convenient, it was hardly behooving for a novice to behave that way. Poor Mother Isabel realized she was the hostess of a house full of illustrious visitors and was overcome at the thought of what Ana would do later on if she started out this way!

Moreover, Mother Isabel had been forced to cope with the question of accepting immediately two ladies-in-waiting of the Princess when permission was to be given by the Provincial Father. With the help of Fr. Baltasar, Prior of the Discalced Friars in Pastrana, it was possible for the two to be accepted.

But try as the heart did to discover equilibrium and serenity, it was not possible for Ana to become a nun without a true vocation. She had brought along her ego into the convent, keeping it by her side constantly. The Princess stood alongside the novice, rendering it impossible to walk down a path reserved only for God and the soul.

Ana committed both spiritual and exterior blunders due to her character and background. She even ended as a victim of her misunderstandings so that she would pout, unconscious of her own fault in the matter. Feeling misunderstood, the spoiled child in her would be offended inwardly, and irritation was the next step.

Mother Isabel unhappily noted the change of feelings in her troublesome novice. To hurt the Princess was not desirable since they were bound in gratitude to her for aiding the Carmelite Reform. On the other hand, if she accepted Ana's attitude, where would be the principle of the Reform if they were to bend to the changing humors of a great lady? Following her sense of duty, the Prioress spoke to the Princess in clear terms concerning the state of affairs.

Ana's reply[1] was terse: "In all my life Ruy Gómez was the only person I have ever obeyed because he was a nobleman and a gentleman, and I do not mean to obey any other person."

Whether these words are authentic or not, that was the situation. The whole thing unfolded by itself. First the Princess left the convent for a small hermitage in the garden, naturally accompanied by one of her maid-postulants. Her heart still sought peace in religious seclusion, but she increasingly felt the call of her social position which bade her return to the palace and take up where she had left off.

Her Carmelite experience ended, her feelings toward the convent were complex—irritation mingled with affection. At first she withheld all material help from the nuns, ordering construction to stop and suspending their annual allowance.

Informed of everything, Teresa suffered from afar, feeling a deep urge to take the community away. Before resorting to such an extreme measure, she sent two renowned priests to intervene, trying to reconcile Prin-

---

1. Documents taken from the Alba archives, as cited by Fr. Silverio, *op. cit.*, IV, VI.

cess Ana to the convent, but their efforts failed. Yet, that refusal cleared the situation from the realm of nebulous misunderstandings. All was clear now. It was impossible for a Carmelite convent to remain in Pastrana.

Providentially enough, there was room for the nuns to take refuge in the new foundation in Segovia. All that remained was the planning of the escape, considering the Princess' temperament which would likely oppose the nuns' leaving "her" convent. Plans were thus made secretly with the aid of two accomplices, the ever faithful Fr. Julian de Avila and Fr. Antonio de Gaytán.

Teresa had already written to Mother Isabel to be prepared for immediate evacuation. This news was received with a sigh of relief, leaving only one final thing to be settled. In a moment of generosity, Princess Ana had donated all her jewels to the nuns. Now that they were about to take flight, the Prioress felt the jewels should be returned to the Princess. But how? Surely she would sense something if the gems were sent to her directly. Instead, Mother Isabel asked the governor and notary public to come to the convent. She deposited the precious load with them.

Now the nuns were ready. Little did the Princess know how fast the nuns' hearts were beating those last few days.

After the Segovia foundation was inaugurated on March 19, Fr. de Avila and Fr. Gaytán arrived. No one knows how, but the Princess got word of the projected flight, so the departure was to appear more or less authorized. Impulsively, the Princess first sent for the chief of police ordering guards to be placed around the convent to prevent the nuns from leaving. The chief diplomatically ventured that there was nothing to do considering the point the situation had reached. Nervously pouting, the Princess reflected that the objection was valid; she was beginning to understand that she would not have her way with those Carmelites. Intelligent, she then put a condition to their departure: that they take along the two maids who had entered the convent with her.

Mother Isabel's righteous reply was that they would be happy to take the one of little means who seemed willing to live in their Order, but not the other, who was well enough off and had not the necessary vocation.

How deserted and sad the convent appeared when all the bags were ready. Thirteen Discalced nuns had lived there for four years, and it saddened them to see the chapel with no Blessed Sacrament.

At midnight, the nuns left in single file, following Fathers de Avila and Gaytán and another priest to the five carts which were waiting farther out in the country. Looking back at Pastrana, Mother Isabel inwardly said farewell to the house and people with whom bonds of charitable friendship had grown. Strangely enough, she also thought of the Princess and of the sorrow she must feel in her ever-reaching, insatiable life. Though the Princess had caused her sadness, there was no bitterness harbored in her thoughts while reminiscing over the period. Princess Ana had been a great benefactress of the Carmelite Reform, and seen at a distance, she seemed more to be pitied than anything else—after all, she represented the vast majority of humans who seek peace in this world when the world can offer only apprehension.

Once the carts had been reached and they started on their journey, the nuns all relaxed in smiles, feeling a great sense of freedom. The trip proceeded well for two days. Then they reached the Henares River where waters were high. A raft was available for passengers and carts, but the wagoners argued among themselves whether it was worth paying to cross over on a raft. It seemed as though those men knew more about the matter, so the priests and nuns did not enter the discussion. Feeling sure they could wade across with the mules and carts, the wagoners decided only the passengers should use the raft. Fr. de Avila remained with the carts to keep an eye on the baggage. All five carts then entered the river and had gotten half-way across when the two mules pulling the first cart balked.

At this point the water flowed rapidly, forming a current. Heedless of the muleteers' shouts, the beasts stood, all more obstinate. It was clear they felt the earth yielding beneath their hoofs, leading them to instinctively draw back. An uproar ensued, and the muleteers decided to turn back. But when they tried to turn back they found that the wheels had sunk in the mud—it was either to go ahead or to remain there.

Fortunately, someone thought of attaching all the mules to the unsteady wagon, so all ten mules together succeeded in pulling the wagon out of the mud and dragging it to the other side. The scene had to be repeated for all the wagons so the men had to ford the river ten times instead of one. This episode gives an idea of what traveling entailed in the days of St. Teresa and how adverse conditions were in the founding of convents.

The joyously warm welcome the party received in Segovia made everyone forget the mishaps. Best of all, Mother Teresa was there with open arms waiting for her "Pastrana daughters." After having undergone many trials, changes of habitat, and even lawsuits, the Segovia and Pastrana families found themselves united in a beautiful, permanent house full of true happiness.

CHAPTER FORTY-SIX

The Discalced Friars in Andalusia

At this point we must leave the boundaries of Old and New Castile for Andalusia where the Discalced Carmelite Friars extended their reform. Fearless superiors had profited by favorable circumstances to found three new monastery sanctuaries almost contemporaneously: "Los Mártires" in Granada, "La Peñuela" in Sierra Morena, and "Nuestra Señora de los Remedios" in Seville. All three flourished. Their foundations furnished, however, the first pretext on which to start the long and dramatic battle between the Mitigated and Unmitigated members of the Order that ended in 1580 with the separation of the two branches.

As a result, every single foundation increased in value, for not only did they count for what they represented, but they also bore testimony to the repercussion of a whole Order's life. If we remember, both Mitigated and Unmitigated families of the Order depended on Fr. Rubeo, the General, who was to be notified and pass approval on any new foundation. Unseparated as they were, the hierarchy remained one, so at times the Mitigated directed the Unmitigated and vice-versa.

The situation became still more complicated when Pius V sent Dominicans as apostolic visitors to the Carmelites of the provinces of Castile and Andalusia in the Pope's intent to reform religious orders. Both of these apostolic visitors had great faith in the Teresian Reform. Indeed, one of them, Fr. Vargas, had conceived the idea of using Discalced Friars to carry out a reform in a mitigated monastery for renewed fervor and stricter observance of the rules.

With the first attempts of founding in Andalusia, Fr. Vargas seized upon the opportunity to carry out his projects. After discussing the matter with Fr. Ambrosio Mariano, a measure was drawn up which delegated Fr. Baltasar of Jesus, Prior of Pastrana, to act as apostolic visitor in Andalusia. Since Fr. Vargas had the right to appoint a delegate, such a provision notably increased the authority of the Reform. The little shoot which had seemed quite insignificant now looked upon the Mitigated as a branch. Not only that, but on August 4, 1573, Fr. Baltasar sub-delegated the same office to Fr. Gracián of the Mother of God, a young Discalced Friar just graduated from the University of Alcalá with a brilliant record. Gifted with great intelligence, gentle manners, virtue and human qualities, he personified the hopes of the Reform.

In Avila, meanwhile, Teresa had finished her term as prioress. While still in Segovia before her return to Avila, a young woman, Catalina de Godínez, and her sister, María de Sandoval had repeatedly requested her to found a new convent in Beas de Segura. The parish priest and other reliable people backed the project.

Teresa now found herself in a delicate situation. Fr. Rubeo had disposed that no new foundation would be refused her as long as the Provincial gave his approval. However, the Provincial, Fr. Fernández, though a supporter of the Reform, advised the suspension of new foundations in order to strengthen those already existing.

But the invitation from Beas represented the epilogue of such a heart-warming, supernatural episode that it seemed a pity to refuse. The letters from the two young women fully explained their desire for a foundation, so Teresa sent them all to Fr. Fernández, saying that though their General had said no new foundations should be refused, he should decide what he thought best.

In the *Foundations* Teresa comments, "When God wants something we all become instruments in the cause." In elaboration of this concept she cites the marvelous story of Catalina Godínez and María Sandoval, other representatives of sixteenth-century mysticism. Teresa greatly admired the hard life Catalina led, feeling maternal love for this young lady who invoked her help from afar.

Catalina was the daughter of aristocratic, well-to-do Sancho Rodriguez de Sandoval and Doña Catalina de Godínez. At fourteen she was a self-assured, well-loved and pretty girl. Matrimony was a frequent subject in the Sandoval household because girls married early in Spain, and Catalina did not lack suitors. Greatly affected by titles and wealth, she found that what her various suitors had to offer seemed too modest. Thinking over her latest proposal of marriage, she thought: my father is so easily contented to think that a mere first-born could be enough for me! Instead I want my nobility to start with me! As these thoughts passed through her mind, her glance fell on the crucifix, and she stopped short, gazing at it for a long time.

This made her change her train of thought. There was Christ, bleeding from five wounds with his head bowed in agony. He had given his life for all humanity, even for her. The Lord of the universe was poor, humble, detached from worldly goods, deprived of comforts and opposed to flattery and honors.

As Catalina slowly delved into the mystery of Christ and His passion, she suddenly felt a freedom of thought, torn from the shackles of a thousand frivolous phantasms. St. Teresa later described ''a light like a sun's ray penetrating a dark room suddenly flash in her soul, permitting her to see the truth. God suspended her soul in order to have her understand her wretchedness so well that afterwards she wanted everyone to know it, too. A consuming desire to suffer for God overcame her; she would have gladly borne all the torments of the martyrs. She also felt a deep humility and disdain of herself, and if it were not that God would be offended, she would have wished to be a great sinner so that everyone could abhor her. So began her abasement with a great longing for penance which she later put into practice. Vowing chastity and poverty, she would have wished to be dragged among the Moors as a slave so she could live as a subject. The strength of these virtues in her proved she had received extraordinary grace, as we shall soon learn.''[1]

So much love for God was infused into her during that instant of light that the girl's life changed radically. A tremendous clash was heard in the room as though all the walls were falling, and Catalina even heard moans. ''Like a roaring lion,'' says the liturgy. That unaccountable noise had been a preternatural manifestation of demoniacal rage at the moment in which the soul was elevated to the state of grace all in one bound. Catalina's father also heard the noise; trembling in bed, he seized his sword and ran to his daughter's room to ask what had happened. Finding nothing, he called his wife to remain with the girl.

---

1. *Foundations*, XXII, also for the following.

Catalina's dominating thought now was to enter the religious life, but her parents were inflexible in their opposition. On St. Joseph's day, after three years of futile waiting, the girl put on a simple dress of monastic cut, and with her mother's permission, went to church wearing it. Her hope was that once everyone saw her dressed like that, no one would dare to take away her dress.

The plan worked. Her mother had always been less opposed to her desire, and when Don Sancho saw the seriousness of his daughter's vocation, he no longer tried her with proposals of marriage. Everyone left her free to live her inner life, but no one spoke of her entering a convent. In Beas, moreover, there were none. Alone, Catalina gave in to her desire for penance, mortifying herself in every way possible. With extraordinary control of herself, she castigated the will and tortured the flesh by scourging and wearing a hair shirt, always with a smile on her face, demonstrating extraordinary command of herself. At times she wore an iron mail of her father's over her bare skin without anyone's knowing it. Her sureness and spiritual serenity astonished everyone, for she was happier than when surrounded by frills.

When governing the house, her humility was so great that to give an order to a maid was a sacrifice, so extreme had her humility become. "Whenever it happened that for some unavoidable reason she had to order the servants, she would wait until they slept to kiss their feet so sorry was she that they, who were ever so much better than she, should have to serve her."

Misfortunes soon set upon her. When she was nineteen, her father died, and the following year, her mother also died. But the fruits of heroism blossom when least expected. Catalina's sister, María de Sandoval, also left the world at the age of fourteen in imitation of her sister.

Catalina fell ill, and after an aggravating illness, a vow, and a miraculous recovery, the two young ladies resolved to found a convent in Beas with their inheritance.

A difficult judicial question had to be surmounted because the town was in possession of the Commendam of St. James of Santiago, who had always opposed the founding of orders or congregations different from their own. Instituted as a military defense against the Moors for that part of Spain, the outpost had been held proudly for centuries, later having freely united their territories to the Crown of Spain. But even Philip II, who personified absolute monarchy, was wont to consult the Commendam before making decisions on its territories.

When Teresa requested the necessary permission of the Carmelite Provincial for a foundation in Beas, he subjected it to the condition that the Order of Santiago also agree to the foundation. That made the obstacle appear insurmountable. But here is where Teresa's comment "when God wishes something, He makes us all instruments in its realization" comes in. Feeling inspired, she wrote to the King about the matter. Upon hearing that the projected convent was to belong to the Teresian Reform, Philip II exerted so much influence on the Order that they ended by giving their consent. How could they resist the will of their King? And that was how Catalina received a favorable reply from Madrid and could effectively invite Teresa.

CHAPTER FORTY-SEVEN

The Mitigated or Unmitigated Controversy Gets Under Way

Now we must remember that Beas is in Andalusia, while Fr. General Rubeo's permission to Teresa to found a convent was only for Castile. Situated only six miles from New Castile's boundaries, Beas was overstepping the demarcation line. Teresa had not realized this because of a geographical error. In the sixteenth century, maps were scarce and inaccurate. This situation permitted Teresa to accept the invitation and to found her new convent without a shadow of a doubt. Only after several days there did she chance to hear that the city was in Andalusia. Though intensely disturbed, she certainly would not retract what had been accomplished.

Fathers Gracián and Ambrosio Mariano were also in Andalusia busily settling a new foundation near Seville. The sanctuary had risen around a beautiful picture of the Madonna dear to sailors. The church was tiny, but it could be seen from afar as it was on a high embankment. The crews of the ships that passed nearby on their way to the Americas would gather on deck shooting artillery and saluting the sanctuary. The men must have reflected either on what was in store for them, or, if returning from the solitary Atlantic, rendered thanks to the Virgin.

Since Seville's port constituted a platform for trans-oceanic traffic, Fathers Gracián and Mariano found the offer to establish a small community in the service of the Virgin most advantageous there. And the community moved in on January 5, 1574. But a fundamentally important misunderstanding soon caused unpleasant effects. A commission of Mitigated Carmelites demanded to know what right they had to found a Reformed community in Andalusia. The question proved all the more embarrassing since this was already the third Discalced foundation set up in Andalusia without the direct consent of the Father General. Fr. Gracián's explanation of having done so with the authority invested in him as apostolic visitor, subdelegated to him by Fr. Baltasar, greatly surprised the inquisitors but did not entirely convince them.

The situation involved the germs of an important conflict which unfortunately burst out, due in great part to the disadvantage created by the distances between the various parties. The difficulties of meeting and speaking at opportune moments placed each side in a dangerous position.

What had happened was that newly-elected Pope Gregory XIII had revoked all powers invested in apostolic visitors to Spanish Carmelite monasteries through the suggestion of Fr. Rubeo, who had exposed what a difficult situation the Carmelites were in, having to obey non-Carmelite apostolic visitors. The revocation having taken place on August 13, 1573, Fr. Vargas' commission and subsequent indirect delegation were void.

But Fr. Rubeo did not make the papal document known immediately, having intended to announce the order with more solemnity at a Carmelite general chapter meeting to be held in Piacenza, Italy, the following spring. Indiscreet reports, however, escaped and the court of Spain got an echo of it. Having asked the late Pope Pius V to send apostolic commissaries, the King was indeed an ardent supporter of the reform of religious orders, and now sought a way to conceal the grievous provision.

Meanwhile, matters became still more complex because the Mitigated Carmelites in Seville complained to Fr. Rubeo of their being subject to a twenty-eight year old Discalced Carmelite as apostolic visitor, who, according to them, lacked even experience and adequate qualifications; at the same time, they were denouncing the "abuse" committed by the Discalced in founding in Andalusia.

In view of such circumstances, Fr. Rubeo changed his feelings toward the Teresian Reform. When he had passed through Spain seven years earlier, he advocated reform, deeply admiring Teresa. But those days were gone, and now Fr. Rubeo considered the Reformed religious as undisciplined and rebellious. Never having met Fr. Gracián, he could not admit that anyone should act as he did on his own authority in such delicate matters as foundations. Neither Teresa nor Fr. Gracián knew of this change of spirit, whereas Philip II and Papal Nuncio Ormaneto, who sided fervidly with the Teresian Reform, knew what state affairs were in.

In collaboration with Nuncio Ormaneto, Philip II summoned his special council justly attributing grave importance to the matter. Just then, a priest by the name of Juan Padilla, another fervent Reform backer, happened to pass by and was able to explain clearly the situation in Andalusia. He related that since Fr. Gracián no longer felt sure of his authority, no new effective reform measures were being taken. However, Padilla continued, no one better than Fr. Gracián was qualified to carry out the great undertaking of reform, for his keen intelligence, affable manners, profound spiritual and humanistic qualities made him the best religious man for the task.

These bits of information served to confirm Philip II's private council in its conviction to support the Discalced Order. On the other hand, everyone regarded the Mitigated Carmelites with respect. The problem then was how to strengthen Fr. Gracián's position in the eyes of the Mitigated Carmelites enabling him to act with more assurance. Juan Padilla thought of the solution: have Nuncio Ormaneto exercise his prestige over all the religious orders in Spain and nominate Fr. Gracián as apostolic visitor in Andalusia with full power over both Mitigated and Unmitigated Carmelites while the King's immense authority would guarantee the nomination.

In fact the papal bull revoked only those powers belonging to apostolic visitors, not in the least limiting those of the Nuncio. Feeling he was within his rights, Nuncio Ormaneto used his authority and nominated Fr. Gracián as apostolic visitor. Such an important appointment necessarily entailed a trip to Madrid on Fr. Gracián's part. The King already knew Fr. Gracián's father and brother because they were court officials, but he wanted to meet the religious man to evaluate better his capacities.

Invited in February, Fr. Gracián first completed his lenten cycle of sermons before taking leave on April 3. He went out of his way to Beas to meet Mother Teresa whom he had long desired to meet and from whom he now sought advice. The two discussed their problems at length during the month Fr. Gracián remained in Beas awaiting Fr. Ambrosio Mariano. Teresa rejoiced in seeing he was the man needed to fortify the growing reform because the eight Discalced monasteries existing had no underlying uniformity regarding development of the rules. Each monastery was quite autonomous in doing what it thought best even though true ascetic superiority reigned in them all. But the practice of their extraordinary fervor through penances and mortifications was not controlled, and in this lay the weakness of the Reform. In Fr. Gracián, Teresa saw just the person who could draw up the Reform's constitution.

An important decision was also made at that time. Several requests for new convents had reached Teresa, for which she thought she would go to Madrid and later to Caravaca. But Fr. Gracián said he preferred the next foundation to be set up in Seville where the Discalced Friars were already well established. Objecting that she did not feel authorized by Fr. Rubeo to open convents in Andalusia, Teresa added that such patronesses as the King's sister, Juana, and Doña Leonor de Mascarenhas awaited her in Madrid. Fr. Gracián's only reply to this was: "Ask the Lord which is the better road, that to Seville or that to Madrid."

When he asked several days later what the Lord's reply had been, Teresa simply said, "Madrid."

But Fr. Gracián smiled as if to say he was not convinced and concluded, "Notwithstanding this, I firmly believe it is better to open a foundation in Seville."

Teresa, true to her character, replied, "Very well."

The decision made, preparations were immediately begun. Her health was not good, and the heat was unbearable. Thoughts of the hot Andalusian sun frightened her, but she continued her preparations nonetheless. Observing Teresa's fervor, after two days Fr. Gracián felt compelled to ask, "How can you obey with no resistance whatever when my words are only an opinion and yours are from sure revelation and they do not coincide?"

The reply Teresa gave typifies her method, "If I obey my superior, I am sure of not erring, whereas how am I sure of not being deceived if I follow my inner revelation?" Fr. Gracián could only bow his head at such great loftiness.

Several hours later, a supernatural locution confirmed her action. "You have done well to obey," the Lord told her. "The affairs of the Reform and the foundation in Madrid will not lose anything. Go to Seville. You will succeed, but you will have to suffer much."[1]

Fr. Gracián then continued his trip to Madrid where the Nuncio awaited him, and Teresa started off to Seville on May 8, together with six nuns. Among these was María de Salazar, a protégée of Duchess de la Cerda, who had been enchanted by Teresa back in Toledo. Now she was María of St. Joseph, and the designated Prioress of Seville's new convent. Fathers Julian de Avila and Antonio Gaytán were again in the company of travelers together with Friar Gregorio Nazioncieno, wagoners and muleteers.

The journey to Seville turned out to be Teresa's most picturesque trip, not only because of the scenery, but also because of the quaint adventures happening along the way. The panorama was majestic, but the heat was suffocating. Rain was badly needed everywhere. The jolting inside the wagons was penitential, and breathing was difficult because the vehicles were too well covered and holeproof; air couldn't circulate inside. During the hottest hours of the day which the saint described as a "sort of purgatory," the travelers felt as though they were breathing in an oven. And yet, the group was in high spirits according to María of St. Joseph's account of the trip.

---

1. *Año Teresiano*, Tomo IV, April 3.

"We were continually joking, for we would compose rhymes about what was happening. Mother Teresa excelled in this and kept us happy."[2]

But the fatigue and heat caused Teresa another of her characteristic attacks of high fever. Immediately taken to a comfortable hospital, she was given every possible care. "I had never had such a high fever before. While I was unconscious, the others felt I had fallen into lethargy. The sisters would sprinkle water over my face, but I felt no relief because the water was hot." Water, by the way, cost more than wine.

"I cannot omit telling of the inn we found. We had a little hot room with no windows, and if we opened the door the strong Andalusian sun cooked us. They put me on a bed that was so lumpy it might have been made of sharp stones. I could not be comfortable in any position on it. I would have preferred the floor to sleep on. Finally, I thought it would be better to get up and leave that horrible room and face the sun outside. How will those wretched souls condemned to hell ever be able to bear not even changing position?"[3]

This had occurred perhaps in consequence of the adventurous crossing of the Guadalquivir River. "The raft which was carrying our wagons was unable to go straight across the river along the guiding cord, but was obliged to go in an oblique line. The rope was held obliquely as well, but it seems that those who were holding it somehow let go, and the raft with its cargo were at the mercy of the current with no rope to hang on to and no oars. The boatmen steering the raft distressed me more than anything else. We began praying while the others screamed. A man watching from a nearby castle sent people to help us. At that time there was still one rope attached to the raft, and the men held

---

2. *Book of Recreations*, IX.
3. *Foundations*, XXIV, also for the following.

on to it with all their might, but the violence of the
current was too much for them, and some even fell
from exhaustion. The boatman's son, a boy of ten or
eleven, made me feel so deeply sorry for him that I
shall never forget him. It was plain to see he was
suffering ever so greatly to watch his father in such
torment that I praised the Lord for that capacity of
feeling."

Providentially enough, the raft struck into a sand
bank. It was already night before all were ashore so
they knew not how to continue in the dark, but one of
the men, sent by a courteous gentleman onlooker, led
the group onto the main road.

In Cordova, their passage through the city was a
succession of embarrassing adventures. On Pentecost
morning, the group started before dawn in order to
arrive at a church where Mass could be celebrated and
participated in without a flock of curiosity-stricken people gaping. Much to their dismay, however, the wagons
and mules were forced to halt before the bridge which
leads into the city. No wagons could cross the bridge
without the governor's permission! Fr. Julian de Avila
ran to the governor's palace, but at that hour everyone
was still sound asleep. The gatekeeper was slow in
awakening, and after that, the governor kept Fr. de
Avila waiting a long time before appearing.

Early-risers and travelers, meanwhile, had gathered
about that strange apparition of covered wagons, everyone desiring information about the identity of the occu-
pants. The hissing replies of the wagoners only enticed
them the more until finally someone raised a tip of the
canvas, discovering a double row of nuns wearing
white cloaks and black veils over their faces. Their
attire was superb, and those simple people of Cordova
had never seen nuns dressed like that before.

Fr. Julian finally returned, waving the permit. The
row of wagons crossed the bridge to the other side

where there was a church in which Mass could be celebrated. Now late, there was a crowd on the square waiting to enter the church for Mass also. Momentarily frightened, Teresa imagined the harsh comments their group would cause, and this feeling prompted her to say it might be better to forego Mass for that day to avoid undue publicity. But Fr. Julian opposed her reaction, and "since he was a theologian," the nuns acquiesced. So the nuns filed out of the mysterious covered wagon.

In the confusion that accompanied the religious to the church, the sharp-tongued Andalusians all made their personal comments. Poor Teresa writes that her blood sank so low that her fever left her, and that the noise was so great it was as if bulls had entered the square. Fortunately, someone led the nuns into the sacristy, closing the door so that they could breathe more easily. Fr. Julian offered Mass and administered Communion to the nuns, after which the caravan again set off.

While passing through a wood on Pentecost Monday, Teresa spent several hours in a prayer of gratitude for the grace our Lord had bestowed upon her several years earlier on that day. Searching in her impulse of gratitude for some offering in return, her thoughts lingered on an obligation so binding that the more she thought of it, the more she trembled. Having already offered everything that she could, all that remained was her freedom of will, and now she even felt obliged to bind that still more than her monastic vows had done, still more than by the vow she had made of doing all as perfectly as possible. Her new yoke was to consist in vowing that she would never conceal anything from her superior, Fr. Gracián, always obeying him in important matters, naturally, if not contrary to the obedience to which she was already under oath.

The offering was supreme, and the saint herself trembled while pronouncing the vow: "...on the one hand I felt as though it was nothing, but on the other hand, the thing appeared very difficult. I saw that I would never again have either external or internal freedom, for which I felt a profound abhorrence. Except for the agony of leaving home, no other act has cost me so much. I no longer thought of Fr. Gracián's merits nor of my affection for him, but I considered him a total stranger and wondered only if the Holy Spirit would accept my promise. After some anguish our Lord filled me with faith—I knelt and promised to do all my superior would order me to do until death."[4]

This act admirably crowned the long sacrifice which Teresa's life had always been, and it engendered deep peace within her.

The trip continued with the hot Andalusian sun burning the vegetation all around. One day while the nuns were resting at noon, savage and brutal shouts were heard nearby, and a strange and frightening scene took place. About forty men divided between soldiers and peasants were fighting, and the danger of bloodshed was imminent. Outwardly calm, Teresa disentangled the nuns clinging about her in fright, walked straight into the middle of the quarreling men and said: "Brothers, I beseech you to remember God is present and will judge you." The appearance, the voice and Teresa's face made such an impression on the men that each put away his sword shamefacedly.

The caravan finally reached Seville after such a chain of adventures and with but one small coin remaining.

---

4. *Spiritual Favors*, XLI.

CHAPTER FORTY-EIGHT

The Seville Foundation

"On our arrival in Seville we went to the house Friar Mariano had rented for us, expecting everything to be ready for us, knowing how the Archbishop favored the Discalced Order since he had written me several kind letters."[1]

Teresa had hoped to go through the actual foundation ceremony immediately and then be able to enjoy a period of retirement together with her daughters in cloister. In addition to the thirst for silence and contemplation, her tired body needed a period of rest. But each time Teresa tried to make arrangements for bringing the Holy Eucharist into the tabernacle, Fr. Mariano would evade setting the date, procrastinating with one excuse or another. Suspecting something awry, Teresa finally found out that it was because the Archbishop was opposed to the new convent!

The truth was so unexpected that she could hardly believe it at first. She had come from so far, having suffered intensely to get there, believing not only that

---

1. *Foundations*, XXIV.

she acted in accordance with the Prelate's wishes, but even feeling she was doing him a favor—and now the surprise was almost too much to bear. Fr. Mariano had not had the courage to tell her, for he knew how grieved she would be.

Tempted to take her nuns back to Beas and from there to Caravaca where a foundation was earnestly requested, she was dissuaded from doing so by the friars. Everyone knew they were in the city by now and to withdraw would have caused general disappointment. Put in that light, the situation seemed worth a struggle, and Teresa decided to wait and see what could be done.

Though a firm supporter of the Reform, the Archbishop refused on general principles. He was opposed to new convents, all the more those founded in absolute poverty. Seeking a compromise, Fr. Mariano proposed that Teresa found the convent on a self-supporting basis.

"And how are we to provide an income when we possess only one coin? Anyway, even if you should find the means, I would not accept. My plan is to establish foundations in absolute poverty wherever a city is well-populated and rich. We accept income only in small, poor towns which cannot support us, for in such cases we would not show charity if we went out and asked for charity. But Seville is a city of commerce and wealth!"

Fr. Mariano understood the matter was closed. On the other hand, it was necessary to procure any help whatever for the nuns who were left with but one coin, the clothes on their backs, a few tunics and hoods and the cloth that had served to keep out the sun and curious eyes. Antonio Gaytán had been forced to borrow money from a friend in order to send the wagons and mules back. Such dire circumstances made Fr. Mariano use insistence to obtain a temporary permit from the Archbishop. Mass could be said in the convent on May 29, 1575, but no bells were to be rung nor other signs of external festivities to be shown.

The concession was most consoling, yet things remained at more or less the same point with Teresa suffering greatly. From Madrid, Fr. Gracián sent letter after letter to the Archbishop, and Fr. Mariano expected to be summoned for the permit from day to day, but all remained stationary. Teresa would have written to the Archbishop herself, but Fr. Mariano would not hear of it, because surely her request would gain nothing if in so many years of government His Excellency had not permitted the establishment of even one convent. Fr. Mariano's hopes lay in Fr. Gracián's action, who deeply regretted having insisted on the trip. The Archbishop on his part treated Teresa with special respect, sending emissaries to announce an imminent visit from him personally.

While impatiently awaiting the announced visit, friars of the Mitigated Carmelite Order arrived to ask whose permission the sisters had to found the convent. Upon presentation of the Father General's certificate, the friars left, little suspecting the Archbishop to be unfavorable. That certificate, dated April 5, 1575, was one of the last Fr. Rubeo had granted in which no geographical limitation was specified.

The first month passed with great suffering for both the Mother and her daughters. Sr. María of St. Joseph tells in her book that their poverty was so great that most of the time they ate nothing but eggplant and bread. Once they had but one loaf of bread which they divided and made to suffice for the day. Since they were unknown in the city, no one came to offer anything. Whatever money came in was spent on such indispensable things as the cloister grille and revolving shelf, called a "turn."

Doña Leonor de Valera was the first to be moved to pity, and she helped the nuns generously all that summer until her financial ruin later that year forced her to stop. Afterwards, two of her daughters entered the convent.

A pious woman, Doña Leonor did not care to let it be known that it was she who was providing all the kitchen utensils, linens, and necessities to the poor nuns, so she sent donations through the hands of a tertiary. This woman, however, usually cared for wayward girls in an effort to put them on the right path. While carrying all those things to the nuns, the woman thought to herself: who is more in need, the nuns who, though suffering, are at peace with God, or those unfortunate women who will lose their souls if they do not repent? Her rationalizing easily brought her to the decision to assist the latter of the two groups of women. Meanwhile, hunger continued to be the daily routine in the convent, and the nuns did not know of the existence of Doña Leonor. The best part of the incident is that the friend would often visit Teresa.

This continued for several months, but the practice finally became known. Precise orders were given, and the articles all reached the nuns from that time on. The situation steadily grew better. Other benefactors joined to help maintain the nuns, even the Archbishop himself. His visit to the convent had changed his mind, and he was now all in favor of the Discalced nuns.

In a letter to Gaytán, Teresa wrote how the Archbishop did all that she requested of him, kindly giving the nuns wheat and money. She reported the heat as terrible, but her health good, for the nuns had a large canvas over their yard which she said "is better than bearing the sun in the open countryside."

But a new storm was soon to break. As the nuns became better known, more and more postulants arrived. Finding most of them inadequate, Teresa selected candidates carefully. For instance, she was inflexible in refusing two influential women whom the community wished to have taken in.

A sort of "local saint" was admitted. However, she would not adhere to the schedule, menu, and community exercises, and gave excuses such as poor health, excessive heat, and the like. Teresa would tell the others to be patient with her, certain that she would later improve. But that woman of forty who was canonized in the minds of half the city would not allow her strong character to be broken by monastic life. One day she decided to leave. Once out, she went directly to the Inquisition officials and denounced the convent. Another denunciation arrived simultaneously from a good, but narrow-minded priest who interpreted the nuns' habit of opening their souls to their Mother Superior in search of counsel and spiritual direction as a confession. It was indeed a serious matter for a budding convent, not yet formally founded and in need of public approval, to have to answer to the Inquisition.

A few days later, several austere-looking carriages brought a group of prelates and laymen to the convent. All the nuns but Teresa were terrified, for those were the men who would decide whether they would lead a tranquil life in the convent or go to prison. Coincidentally, Fr. Gracián happened to arrive from Madrid at that very moment while the men of the Inquisition were minutely inspecting the rooms of the cloister. He sent for Mother Teresa. The latter appeared, cheerfully regretting there would be no possibility of being burnt at the stake because there was nothing to be found against the faith. Fr. Gracián was not relieved, however, and said the inspection was probably to be connected with the absurd denunciation of the abuse of the Sacrament of Reconciliation of which Teresa probably knew nothing. She again reassured him, however, that nothing would come of it.

Inside, the inquisitors were questioning the nuns: Is it true that you reveal your soul to your Mother Superior? Yes, but Mother does not give us absolution. This ingenuous reply made the inquisitors laugh. Continuing, those men saw that the accusations against the nuns were false. Indeed, their esteem for the Order grew, and they left with a happier spirit.

The Inquisition nevertheless wished to know the character of the reformer because Teresa's autobiography had passed into its hands after the Princess of Eboli had lent it to her servants. After careful examination, the verdict concerning the book was favorable. Teresa was greatly relieved to hear of this when she was in Seville, because it increased her confidence and gave the book greater value. After the incident of the denunciation of the outgoing novice, Teresa's name again came to their attention, so she was asked to write reports of her mental prayer. She wrote two while in Seville, both directed to Fr. Rodrigo Alvarez, her examiner. His opinion was so laudatory that the court's verdict was strongly favorable to Teresa and even accompanied by words of esteem.

But the nuns were still not in their own house, and the foundation was not permanent.

It was now that Teresa received the unexpected news that her brothers, Lorenzo de Cepeda and Pedro de Ahumada, and the former's three children had just returned from the Indies. Shortly before embarking in Panama, Jerónimo Cepeda, another brother, had died, and during the trip Lorenzo's fourth child had died also. The men had been gone thirty-four years so excitement over their return was great, and as a climax they would disembark at Seville. In a letter to her sister Juana, Teresa wrote, "They will be here in three days. How magnificent are the works of God—those who were so far from me are now so near!"

Nine-year-old Teresita captivated Teresa of Jesus by her gentle manners, intelligence and speech, and it was Teresa's desire to protect her by having her come into the convent. After long documentation, the little girl was admitted. Teresita became the darling of the convent. During recreational periods she would talk of the Indies, the sea, and at times, of her little brother Esteban's fate in the great Atlantic tempest.

Lorenzo was happy to see Teresita surrounded by serene faces, and in gratitude wished to help alleviate the convent's situation. He toured Seville, visiting every house that was for sale, trying to find one suitable for a convent. Only after several months could he find one. After making a heavy down payment, he guaranteed to pay the rest himself. However, certain misunderstandings regarding notarial fees and taxes caused delay of the final payment so the law was sent in search of him. A stranger in Seville, he knew no influential men to intervene on his behalf, so he took refuge at the convent where no one could pester him since he was in a sacred place.

The situation was unpleasant for everyone concerned. Fr. Pantoja, the Prior at the Carthusian monastery, called as mediator, settled the question. After months of restoration, creating months of sharpened conflict between the two branches of the Carmelite Order, the community moved into its new residence on June 3, 1576.

The Archbishop[2] who had been opposed to adding another convent placed the Blessed Sacrament in the chapel himself, following one of the most grandiose processions Seville had ever seen. He had given orders for the streets to be hung with tapestries, and all religious congregations and clergy were commanded to

2. *Histoire de Sainte Thérèse,* par une Carmelite de Caen, II, XXXII, also for the following.

take part in the procession. Even the Carthusian Prior who never made public appearances carried the Holy Eucharist under the canopy through the city. Hymns of gratitude and joyful music pervaded the city while tears ran down the veiled faces of the nuns.

Fr. García Alvarez had prepared the new convent, complete with altar decorations and festoons and went so far as to have a fountain spurting perfumed water. The Archbishop arrived at the same time as the procession, to take the Holy Eucharist and place It in the chapel, after which he went to visit the nuns. Teresa, kneeling, met him at the cloister door to ask his blessing, but much to everyone's amazement, the Archbishop humbly knelt before her, "the first pontifical head to bow before the great saint." Referring to this episode, Teresa would tell her daughters how confused she became.

In her *Foundations,* chapter twenty-five, she writes, "My daughters, you now see that everyone honors the poor Discalced nuns, whereas before it seemed there was not even a glass of water for them from that prosperous river."

A city known for its great festive spirit, Seville celebrated the event boisterously with cannon balls and fireworks. A fire threatened to spoil the celebration because a box of gun powder caught fire and reached the drapery hung at the convent portico—cloth which Fr. García Alvarez had borrowed for the occasion. Amazingly enough, there were no victims nor was there damage done, so the big day ended joyfully with the nuns inside their convent beginning their life of retirement and prayer.

CHAPTER FORTY-NINE

Open Conflict Between the Two Carmelite Families

The controversy between the Mitigated and Unmitigated Carmelites is a long story. Juridically it was a contention between authorities. The King of Spain sided with the Papal Nuncio Ormaneto, who wanted Fr. Gracián of the Reform to be apostolic visitor with jurisdiction over the Mitigated Friars. The fundamental reason for this was that religious reform was desired, and Nuncio Ormaneto was acting within his powers as representative of the Holy See.

On the other hand, Fr. Rubeo, the General of the Carmelite Order, did not recognize Fr. Gracián's appointment in 1576 because he had been ordered by Gregory XIII to revoke commissaries and apostolic visitors. In view of this, he had nominated an austere and capable Mitigated Carmelite Friar, Fr. Tostado, at the General Chapter meeting in Piacenza in 1576.

So it was that the controversy arose over the legitimate nomination of the apostolic visitor, a question of vital importance because the office entailed important consequences on the life of the Order, especially in respect to the Teresian Reform.

In truth, the episode fits in as a particular aspect of the reform Pius V had undertaken to accomplish in religious orders in general. It must be said, however, that the Mitigated Rule was and has remained a most meritorious Order and that everyone on both sides acted with honesty and good intentions, each convinced of his own genuine right. To Fr. Rubeo, the Discalced Friars appeared as insubordinate, and Fr. Tostado treated Fathers Gracián, Antonio of Jesus, Ambrosio Mariano, and John of the Cross as rebels.

———

While in Seville in December, 1575, Teresa had been ordered to remain in one of her convents. As always, she met this new tribulation added to those already on her shoulders with admirable serenity. Indeed, she even asked Fr. Gracián to decide in which convent she should be. The choice was between Toledo and Avila, and Fr. Gracián decided on Toledo, which made Teresa feel that every hope of comfort which she could have received in her hometown, Avila, was gone.

In January, 1576, Teresa wrote the following letter to Fr. Rubeo which is a true example of dignified humility.

"My most Reverend Father, the order by which the General Chapter prohibits my leaving the house of my choosing has just become known to me. Fr. Ulloa was to communicate the order to me as soon as Fr. Angel de Salazar had communicated it to him, but fearing my great sorrow, he decided to keep it from me as long as possible. But, having heard hints of it, I have compelled Fr. Ulloa to notify me of my condemnation, a month late.

"I assure you, my Father, that I would have considered this order as a great favor and recompense if you had written it to me in one of your letters, saying, for example, that in view of my poor health and weariness from long suffering, you ordered me to retire. Proof of my truthfulness is that I am most content to be able to live in peace, even if the order has reached me in another light. Though your order fills me with joy, my filial love for you makes it become difficult and depressing because you give it to me as you would to a very disobedient person. At least, this is according to Fr. Angel Salazar's version of it, who, thinking he was imposing such a violent constriction on me that he wrote I could appeal to the Pope—just as though this were not an advantage for me! But even if it were not, and I were to feel every affliction in the world, never would I think of disobeying you. God does not wish me to obtain the least amount of happiness against your will. My most Reverend Father, I can indeed say, and God knows it, that what has consoled me through my apprehensions, afflictions, contradictions and toil which I have borne in the past has been the knowledge of obeying you and feeling your satisfaction in me. Even today I find satisfaction in doing what you tell me to do. I would have obeyed immediately, but the Christmas festivities being near, and the journey being long, they have not permitted me to leave, deeming it against your intentions to impair my health. That is why I am still here at the end of winter. The favor I ask of you is kindly to continue writing to me wherever I may go. Since I shall no longer be active, thanks be to God, I fear you will forget me. But even if my letters should tire you, I shall think of you and never stop writing for my own peace of mind."

It was painful to leave her daughters in Seville after having battled together and borne each other's afflictions for a year. In recompense, the trip was peaceful and brief. In Toledo a small unadorned cell with a window overlooking the garden awaited her—just what she needed to aid her retirement. She would soon pray and write there, forced to write in defense of her reform.

Before Teresa's leaving Seville, the nuns had begged their Mother to pose for an oil portrait painting to be executed by Friar Juan of Misery. Reluctant as she was, Fr. Gracián ordered her to consent. Definitely no masterpiece, it is the only painting made of the saint directly. Her laughing exclamation of the picture was, "God forgive you, Friar Juan, after having made me suffer so long, you have made me ugly and bleary-eyed!"

CHAPTER FIFTY

The Great Dispute Continues

The unpleasant situation between the Mitigated and Unmitigated Rules of the Carmelite Order continued. In 1576, Fr. Tostado held a chapter reunion excluding those of the Reform. A few months later, Fr. Gracián organized one for only those belonging to the Reform. But it was the death of Nuncio Ormaneto which made the contest reach its climax. The successor of the great protector of the Teresian Reform was Bishop Filipe Sega, a man who clearly sided with the Mitigated Carmelites.

Fr. Tostado and Bishop Sega had never met Fr. Gracián and barely knew the others. Those of the Reform were thought of only in terms of obstinate, disobedient religious. They had not the slightest notion of what the Teresian Reform consisted in and what sacrifices it had cost. With harmony of the Carmelite Order in mind, they decided the best system to use would be resolute conduct: immobilize the dissenters with no possibility of resisting, the monastic prisons helping in this sense.

In no time at all, Fathers John of the Cross, Gracián, Antonio of Jesus, Juan of Jesus and Ambrosio

Mariano found themselves imprisoned, either in Avila or Madrid as a consequence of the Papal Nuncio's honest but prejudiced mind. He considered these men as adversaries with evil intentions.

Fr. Juan of Jesus started writing letter after letter to Bishop Sega to ask for an audience. After some time he was called. Asked what he wanted, Fr. Juan said he wished to confide secret matters of the Discalced Carmelites. Given permission, he began by speaking of Teresa of Jesus, but Bishop Sega interrupted, saying, ''I don't want to hear anything on this point. That nun is unstable, disobedient, and dares to teach as a doctor of religion notwithstanding St. Paul's prohibitions.''

Profoundly saddened and offended in his filial respect for Teresa and love for truth, he continued in a humble but firm tone, prompted only by the spirit of justice and dignity. He briefly outlined the personality of the saint motivated by love and above earthly contentions, illuminated as she was by extraordinary gifts. The virtues of humility, prudence and wisdom were in her, in proof of which Fr. Juan cited facts and words of the saint.

It was the first time anyone who really knew Teresa of Jesus had spoken to Bishop Sega, and he listened mutely, mentally discerning whether the friar had been hypnotized by Teresa or if he spoke with sincerity. The whole story certainly bore supernatural marks, and he asked how the Reform had become established and diffused. When the Nuncio took leave of Friar Juan, his expression had changed, and his words were gentle.

Unfortunately, however, misunderstandings again arose, and everyone's hopes fell once more. The situation led certain Discalced Friars to commit an error. Deeming themselves definitely outcast by the Nuncio, they called a second chapter meeting in October, 1578, resolving to put an end to the long conflict.

Without stopping to think whether they had the power to do so or not, they decreed the Reform a separate province despite Teresa's opposition to the meeting. Fr. Antonio of Jesus was nominated Reform Provincial while two others were sent to Rome to tell of the election and obtain recognition of it.

The Papal Nuncio's reaction was immediate. Those of the Reform had been led to action exasperated by their suffering, but the Nuncio also felt tired of this drawn-out affair and therefore decided to put an end to the quarrel. To him, the Almodovar chapter meeting was nothing but an open act of unjustified independence, clouding over the horizon just as it was beginning to clear. Thus, on October 16, 1578, he ordered all participants interdicted with monastic imprisonment.

Along with the others, Teresa received orders to return to Toledo from Avila where she had gone in the meantime, and never to leave the convent of Toledo again. They were all put under obedience to the Mitigated Rule and deprived of admitting new novices into their monasteries.

This was the Reform's most crucial moment for this time the prohibition included all Reformed monasteries and convents. When Teresa got word of these provisions in December, at St. Joseph's in Avila, she seemed for the first time to become depressed. She spent the day in isolation and fasting.

"After long hours of agony, Sr. Ana of St. Bartholomew softly knocked at her door. No one had dared speak a word to her since that morning out of respect for her sorrow, but night was coming on, and the great Christmas Office would soon be sung. Sr. Ana begged her to go to the refectory, which Teresa did. After taking Teresa's frugal supper to her, Sr. Ana withdrew from where she saw the Divine Master go near the table, bless the saint's bread and give it to her, encouraging her to eat for His love."[1]

After that Teresa was up again. A host of letters left the convent addressed to Court, the Council of Castile, monasteries in Andalusia and Castile. She was out to defend the cause of justice. If the Discalced Friars had erred in lack of discipline and prudence, the Nuncio's provisions were excessive. She did not criticize his disciplinary sanctions outwardly because she understood that a superior should be strong, but the decree could not remain this way, as lightning bolting the rebels. Teresa still had friends and protectors: now was the time to call for their aid en masse.

She could no longer write to Fr. Rubeo because he had died in Rome some time before. News of his death had caused Teresa to weep bitterly. In a letter to Fr. Gracián on October 15, she had written: "The loss of our Father General profoundly afflicts me; I have been crying over it the whole day. How the thought of the troubles we caused him saddens me because he certainly did not deserve them. May God forgive those who kept us from going toward Him." Passing over those last misunderstandings and mortifications, she remembered that back at St. Joseph's in Avila, Fr. Rubeo had understood her, treating her as a daughter when almost everyone was still opposed to her.

Together with the loss of Papal Nuncio Ormaneto and Msgr. Covarrubias of the Council of Castile and Teresian Reform protector, the saint felt very much alone on her side of the battlefield. All the others were either exhausted with depression or in chains, and no words of mutual encouragement could pass between their solitudes. Indomitable, Teresa felt the full responsibility of trying the defense by multiplying her efforts in writing letters, reports and mystical works. In fact,

---

1. *Histoire de Sainte Thérèse,* par une Carmelite de Caen, II, XXV.

Teresa had written her masterpiece, *The Interior Castle,* in 1576, during her first confinement in Toledo. Moreover, she had recourse to her prayers and to those of her daughters.

In Madrid, meanwhile, something happened which produced serious consequences. Don Luis Mendoza, Count of Tendilla, protector of the Discalced monastery in Granada, had granted drinking water to the friars in his capacity as mayor of the city. His faith and admiration for the "contemplatives" constituted an important motive in him, so much so that he considered the Nuncio's severity toward the friars as a force that struck him personally in his work and foundation which he protected vigorously. When he heard that Fathers Gracián, Antonio and Mariano had been imprisoned, he asked for an audience, formally requesting their momentary release, supplicating the Nuncio to hear them personally before taking drastic measures.

The request seemed reasonable enough, but by this time the Nuncio was oriented differently. He no longer trusted the "rebels," believing them capable of simulating humility before him, promising what he wanted only to start their actions of independence again. How could he make them return to their enclosure after their having behaved perfectly, without their allies crying out injustice and cruelty because he would not accept their protests of submission to the Mitigated Friars?

That was why Bishop Sega deemed it wiser to deny the audience Don Luis requested. The Count of Tendilla insisted, showing deep discontent in his voice, but the Nuncio only replied all the more firmly. Then the Count lost his control and arose, shouting everything that came to his mind. Deed after deed spilled out in detail, just as in a convincing, pitiless accusation against the prelate on Reform questions, using harsh and scolding words. The Nuncio remained impassive throughout the outburst. No one, not even the King, had the right to be disrespectful to a Papal Nuncio. Even if Tendilla was fired by the best of intentions, he was interfering in purely ecclesiastical matters, claiming to impose his way of governing religious congregations.

When Tendilla finished his outburst, Bishop Sega merely raised his arm to show Tendilla he should depart, which the Spaniard did without even saying goodbye.

The next day the Nuncio asked and obtained an immediate audience with the King.

CHAPTER FIFTY-ONE

Reconciliation

Bishop Sega went to Philip II to protest against Count Tendilla's insults, feeling it his duty to uphold the dignity of his office. Expressing his complaint, the Nuncio formally asked amends. He knew how inflexible Philip could be, but always righteous and just. The two men had been of different opinions in certain matters, but each deeply respected the other, knowing that neither acted against his conscience. It was a difficult situation for Philip because the Nuncio was drawing into play the thorny question so near the King's heart. Absolute master of half the world, he had to permit faithful friends of his whom he loved to be thwarted. He could have intervened with greater material force, but the respect his conscience dictated regarding the limits of his own power prevented him from doing so. He was well aware that at times he had been forced to overstep the boundaries of his command into ecclesiastical jurisdiction for the sake of the Teresian Reform, but his conscience had secretly troubled him. On the other hand, he was convinced of having acted justly because he knew that neither Fr. Tostado nor the Nuncio had exact and sufficient knowledge of the state of things.

Furthermore, that very morning Philip had received a letter from Teresa which had moved him deeply. The King's reply to the Nuncio was rapidly calculated, but important.

"Count Tendilla must make amends, Monsignor. He will learn that no one in my kingdom can be disrespectful toward the Pope's representative with impunity. However, I, too, know of the existing hostility between the Mitigated Carmelites and those of the Reform, and there are many reasons to believe that it is all based on misunderstandings. Those of the Reform lead saintly and austere lives. We must protect virtue, Monsignor, and instead I hear that you do not like the Discalced Carmelites, and you make them feel your hostility too much."[1]

The Nuncio politely thanked the King and left. His mission had succeeded: amends would be made in honor of the Holy See. And Philip's speech had struck him to the core. As is likely to happen to many a stubborn mind, a single word can serve to break the ice. To his amazement, the King's words resounded those of Friar Juan of Jesus; both had spoken so ardently of Teresa. The thought occurred to him that perhaps he had been mistaken all along.

Don Mauricio Pardos had been appointed to reprimand Count Tendilla and to demand the amends requested by the Nuncio. The Count admitted his guilt, but he wrote to the King explaining how his excessive behavior had been caused by Bishop Sega's strange attitude toward the Reform fathers whom he revered and loved. In support of his justification he added an exact account of all the vicissitudes the Discalced friars

---

1. *Histoire de Sainte Thérèse,* par une Carmelite de Caen, II, XXVI.

had gone through up to then. All the King did when he finished reading the letter was to send it to the Nuncio without any further explanation or comment.

It was the first time that the complex affair appeared to him in all its contrasting phases. The Discalced were no longer mere rebels and intriguers. Even their imprudent acts took on a light of pathos heretofore unsuspected by the Nuncio. Those so-called rebellions lost their sense of gravity when seen only as the result of exasperated inner aspirations. Both sides had been led by honest intentions throughout the whole controversy. What was basic was misunderstanding.

And now Teresa suddenly took on a new light. She who earlier had appeared as an ambitious woman had nothing for which to be reproved. She had always obeyed her superiors, and a harsh word had never been uttered by her throughout the whole combat.

When Count Tendilla went to excuse himself formally before the Nuncio, Monsignor insisted on being the first to apologize.

"I want to confirm the righteousness of my intentions in this matter: proof of this lies in the fact that I would be happy if the King would nominate some arbiters to judge the whole thing with me. All I desire is to see virtue glorified and evil punished."

Philip accepted, nominating four assistants to judge the case, among whom was Dominican Fr. Pedro Fernández, one-time Carmelite visitor who had seen the controversy form from the very beginning.

In a letter to her Madrid defender, Roque de la Huerta, Teresa wrote: "May our Lord reward you for the good news you send me. My worries are over if these two venerable Dominican priests are to be the Nuncio's assistants. I know that what they order will be done only with the greater glory of God in mind, and we desire nothing else."

On the first of April, 1579, the Nuncio published a brief exonerating the Discalced religious from Mitigated Carmelite jurisdiction and nominating Fr. Angel de Salazar superior. Everyone was happy.

In her letter to Fr. Gracián, Teresa wrote: "My Father, could we have desired anything better from Monsignor Nuncio? He has shown us meritorious to all. Your hope for new troubles makes me smile. For the love of God, do not ask for them yet, for you will not be the only one to bear them. Let's breathe easily at least for a few days."

Fr. Salazar sent Teresa a kind letter which served as a liberating message, for it meant that Teresa was free to go wherever the necessities of her Order called her. An atmosphere of complete peace reigned. Fr. Salazar even took Fr. Gracián as his personal secretary and assistant. Happy messages in praise of the Lord passed between many Carmelite communities.

But Teresa knew that definite order in Reform matters by supreme Roman sanction would be prudent and perhaps necessary. The Reform was to be erected in a separate province, therefore a delegation was to be sent to Rome for this purpose. Mother Ana of Jesus offered the entire dowry of one of her novices so plans for the trip could be made. Fathers Juan of Jesus and Jaime of the Trinity were wisely chosen. They left concealing their true mission under the obvious pretext of obtaining a marriage license for Don Francisco de Bracamonte who wished to marry a cousin, in order not to revive discussions which could have endangered those advantages already gained.

A whole year was needed to collect all the documents, various papers and testimonies. Meanwhile, the Mitigated Carmelites met to elect their new general, and their choice fell on Fr. Cafardo. But the committee of Reformed Carmelites in Rome had presented their request for recognition as a separate province before the election had taken place. Pope Gregory XIII submitted the matter to the religious congregation, and in particular Cardinal Peretti who was to be the future Sixtus V. His penetrating eye disentangled all the contradictions, catching the truth at its core: two separate families of religious, both equally respectable, were fighting for freedom from interference from each other. In view of this, he could only approve Teresa's thesis, and the congregation followed his advice.

But Pope Gregory XIII was prudent and deemed it just to ask the opinion of the highest Carmelite authority. The chapter laid the whole thing into the General's hands as an act of deference to their newly elected head. An objective, intelligent man, Fr. Cafardo could not think of denying what the Discalced reasonably requested. On the other hand, he felt it his duty to safeguard the honor and prestige of the Mitigated Carmelites so he resorted to an arrangement by which the two branches would be finally separated. The complication, however, would be that a Discalced Provincial would alternate with a Mitigated one in governing over the Discalced. Cardinal Peretti was pleased with the compromise, brought it before the Pope and obtained his approval. When the two Reform delegates got news of this they immediately saw how the bond could give rise to serious annoyances. Fr. Juan of Jesus futilely protested to the Cardinal and others of the congregation, all replying that it was too late to change the Pope's mind.

However, just before the two disillusioned friars were to return to Spain, they providentially met Msgr. Spinola who was an astute Vatican clerk. He knew the Sacred College of Cardinals well, and knew that the Pope greatly esteemed Cardinal Sforza. Altogether favorable to the Discalced Carmelites' views, he asked why they did not try to get Cardinal Sforza's support, for only then would they completely succeed in their mission.

But how to approach such an illustrious person? Both friars thought of a Spaniard who was a papal guard and an acquaintance of theirs who might help them. After having heard all the explanations of the question at hand, Robostalto referred all to Cardinal Sforza who, while listening carefully to the complicated narration, placed everything in its correct proportion. It was evident that the separation between the Mitigated and Unmitigated was to be complete. The only bond between the two could be in the person of the Father General.

The next day Cardinal Sforza went to Gregory XIII presenting his point of view on the subject. Sforza's argument was that the matter of the separation had been treated already by various authorities, and each brought forth new solutions. In order to avoid dissatisfaction in the future, the best measure would be to have the question settled definitely in the consistory. This supreme irrevocable verdict would serve to create permanent peace in the Order since the Mitigated and Unmitigated could then follow their own paths in certainty. Gregory XIII agreed to judge the matter in the consistory.

Two days later, Teresa's Reform was being discussed in the very heart of the Catholic world. Gregory XIII rendered justice to that which Teresa of Jesus had undertaken twenty years earlier amid the scorn of an entire city. The Pope ordered all Discalced monasteries and convents to form a separate province and to be governed by a provincial of their own rule and election. The brief was dispatched on June 27, 1580.

Only twenty years earlier three professed nuns, one novice, and one boarding school girl had grouped together to become the seed that was to produce such a majestic tree. Certain it is that if the physical world gives rise to stupendous phenomena, the spiritual world presents the most significant of events. What was characteristic in the Teresian Reform was its lack of human attraction. It was imbued with every element that repulsed human frailty—seclusion, fasting, total renunciation, mortification, solitude, silence. Continual prayer elevated members to a privileged spiritual level. Such rapid diffusion of these characteristics— unapproachable to the mediocre—splendidly shows the power of the grace of God.

CHAPTER FIFTY-TWO

The Foundations and *The Interior Castle*

Before continuing with the narration of events, let us pause to consider two great works of St. Teresa, *The Foundations* and *The Interior Castle*.

The Foundations is the story of Teresa's external activity in establishing the Reform convents. It is a true and lively account which relates even the details in a sure and careful manner. She had begun it out of obedience in 1571-1572 and again in 1575-1576 in Toledo by the order of Fr. Gracián. A picture of reality is presented in this book with sublime circumstances alternating with small painful and amusing incidents. All that counts is the truth. Her strokes are genuine with a special verve that is dignified, slightly ironic, but always cordial, and equally sincere toward her reader as toward the people described.

Teresa's literary and psychological style can only be traced to her spirit, to her superior practice of charity. No matter how hostile, narrow-minded and mean the people she met, she remained calm, understanding and full of affection. This is what was found written in her prayer book:

> "Let nothing trouble or sadden you,
> All passes, but God does not change,
> You will conquer all with patience;
> You lack nothing if God is in your heart,
> His love is enough."

The second book reflects the contemplative side of Teresa's life, transporting us to head-spinning heights. No one else has combined the travails of active life with the summits of contemplation to such a degree. It is her most organized work, written better with a definite plan, which treats seraphic arguments and codifies the most difficult and elusive of subjects. The book belongs to that most restricted group of masterpieces of human creativity such as those of St. Augustine and St. Thomas, Dante and Bach. Parsifal was too human to be placed in this category and neither can Michelangelo's gigantic visions, which were too dramatic, be admitted to this level.

Just as her other books, this, too, was written under obedience. While discussing prayer with Fr. Gracián in Toledo one day, Teresa exclaimed, "Oh, how that is well explained in the book of my life which is now in the hands of the Inquisition!" Fr. Gracián replied, "Since that book is no longer to be had, try to remember all you wrote in it, add more and write another book, treating the subject in general without naming the person to whom these things have happened."

Not expecting this from her superior, and feeling the bond of obedience upon her, Teresa's face clouded and she begged Fr. Gracián not to impose this command on her, but to permit her to weave and pray along with the rest of the community. The friar would not retract his disposition and even told Teresa's confessor about it so he could persuade her all the more and add his command as well.

She was to be objective, expose her inner experiences as in a treatise and reveal the most unbelievable true gifts of God from a general point of view. It was a grave, almost superhuman task, but she overcame her fright by obedience and faith in God. It was Holy Trinity Eve, 1577, and Teresa had resolved to start her work, but think as she might, no acceptable opening idea came to her when suddenly a vision enraptured her. There appeared before her a block of crystal in the shape of a castle divided in seven apartments. The seventh, in the center, was inhabited by the King of Glory of such radiant splendor that all the other apartments were illumined by its light. Those closer to the royal apartment received stronger light, but the rays did not pass the castle walls which were surrounded by heaps of rubbish, toads, snakes, and other poisonous animals moving about in a frightful darkness.

The crystal was the vision of a soul in grace. While the saint was enraptured by the sublime spectacle, everything suddenly turned black and the venomous beasts entered, bringing ruin to the castle. The soul had fallen into mortal sin.

Teresa remembered her vision and saw that it contained the design for her book which she began the next day.

"It may seem erroneous to speak of entering the castle if the castle is our own soul; there should be no need to enter it since we are already there. However, the great difference lies in how we are in it because many souls linger only in the outskirts with the guards, not caring to go farther to see what is in the splendid apartment and who lives there. Books on prayer advise the soul to enter into itself, and that is exactly what I mean.

"A great theologian was telling me recently that those souls without prayer are as crippled bodies unable to move their arms and legs even though they have them. Some souls are so ill and accustomed to living among external things that they cannot be cured, unable as they are to enter into themselves. In continual contact with the beasts about the castle, they have become so similar to them that they can no longer overcome themselves, notwithstanding their noble nature and their having to do with God. If these souls do not try to understand their immense misery and do not correct themselves, they will become statues of salt just as did Lot's wife for having turned backwards.

"As far as I can understand, prayer and meditation open the castle door. Mental prayer is no better than vocal prayer because there must be meditation in both cases in order to be called prayer. I do not call prayer what someone does who considers not with Whom he is speaking. Even this may be valid prayer if the appropriate reflections have been made other times. But if someone has the habit of speaking to God as if to a slave without reflecting whether what he says is good or bad, content with whatever comes to his mouth perhaps from memory, this, to me, is not prayer, nor does God like Christians to be this way. Faith in the goodness of God and your constant contact with interior things, Sisters, make me hope this will never happen to you.

"So let us not speak further of these paralytic souls who are in serious danger if God does not command them to arise as he did to the paralytic who had been waiting at the side of the pool for thirty years. Let us speak rather of those who at last enter the castle. Though engulfed by duties in the world, their desires are good, they ask God's help from time to time and fleetingly reflect upon themselves. They do pray several times a month, though distracted by business or private affairs according to the saying 'your heart is where your treasure is.' However, they decide to free themselves from these bonds every now and then, realizing that the road they are following does not lead to the castle entrance.

"They finally reach the ground floor rooms, but dragging a host of tiny lizards and other small animals which block the view of the castle's beauty and do not permit peace of mind. Nevertheless, those souls have gone a long way simply in entering the castle."[1]

This was the opening theme. The little lizards symbolize the obstacles the world puts before those desiring to enter the castle, the door to which is prayer.

"You must not imagine these apartments lined up side by side. Instead, they are all grouped about and above the King's apartment, illuminated by the brilliant sun shining in the middle. Things of the soul must always be considered with much breadth and magnificence, not fearing exaggeration because the soul's capacity surpasses all human imagination. It is very important that a soul in prayer be left free to circulate as it wishes and not be restricted to one room. God created it so great that it must not be forced to remain in the same place too long, even if within its own knowledge."

Those souls which are still battling temptations are in the first three apartments. There lizards crawl everywhere, and vigilance must be constant.

"How important is a knowledge of ourselves! Follow me well, daughters! It is so necessary that not even those who are already admitted into God's apartment can afford to forget it. Furthermore, they couldn't forget it even if they cared to because just like the bee, only humility can manufacture that honey without which comes perdition. The bee cannot omit sucking

---

1. *The Interior Castle*, I, II, 6, 7, 8, here and for the following.

flowers, nor can the soul full of self-knowledge omit considering the greatness and majesty of God. This is where it discovers how wretched it is, and those filthy beasts will be of less trouble than in the first rooms where knowledge of ourselves is exercised."

Retirement in prayer, then, serves to make us contemplate the greatness of God, thereby witnessing our own miserable nature and understanding ourselves. God grants periods of consolation and aridity in the soul's effort to ascend through "prayer, retirement, correction of its own defects and organization of its spiritual life."

———

In the fourth mansion the atmosphere is cleared of all inner resistance. The degrees to pass are now clearly mystical because in addition to possessing ordinary grace, the soul is completely governed by God. It is only fitting to note that Teresa's mystic way of reaching sanctity is sure, no other being so clearly expressed.

God progressively intervenes with the gifts of the Holy Spirit, invading the soul with love, and the soul surrenders humbly. By occupying the soul's topmost faculties, God leaves the inferior senses free to live naturally. This is "prayer of divine taste" which she has elsewhere called "prayer of quiet," and the whole fourth residence symbolizes this degree of prayer and is described in great detail. God's action overcomes the soul's superior part just as the sun lighting a mountain top leaves the sides and valleys dim or black. This constitutes the night of the senses and the quiet of the spirit. The presence of God is manifested by a blinding light bearing with a delightful passiveness. The soul respects God's actions in prayer joined to peace, silence and moderate action. Capital spiritual sins become destroyed while the wisdom of the Gospel is revealed.

Full union is obtained in the fifth mansion. Here God occupies not only the soul's tip, but all its spiritual faculties, will, intellect and imagination, leaving only external senses apart. The saint describes this state as "religious death." The soul is dead to the world in order to live better in God. But it is a delightful death. No longer actively united to its body, the soul lives better in God. The body has barely enough life to breathe. The will is almost habitually conquered, for the soul lives in obedience. This spirituality is full of that wisdom which binds the will to its eternal undertaking: "the church."[2]

A still higher step in mystical union with God is obtained in the sixth mansion. The theme here is the soul's engagement with God in preparation for the seventh, supreme residence where "spiritual marriage," the full and uninterrupted union with God takes place. Union is already complete in the spiritual betrothal phase because God occupies the senses of the soul along with its spiritual faculties. But union here is temporary. Teresa describes the "engagement" as ecstasy, rapture and spiritual flight.

The doctrine exposed corresponds to that of her *Life*, which demonstrates the clarity and sureness of the phenomena and the lucidity of introspection and exposition. Here the subject is treated more scientifically without the loss of the enthusiasm of personal experience. The saint does not name herself, but it is most obvious that she is the protagonist. All we need do is compare the description of rapture already read in the *Life* with this one in *The Interior Castle* where she writes, "...breathing stops and there is not the strength to speak, notwithstanding the fact that the other senses may have more strength. At times, however, every

---

2. See Fr. Marie-Eugene, *Je Veux Voir Dieu,* I, III. This work constitutes a great contribution to the *Castle's* interpretation.

sense is lost immediately: the body turns cold and appears dead, so much so that it is not even known if it still breathes. But this degree does not last long because the body revives as the great suspension releases hold, but the body only returns to die to give more life to the soul. This great ecstasy, however, does not last long." [3]

The effects of rapture are thus described: "Oh, what confusion the soul feels returning to itself! What burning desires to serve God in whatever way He wishes! If only one could have a thousand lives to use them all in God's service with everything on earth being tongues to praise Him. There is impetuous desire for penances, but there is not much suffering in carrying them out since our great love keeps us from feeling what we do.

"Another type of rapture is what I call the 'spiritual flight.' The soul feels taken up so impetuously as if the spirit were being stolen, and great fear is felt at first. This is why I say that whoever receives these graces must be courageous, have much faith and completely abandon himself to what the Lord wishes. Can you imagine the fright of having your soul and sometimes even your body snatched away without knowing who is taking it or where it is going and how? The action is so sudden, we are not yet certain it is God. Is there any means of resisting? No, in fact I know from someone that it is worse if you offer resistance. That great God who holds the ocean's waters within its boundaries seems to permit a powerful wave to raise the soul's boat high up. No matter how hard the pilot tries to stop the boat he cannot. The spirit has a definite feeling of separation from the body in this 'flight.' Though not dead, the body cannot say if the soul is still within it. Being transported in a very different land, it sees unimaginable things in an incomparable light. Infinite

---

3. Here and for the following: *Interior Castle*, IV, V, VI, VIII, IX.

secrets are revealed in an instant. The soul is as a rifle ball shot silently, so clear in movement that illusion is impossible."

There are numerous passages relating the identical phenomena already affirmed in her *Life.* The following description of the intellectual vision can be compared to the one in her earlier book: "When the soul is not in the least intent on receiving such graces, undeserving as it feels, it perceives our Lord Jesus Christ near without seeing Him. This is not like an imaginary vision which passes quickly, but lasts days and may even last more than a year."

All this takes place in the sixth mansion which is a preparation for the spiritual marriage. Her *Interior Castle* which is truly a poem of sacred love reaches its climax "when the soul is introduced into the seventh mansion where the three Persons of the Holy Trinity are revealed to it in an intellectual vision as a show of truth in the midst of a fire, just as a brilliant mist falling over the spirit.[4] The three Persons are distinctly seen, and by means of the special grace the soul receives, it recognizes with certainty that all three are but one substance, one power, one wisdom, one God. What we believe by faith is *almost* seen, though not through the bodily or mind's eyes because this is not a vision of imagery. Here the three Persons communicate with the soul, fulfilling the words of the Gospel which say that God in the Holy Trinity will inhabit the soul that loves Him and observes His commandments.

---

4. Teresa uses the terminology set up by theologians of mysticism who divided the soul in three parts: the lowest was the sensitive or animal part; the middle consisted of three spiritual powers: the intellect, memory and the will. In the topmost part lies the soul's essence, from where the powers originate; it is here that God dwells by means of grace. This supreme essence is in the center of the soul. That is why she refers to the middle and supreme parts of the soul as "the spirit of the soul."

"The Lord appears in the center of the soul in a still more delicate manner than in the other mansions, just as He appeared to the Apostles without passing through the door. It is such a great secret, so intensely delightful, so sublime and sudden that I know not what to compare it to. The Lord must wish to show heaven's glory to the soul, but in a much more elevated manner than in any other spiritual vision. All that can be said is that the soul, rather the spirit, becomes one with God. At least that is what we come to understand. Himself a Spirit, the Lord permits certain spirits to see how much He loves them so they can praise His majesty because He becomes so united to a creature that He would never be separated from it."

The effects of the spiritual marriage are worth quoting: "First of all, a deep forgetfulness of one's self, so much so that one doubts one's existence. So changed, the butterfly is dead, delighted at having found repose with Christ abiding in it. Let us see how differently it lives now to learn the effects of the grace it has received. First of all, a deep forgetfulness overcomes it so it no longer believes it exists. Completely changed, it no longer recognizes itself, thinking not of heaven which awaits it, nor life nor honor, but only of contributing to the greater glory of God, ready to give up its life for this. Otherwise, it feels it no longer exists. Nevertheless, it continues to sleep and eat, even if with great difficulty, and continues its duties. The second effect is a great desire to suffer, but there is no anguish present now. There is but one immense desire to do God's will. To suffer or not to suffer is the same.

"If someone persecutes the butterfly, it is filled with joy. Such peace reigns within it that not only does it not feel in the least resentful toward that particular person, but it actually feels special affection for him, trapped as he is by some affliction.

"But what is more surprising is that whereas previously these souls were tormented by the desire to die and go to God, now they only wish to serve and glorify Him so they would live many years amid great labors just to have God praised even a little. For the moment, they neither care nor desire the glory of the saints; their glory is in helping the crucified Lord, especially since they see how much He is offended, and how few really seek His honor above all things.

"They are no more afraid of death than of a gentle rapture. It is stupendous to know that the Author of these sweet feelings is the same who once gave them such excessive desires. May He be forever praised! In short, these souls no longer desire spiritual consolation because they have God with them, and He lives with them. Since His life was one continuous martyrdom, it is logical that He make their lives similar to His. These souls are detached from everything. They are neither arid nor inwardly harrassed, wishing only to praise God. When they become distracted, God Himself recalls them from within, this being a common phenomenon. The intellect plays no part in this. Just as fire throws its flames upward, no matter how intense the fire may be, so does this gentle movement originate from the center of the soul to awaken its powers.

"God enriches and instructs the soul in this prayer in a completely calm and silent manner, making one remember how not a sound was heard when Solomon's temple was built. In this temple which is God's residence, God and the soul enjoy each other in lofty silence. The intellect has nothing to do. Its Author wishes it to rest and contemplate what is happening through a small opening. At times it cannot even do that because the powers often remain in a stupor, unable to operate."

These effects are the reflection of the divine presence, and St. Teresa reveals them to us proportioned to

the different degrees of this presence. Obscure phenomena become admirably clear, revealing a limpid
logic in God's love. Thus we see how right it is for a
soul that has reached incomplete union to pine for
death, wishing to be dissolved in God. Here there may
be a grain of egoism still, for in its desire for absorption
in God, the soul may be led by a supreme need for
satisfaction and joy. When a soul is already constantly
united as in the spiritual marriage, the love borne is
more nearly perfect, and thus the only aspiration exist-
ent is to serve God without caring about hurrying to get
to paradise. This fact proves that not a bit of human
nature is left, as is behooving to one truly united with
God.

The complete union obtained in the seventh mansion is reflected on the whole soul's crystal. No
shadows remain; the effect is complete. The soul is the
true spouse of the Lord; the pure act of love is constant.

What wealth of supernatural truth is contained in
the exactitude of Teresa's analysis! It is not possible
that any human intellect could have imagined this spiritual castle with such divine majesty, where the human
and the divine correspond ineffably. This very harmony between the divine ray and human reflection
constitutes the veracity of St. Teresa's experience. For
this reason, her *Interior Castle* can be considered the
greatest work written on experimental mysticism.

The book's ending is moving and gives the exact
date of its completion. "My great desire to have a part
in helping you to serve my Lord and God prompts me
to ask you to grandly praise His Majesty in my name
each time you read these pages and pray for the exaltation of the Church and for the conversion of Lutherans.
Beseech the Lord to pardon my sins and to free me
from purgatory where His mercy may perhaps keep me
when you will read this book, if learned men deem it
worthy to be read. If some error is contained therein, it

is because I am not learned. I submit myself entirely to what the Holy Roman Catholic Church teaches. This is how I believe now and hope to live and die believing. May our Lord God be ever praised and blessed! Amen, amen.

"This writing was finished in St. Joseph's Convent in Avila on St. Andrew's Eve, 1577, for the glory of God who lives and reigns forever and ever. Amen."

CHAPTER FIFTY-THREE

Family Affections, Locutions and Another Foundation

It is difficult to speak of family affections when speaking of a Discalced Carmelite nun, but Teresa herself conciliated her monastic condition to her brothers' necessities especially when in Toledo. At the time of that humiliating exile, her two brothers, who had returned from the New World, needed her support in different ways. Back from Peru, Cepeda wished to introduce his two children into Spanish society. More than once his financial help had been providential for his sister's Reform. Unprepared for a true religious life, he felt a deep desire to practice his religion through good works. But his desire overstepped his means. He would overdiscipline himself, practice extravagant mortifications, and pray with impossible assiduity. Under Teresa's guidance he gained equilibrium.

Don Lorenzo's daughter, Teresita, was in the convent of Toledo. Later on, she also went to St. Joseph's in Avila, where she grew up with Fr. Gracián's niece, Isabel Gracián. Both were very gentle and pure, a consolation for Teresa during the struggles of that time.

But Teresa's other brother, Don Pedro de Ahumada, who had also returned from the Indies, caused her deep concern because of his neurasthenic tendencies. His low economic status favored the condition. Impulsive and rather a spendthrift, he had not put anything aside, but to be dependent on his older brother embittered him so much that he appeared ungrateful. Relations between the two brothers grew so tense that a break was imminent, but that was when Teresa stepped in with a letter which is a masterpiece of charity. By showing herself weak, she was more encouraging in her advice to Lorenzo to be forgiving and generous.

"Believe me, God permits that we be tempted by that poor man to see how generous we are. I confess I feel so little sympathy for him that it makes me ashamed. Even if he were not my brother I should feel pity toward him, but I am not very inclined to feel even that. But I consider how I should be to please God, and when I see the good Master between Pedro and me, I am ready to suffer anything."

This preamble is psychologically effective. Continuing, she wrote: "This poor man realizes you are right in being angry with him, but he says he can do no better. He understands he is going astray and must be tired of it. Nevertheless, he says he would rather die than remain as he was. He had even ordered a muleteer to come for him tomorrow morning to take him to Seville, but a whole day of sun would have killed him since his head already pained him greatly. And what would he do in Seville but spend his money and go alms-begging? I shall keep him here until I hear from you even though he is convinced of waiting in vain. Yet, he consents to wait because he has begun to realize what a problem he has created for himself. Please answer immediately. Send two hundred royals for his clothing and food. His extravagance has passed all limits. He will have enough to live on for a year if you send another two hundred so he can go to live with our sister who has invited him. He may even go to his nephew's, Diego de Guzmán, who has sent money for the journey. Next year it will be better not to give it all to him at one time, but pay the people who feed him from time to time because I don't think he will remain long in one place. This is certainly all very sad, but if our poor brother is strange in this way it is clear that, according to the law of perfection, you are all the more obligated to help him, using charity toward him above all others. Believe me that when God grants someone as many favors as He has you, He expects great things from that person, and this is one. Consider this money given to me, as you certainly would give to me if I were in need. Truly, I shall look upon the matter as though it really had been for me. I assure you that it is difficult for me not to be able to help him."

The letter was effective, and Lorenzo sent the money, and even pledged further maintenance. Everyone in the family finally began to understand that Pedro was mentally ill, and he eventually died piously, thanks to Teresa's warm understanding and saving ways.

Teresa's last foundations were those established in Villanueva de la Jara, Palencia, Soria and Burgos. She had aged physically, more ailing than ever, going from one sickness to another, but inwardly always more detached. Near the end of 1577, she had a bad fall down the choir steps and broke her arm. A certain woman from Medina was called to heal the arm, but she arrived several months later. The pain Teresa had felt until then, however, was nothing compared to the pulling the woman and her assistant did in their therapy. The pain was excruciating, but the nuns saw that she bore it all serenely.

In a letter to Fr. Gracián in 1578, she wrote, "I felt the greatest joy in being able to offer that suffering to my Divine Master."

In Avila on Pentecost Eve, 1580, Teresa was praying in "Nazareth," one of St. Joseph's hermitages built in the convent garden. It was here that our Lord appeared to her, dictating four basic rules of the Reform.

"I felt a very great fervor which elevated my spirit. Then I heard our Lord say: 'Tell the Discalced Friars to observe four things, for as long as they do this will their order flourish. First, the superiors must be in good relations with each other, feeling the same way in spiritual matters. Secondly, they should form many foundations, but there should be just a few in each institute. Thirdly, for the good of their souls they should have little to do with laymen. And fourthly, they should teach more through their deeds than through their speech.' This happened in 1579, and because it is a great truth, I am signing my name to it. Teresa of Jesus."

Many years later these words were inscribed in gold in that particular hermitage, and the Discalced Fathers took the rules into their constitution.

Ill as she was, on June 25, Teresa again took up visiting all her foundations. Leaving Avila with her faithful nurse, Sr. Ana of St. Bartholomew, she went to Medina, Valladolid, Alba, Salamanca and Malagón. Then she received an invitation for a new convent from a small community of nine pious women who had united already in Villanueva de la Jara as members of the Third Order. Their life was already Teresian, but they had no fixed rule. They prayed, worked and helped one another, but no one commanded. They lived by their earnings in sewing for outsiders.

Their highest aspiration was to become Discalced Carmelite nuns. They had awaited Teresa for four years, but Teresa had been hesitant in accepting an already formed community of women who were no doubt accustomed to independence. These Tertiaries would form the majority in the new foundation and would be older than the professed nuns and the Mother Superior. What if they should rebel? But one day after Communion she saw that that particular foundation would be pleasing to God.

Now feeling she had hesitated too long, she took four nuns and two priests with her to Villanueva in February, 1580. Bells rang saluting their arrival, and the townspeople were all out to welcome them. There was a solemn procession to the new convent with the Holy Eucharist. Contrary to Teresa's apprehensions, she found all nine novices docile and excelling in all the virtues. They were happy to obey, and had practiced so many mortifications and fasted so much already that they fell in easily with Reform Rules. The more Teresa knew them, the happier she was that she had come to establish the convent.

Witnessing the great poverty of the house, Prioress Ana of St. Augustine resorted to the only practical method she could think of to save her house: she went to a statue of the Child Jesus saying that since He was their chief provider, she would give Him a "royal" on which to gain interest. And indeed, after four centuries, the convent at Villanueva de la Jara is still flourishing.

CHAPTER FIFTY-FOUR

The Foundation in Palencia and Ana of St. Bartholomew

Palencia's new bishop, Alvaro de Mendoza, whom we have met already as Avila's bishop and Teresa's protector, requested that a Reformed convent be set up in Palencia. So Teresa set out, but when she got as far as Valladolid, her health broke down, and everyone thought she would die. She pulled through, but remained extremely tired, even depressed and sluggish. She no longer felt useful and could not take definite action concerning the new foundation in Palencia.

The Prioress of Valladolid, María Battista, was enthusiastic over the projected foundation and tried to reanimate Teresa in every way possible. Strangely enough, Teresa was prey to many doubts concerning the principle of absolute poverty to be adopted. So unlike herself, this reflects a stage of "trying ground" which grace permits certain souls to pass through. Teresa was having again a taste of that arid desert atmosphere. But under that exterior, apparent abandonment, there was still marriage with God.

It is interesting to note that Teresa was being taken aback and frightened by her own work. She felt unfit to establish a new convent, deeming it impossible. Yet she never lost her introspective ability. As always, she masterfully depicted her own state of mind.

''The body subjects the soul to so many needs that it seems the latter should obey the former's laws. One of the gravest miseries of this life is when the soul has not the strength to flee the body's might. Certainly it is painful to suffer atrociously from physical pain, but it is nothing if the soul is free because knowing that all comes from God, it becomes a reason to praise Him. But it is terrible to feel helpless, especially for a soul which desires to dedicate itself entirely to God's service. One can only be patient in this state, recognize one's misery and deliver oneself entirely to God's will to do with as He wishes.''[1]

A Jesuit, Fr. Ripalda, whom Teresa knew, happened to pass through Valladolid then, and she opened her heart to him. He encouraged her, saying it was an effect of old age even though he knew it wasn't so. But it was to persuade her that those fears were not God's. He, therefore, told her to do all she could to go ahead with her foundations, but she was still harassed by irresoluteness.

''After Communion one day, while I was still engrossed in my doubts, resolving never to open another foundation, I begged our Lord for light to follow His will because this latter desire had never weakened in me. And the Lord said in a scolding tone, 'What do you fear? When have I ever forsaken you? I am still what I always have been. Do not neglect to carry out these two foundations!' Oh, great God, how different are Your words from those of men. I became so filled with

---

1. *Foundations*, XXIX, 3, 6, here and for the following.

courage and so resolute that no one could have stopped me.''

In Teresa's case it was her intellectual vigor that led her body to renewed strength. Taking the two nuns whose dowries she would use to buy a house, along with two other nuns, she set off for Palencia on December 28, 1580. Everyone said it would be impossible to live upon alms there, but Teresa knew God would help her. It was cold, and they had to stumble blindly on their way through the fog. Ana of St. Bartholomew, who already had served as Teresa's nurse, was also part of the group.

Let us pause here for a word about Ana's admirable destiny. Of a peasant family, she had always been virtuous, but had never been taught to read and write. She was a humble lay-nun, but now she occupied the enviable post of secretary to the great saint. Her career began one winter evening in 1579 when Teresa was tired and had many letters to write. With compassionate eyes, Ana watched helplessly as Teresa wrote. Teresa, in turn, recognized how full of love Ana's look was, and how incapable she felt. With a smile, Teresa said that Ana could have helped her if she had known how to write. Ana, in return, asked for a written sheet of paper to try to copy. Handing her a learned man's letter whose handwriting was large and clear, Ana could only shake her head as a sign of incomprehension, yet timidly ventured to ask for something written by the saint.

Teresa gave her a sheet of her own writing which, though clear, was rapid and run together. No matter, Ana studied it zealously, sat at a table, picked up a pen, and tried her hand at writing. When she got up, she handed Mother Teresa a copy of her letter to the sisters of Avila in a legible and correct form. From then on, Ana helped Teresa until she wrote all of Teresa's letters, the latter only signing them.

At Teresa's death, Ana went to France, becoming a choir nun under obedience. She became prioress many times and battled to maintain her foundress' spirit in the convents of France. Misunderstood there, she founded a Carmelite convent in Antwerp, Flanders. There by her prayers she twice freed the city from the Prince of Orange and the citizens acclaimed her as the liberator of Antwerp. She died there on June 6, 1626, and she still receives constant devotion. In 1917, Pope Benedict XV announced the beatification of Sr. Ana of St. Bartholomew.

Returning to the foundation in Palencia, we find that the solemn opening ceremony took place on June 1, 1580. The convent is called the "House of Consolation" because there Teresa received the news of the papal bull separating the Reformed Carmelites from the Mitigated. The long battle and infinite anxiety were definitely over, and Teresa felt such a deep consolation that she exclaimed, "My Lord, now I am no longer necessary. You may call me whenever you wish."

CHAPTER FIFTY-FIVE

"And Now, Give Up!"

The first true legitimate Discalced Fathers' chapter meeting was summoned on March 3, 1581, with Fr. Gracián presiding. With the constitutions for both friars and nuns of the Reformed Carmelites drawn up, Teresa's work truly could be considered complete.

Fr. Gracián was elected the new Reform Provincial, and everyone was glad, deeply thankful that all had ended well. Relating the episode in her *Foundations,* Teresa admonishes her future generations "who will find everything easy, to be careful not to fall into imperfection. We must always bear in mind that we are descendents of the holy prophets. How many saints in heaven wear our habit! With the grace of God, let us try to be like them. The battle is short, and the reward eternal, my sisters. Let us pass over terrestrial things which are nothing, concerning ourselves only with what brings us closer to the End which has no end, with the things that help us to love and serve Him who will live forever. Amen. Amen."[1]

---

1. *Foundations,* XXIX, 33.

By this, Teresa shows that she is spiritually proud of her religious forefathers, for she is a Carmelite even in her soul and exhorts her nuns to live up to their heritage. It is here that she utters, "And now, dismiss your servant." She had already said this when she first received word of the papal brief, and she repeated it now that the Reform's autonomy was an accomplished fact. To the Prioress in Seville she wrote, "Now I can say what St. Simeon said because I have seen what I desired in our Virgin Lady's Order, so I beseech you all not to pray for me requesting long life, but that I may go to rest since I am of no more use to you."[2]

But before Teresa died she had to attend to setting up convents in Soria, Granada and Burgos. She even assisted in the opening of second establishments in Valladolid and Salamanca. Moreover, she saw the Discalced Cross in the Portuguese capital.

The foundations in Granada, Lisbon and Burgos were the last three, and all these contained seeds for new expansions. Mother Ana of Jesus was responsible for the opening of the Granada foundation, marking the passage of creative power to Teresa's daughters. Lisbon's foundation represented the missionary inclination of the New Carmel, while the Burgos foundation sums up all of Teresa's activities as a sort of spiritual testament. At Burgos she returned to her early self, battling against misunderstanding and a thunderstorm which caused a serious flood, forcing the nuns to huddle together in a second-story room, abandoned by everyone. But through it all Teresa was serene as always.

---

2. *Libro de Recreaciones,* p. 150 quoted by Fr. Silverio, V, 3.

CHAPTER FIFTY-SIX

The Lisbon Foundation and the First Reform Missionaries

Writing to Fr. Gracián in 1580, Teresa besought him to pray that war would not fall upon Portugal because it was so sad to see Christians kill each other. The Portuguese War did take place, however, but actually only resulted in armed occupation of the old kingdom rather than separate military engagements. A Burgundian dynasty had ruled Portugal from 1147-1580, transforming the simple feudal state into a powerful kingdom. Native land had been liberated from the Moors, and there had been colonial expansion. Don Sebastian, the son of Princess Juana, Philip II's sister, gained the throne in 1557. Of a generous and mystical nature, Don Sebastian was also a daring and enterprising man who declared war on Africa. While battling in Alcazar in 1578, he disappeared with no word ever heard of him again.

The last Burgundian descendent was Don Sebastian's old uncle, Cardinal Enrique. Loving independence, the Portuguese insisted that the Cardinal become king. However, conjectures soon began to be made everywhere concerning the next dynasty, for the

Cardinal was ailing and old. The shadow of Spanish monarchy seemed imminent because Philip II was Don Sebastian's uncle. The Cardinal's death in 1580 marked the end of the Portuguese dynasty.

False "Don Sebastians" turned up from time to time as well as others bearing uncertain claims, so Philip II occupied the land by force, and Portugal could not reasonably resist. Portugal mourned its liberty, and all that the people could do for consolation was turn to the Church and pray for hope.

This is when Teresa's Reform brought new ascetic quiet into the hearts of many Portuguese. Fr. Ambrosio Mariano established the first Portuguese foundation in Lisbon. He was the man best suited for the task both because Philip II admired him and because he was not of Spanish blood which made a good impression on the Portuguese. He arrived with six Reform friars, hoping the Portuguese would have trust in them and help them set up their foundation. He won the people's confidence, however, when he asked Philip II to receive him. When the Portuguese nobility saw that the king of Spain, who was in Lisbon settling affairs, received the friar immediately, they were impressed. The meeting with the king seemed to lead to practical results. The king himself offered to pay for the building of a monastery and church, but Friar Ambrosio feared that what the king ordered would be too costly and refused His Majesty's offer out of love for poverty, saying it would be built from alms and sacrifice. The king was then the first to give his offering of alms which was ample enough to pay for the church and the monastery.

With permission obtained from the Archbishop, Friar Mariano looked about for his site and fell in love with a hill in Pampulla on the outskirts of Lisbon, where a river flowed out to the ocean below. There was so much peace in such a wide horizon that this alone

was an incentive for meditation. Fortunately, the own-
ers were good, holy people and sold the land.

Now it was Friar Mariano, the architect, who was
beginning work. Under his management, the scattered
houses on the hilltop became the new Teresian Reform
Fathers' monastery complete with church. Humility inspired the architect: the lines were clear for practicality,
and the courtyard was constructed to further concentration. On October 14, 1581, the Discalced Friars went
to their new home which was dedicated to St. Philip.
The friars remained there until 1604 when they transferred to a monastery inside Lisbon.

But the Discalced Friars were launched for even
newer horizons. Philip II had often spoken of the Reform Fathers in terms of preaching the Gospel to the
pagans of Africa. Fr. Mariano put the matter up to
Teresa and Fr. Gracián. In this way, Teresa could see,
finally, her childhood missionary dream come true just
before she died.

At 6:00 A.M. on April 15, 1582, Philip II himself
ordered the anchors up for the ship "St. Anthony"
which was carrying the first five Carmelite mission-
aries to Africa. There were six ships in the expedition
led by Admiral Antonio Melo. The nights on the Atlantic were moonless, and one night one of the ships
crashed into the "St. Anthony" with such force that the
crew and passengers barely had time to wake up before
they were hurled into the water. Only two sailors sur-
vived. Though interrupted, the great dream did not end
there.

CHAPTER FIFTY-SEVEN

The Burgos Foundation

Burgos was then Old Castile's capital, rich in prestige but poor in money, and the foundation there caused Teresa considerable trouble. The Archbishop, Cristobal Vela, was bound to the de Cepeda family by Avilian friendship, for the families had been neighbors. A Vela had become Peru's governor and to him five of Teresa's brothers had been drawn, attracted by dreams of glory. Archbishop Cristobal was the son of this very governor. At first, Cristobal had been sent as Bishop to the Canary Islands. Hearing that he did such fine work with the natives there, Philip II asked the Pope to have Vela sent to Burgos as its Archbishop. At the ceremony Vela had spoken favorably of the idea of having a Discalced Carmelite convent established in Burgos, but when he took office and saw there were already many convents dependent on alms, he changed his mind. He had been in Avila in 1561 during the great controversy concerning Teresa's first foundation which lacked sure income and did not want the same to be repeated here.

He, therefore, demanded that Teresa obtain the Municipal Council's consent before going further.

At this point, Teresa must have felt tired of the project, thinking that if the foundation was not to be absolutely favored, it would be better not to establish it. But Doña Catalina de Tolosa, Teresa's last benefactress, was working silently in Teresa's favor. This widow, who at forty-eight was to enter the Reformed Order after her two sons and five daughters had all devoted their lives to Teresa's Reform, persisted in obtaining the difficult approval of the city council, thus making the Burgos foundation possible.

A hard winter had set in when the group started off for Burgos. Everyone who gave an account of the trip mentioned the harsh weather, including Fr. Gracián and Sr. Ana, Teresa's nurse-secretary. A famous anecdote is still told concerning the group's crossing of the Arlanzón River, having to wade through the rushing waters that overran the pontoons. It is said that when Teresa lowered herself into the strong current, she commented, "After so much suffering, Lord, this, too?"

And the Lord is said to have answered, "My daughter, this is how I treat my friends." Teresa is said to have retorted, "That is why You have so few, my Lord."

Those first months in Burgos were uncomfortable and humiliating. Friends finally succeeded in finding a house on the banks of the Arlanzón River. On March 19, 1581, the community moved in. Teresa's account of how she felt on entering into cloister is worth quoting: "No, no one who has not felt it can understand the joy of setting up those foundations when we are in cloister again, far from the people of the world. No matter how much affection may bind us to the people outside, nothing equals the incomparable joy of being alone again. Just as fish in a fish net cannot live unless replaced in water, so it is for those souls accustomed to being in the living waters of the Spouse. Detached from Him in the net of the world, they cannot live until returned to their former state."[1]

When Teresa and her "daughters" had left Doña Tolosa's house for the convent, twelve-year-old Elena had come with them. In April, Archbishop Vela himself presided over the reception ceremony. With tears in his eyes during the sermon, he begged pardon for having made Teresa suffer so much by prolonging the settlement of the foundation.

All seemed well now, until May 24, when the Arlanzón River started to overflow. Everyone around, including other convents, ran for refuge, but Teresa did not see why their cloistered state should be interrupted and would not permit that the Holy Eucharist be left alone. The furious waters, meanwhile, were uprooting trees and tearing away houses. The waters broke very suddenly so that the nuns could only take the Blessed Sacrament and run upstairs without saving anything else.

Sr. Ana relates how "the river had grown so no one could help us, and we could not seek help. The house was old, and each strong wave made it shake as though it would fall. There was water up to the second floor. The Blessed Sacrament had been brought up, and all we did was pray, reciting the litanies. This lasted from six in the morning until midnight without our eating or resting because all our things were under water. Our saint, who felt very weak, at one moment asked if there was a piece of bread because she felt faint. Twelve-year-

---

1. *Foundations,* XXI, 46.

old Elena then went into the water as far as her waist to get some bread for her Mother Teresa. We would have all died if some swimmers had not entered, gone under water and opened the doors to let the water out." [2]

---

2. Found quoted in *Histoire de Sainte Thérèse,* par une Carmelite de Caen, II, XXX.

CHAPTER FIFTY-EIGHT

The Passing

In Fr. Cuivas' deposition of 1585, we read: "Those spiritual contacts that I had with Teresa of Jesus confirmed my belief that she was a great servant of God. In particular, she told me that of the many things which had passed through her soul in the past as visions or revelations, only the presence of God remained, meaning that the other visions and revelations had ceased." Teresa was living in a state of continuous "spiritual marriage"; the highest degree of prayer was constant.

It is marvelous how she could go about her duties and contacts with people in an outwardly normal fashion. In August, 1582, we find her, shrewd and wide awake, in Valladolid where she had to deal delicately, but firmly, with her nephew's mother-in-law, an aristocrat with influential relatives. The woman was a fearful opponent, but Teresa had to argue with her about her brother Lorenzo's inheritance, for he had died in 1581. Francisco, Lorenzo's son, had married Orofrisia de Mendoza y Castilla, and the young couple spent so much that they were in a bad state economically. Now Lorenzo's will entitled Teresita to a good part of her father's wealth, which was to go to St. Joseph's Convent in Avila. Teresa, who had had to battle for five years to found the convent in absolute poverty, now had to defend Teresita's, and in turn, the convent's right to the money.

Lorenzo had expressly willed that his daughter was to have part of his wealth, and Teresa held that his will should be respected. Doña Beatriz, however, would have waived the will and convinced Teresita to renounce her rights. Her argument was simple: Teresita had chosen to be poor out of spiritual taste; her brother instead was living in the world and could not keep up with his social position. Therefore, Teresita would do better to renounce her share in his favor, thereby saving the dignity of their name and the happiness of the couple.

Teresa was naturally not of the same opinion, and after prolonged discussions, an agreement was reached, permitting Teresa to continue her trip. She arrived in Medina in September, 1582. There, Fr. Antonio of Jesus insisted she change direction: no longer go to Avila for Teresita's reception ceremony but go to Alba where the Duchess was waiting to speak to her.

Obedience then cost her great effort, but obey she did. She felt that the command was dominated by too human motives to waste her time and energy on. Teresa abhorred being considered a saint, and she felt the argument of refreshing the tired spirit of a great lady too weak to make her change her course. Why should Teresita be forced to wait to pronounce her religious vows?

Teresa's secret had been obedience, so she left for Alba on September 19, feeling ill with a slight fever. She was traveling by coach so Fr. Antonio felt she was receiving every possible care. When they stopped to spend the night, she felt terrible. She asked Sr. Ana to give her something lest she faint, but all the poor nun could find were dried figs. She had the village searched for eggs, but there were none. Sr. Ana started to cry, and Teresa consoled her by saying that it was all right because the figs were good.

When they reached Alba the next day, Teresa went directly to bed saying, "Good Lord, how exhausted I feel! I haven't gone to bed at this hour for more than twenty years!"

The rest seemed to bolster her, for she got up as usual and visited the convent, leading a normal life for the next few days, receiving Communion daily and going to choir prayers. She even settled petty disturbances that were upsetting the nuns, received several visitors—the Duchess of Alba being one of them.

On St. Michael's morning, however, just after Communion, she spit blood and was immediately put to bed. She requested that Fr. Antonio be called to hear her confession. When he saw the state she was in, he felt grief-stricken with the thought of having been the principal cause of her illness. But Teresa consoled him by saying that he should not wish her to remain longer on earth because she was no longer necessary in this world.

Holy Communion was administered to her on October 3 at five o'clock in the afternoon. All the nuns of the convent were around her, and she spoke to them calmly. "My daughters, pardon the bad example I have given you. Do not learn from me, for I am the greatest sinner in the world, and I have observed the Rules and Constitutions so poorly. For the love of God I ask you, my daughters, to observe them with much perfection and may you always obey your superiors."

When the Holy Eucharist arrived, it seemed she wished to prostrate herself on the floor, but unable to do this, she knelt on the bed to receive the Host. Tears streamed down everyone's face while Teresa's lighted up with joy and she exclaimed: "My Lord and my

Spouse! The desired hour has come; it is time that we see each other, my Beloved and my Lord. It is time to go. Your will be done. It is time that I leave this earth so that my soul may rest in You whom I have so desired."

She continued murmuring words of prayer, her conversation with God never ending. The most salient and oft-repeated of these aspirations was: "After all, Lord, I am a daughter of the Church," as though she were arguing with God persuading Him to forgive her.

At nine o'clock that night she received the Anointing of the Sick. Shortly afterwards, Fr. Antonio asked if she desired to have her body transferred to Avila or to remain in Alba. Marveling at the question, Teresa replied, "You ask me this, Father? Do I have something that belongs to me? Will they not give me a little piece of earth here out of charity?"[1]

She spent the night in agony. In the morning she turned on her side toward the nuns, holding a crucifix in her hands, and remained peacefully in that position all day. From time to time expressions of concentration and prayer would pass over her face as though she were answering inner calls. It was October 4, 1582, St. Francis' Day, when, at 9:30 at night, she uttered three soft groans, smiled briefly and died.

---

1. The Testimony was given by Sr. Mary of St. Francis; cited by Fr. Silverio, V, XII.

CHAPTER FIFTY-NINE

Altars

Teresa of Jesus' prestige and veneration after her death was immediately obvious, first, for her intercession with God in heaven, and secondly, for the memory of her holy life on earth. Papers were collected preparatory to introducing the cause of her beatification as early as 1592 by Fr. Gracián who was in Rome that year. In 1595, Philip II requested the Apostolic Nuncio to gather ample information in the sixteen cities where Teresa had lived or where people who had known her personally still lived. The sixteen sets of materials were sealed and sent to Rome in 1597, together with letters from Philip II and Empress María.

Meanwhile, letters had gone to Rome asking for Teresa's beatification: the Universities of Alcalá, Salamanca, and Coimbra, city councils, leading aristocrats, the King, princesses, provincial councils, bishops, all sent letters to Rome in favor of Teresa. With this imposing testimonial, Paul V ordered the Bishops of Avila and Salamanca to gather canonical information concerning the sanctity and miracles of Mother Teresa. After the first inquiries were completed, the Pope appointed the

Cardinal of Toledo and the Bishops of Ávila and Salamanca to gather further information. These second inquiries finished, the documents were sent to Rome on
June 16, 1611, where, meanwhile, hundreds of letters
from influential people had poured in, all requesting
that Teresa of Jesus be exalted on the altars. Margaret
of Spain had written in 1607, Sigismund of Poland in
1608, Philip III of Spain in 1610, Archduke Albert and
Isabella in 1611 and the governors of the Netherlands.
The general chapter of the Italian Congregation also
sent in its petition in 1608.

All the documents were examined by Cardinal Lan-
cellotti and declared valid on November 10, 1612,
maintaining Teresa of Jesus sufficiently recognized to
have led a pure, righteous and holy life, full of virtue as
behooves a servant of God. The case next passed to the
Holy Tribunal which issued a favorable verdict concerning the miracles and holy life of Teresa of Jesus.
The Congregation of Ceremonies also passed a favorable sentence.

In the Quirinal Palace on April 14, 1614, the Pope
listened to the reports of Cardinals Galli and Lancel-
lotti, after which he declared Teresa beatified as a servant of God. Through a special concession of the Holy
See, the feast of the great Reformer was celebrated in
the Carmelite church, Holy Mary of the Scala, in the
presence of twelve cardinals and great throngs of
people.

More than twenty cities celebrated the event in
Spain. Hardly had the echoes of the celebrations died
away than the canonization process went into effect. At
this point, not only did the Spaniards renew their petitions to have Teresa definitely exalted, but even French
royalty joined the choir of acclaiming voices. There
were now many French Catholics enthralled by the
mystical revelations of Teresa of Jesus. Her books had
been translated into several languages, French being

one of the first. Besides, France already had ten Reform monasteries and convents, ever since Mother Ana of Jesus brought the first Discalced nuns to Paris in 1604. That was why Louis XIII wrote to the Pope in January, 1615, saying that since the holy life of Teresa and miracles which God had worked on her behalf were known to everyone, and her veneration had reached such a point that many Reform institutes had already been founded in France, would not His Holiness accept his petition to have Teresa canonized?

Again in 1617, Louis XIII wrote, along with María de Medici, Princess Isabel, Spain's future queen, and Archduke Albert of Belgium. Four years later, Emperor Ferdinand II wrote, as did the kings of Spain, France, and Poland and many others.

Meanwhile, Paul V had died, and his successor, Gregory XV ordered the processes to continue. In January, 1622, the Congregation of Rites declared the virgin of Ávila admissible to the catalogue of saints. On February 24, all the cardinals, archbishops and bishops that were in Rome voted in her favor. On March 12, the Pope called Teresa of Jesus a saint along with four other famous beatified men: Isidore, Ignatius of Loyola, Francis Xavier, and Philip Neri. It was the first canonization ceremony to be held in St. Peter's Basilica in such an august manner, and from that time on the ceremony became a Church custom.

Among the five, Teresa represented the summit of contemplative life and the value of silent monastic immolation.

Teresa's spiritual value is superiorly contemplative, but she was also exalted because she combined so perfectly Mary's duties with those of Martha in her own private life. Ascetic and mystic elements were well balanced in her so her humanity was not lessened. She was such a many-sided personality that different scholars have studied her from many aspects. Some have seen her intellectual power, others her virtues, her intense mortifications, her energetic character, her clear judgments, her surety of decisions. Contemplatives have exulted in the delights of her mystic life, while men of action have chosen her energy. The cultured referred to her writings as naturally elegant and fresh.

But everyone had to admire her gift of love which had both ascetic and mystical qualities. The faculty of love had been conquered by grace and with God's help the loving of one's neighbor, especially one's enemies. The other faculty of loving she received from above was as a flame infused which burns toward God, consisting entirely in a mystic privilege.

Though these mystical moments of love are impossible to narrate, it is those very conversations of love that Teresa has given us which are the most capable of revealing God within human limitations.

Bibliography

(English authors or translated works)

EDITOR'S NOTE: Instead of the 14 pages of the bibliography that the author published in his Italian edition, which is only a resumé of the one published by Fr. Otilio of the Infant Jesus, OCD, with his Spanish edition of the works of St. Teresa (Madrid: BAC, 1951. Vol. I., pp. 23-127), we reproduce here the English Teresian bibliography prepared for the first edition of this book by Fr. Otilio at our request.

I. Bibliographies

Curzon, Henri de. *Bibliographie Teresienne.* Ouvrages français et étrangers sur Sainte Thérèse et sur ses oeuvres. Bibliographie critique. Paris: Libr. des S-P., 1902. 67 pp.

Otilio del N. J., OCD. *Bibliografía Teresiana.* Obras Completas de Sta. Teresa de Jesús. Madrid: Biblioteca de Autores Cristianos (BAC), 1951. t. I. pp. 23-127.

Valenti, José Ignacio. *Estudio Critico-Bibliográfico Sobre las Obras de Santa Teresa de Jesús.* Reus: Tip. Sanjuán Hnos, 1916. 38 pp.

II. Biographies

Auclair, M. (Pond, K.) *Saint Teresa of Avila,* by Marcelle Auclair with a Preface by André Maurois. Trans. from French by Kathleen Pond. New York: Pantheon Books, Inc., 1953. XVI. 457 pp. (Paperback ed. New York: Doubleday Doran, Inc., 1959. 480 pp.)

Barden, M. M. *Saint Teresa Mirrored in Her Letters.* (Apud: *Thought,* 7 [1932-1933], pp. 225-239.)

Bertrand, L. (Hazard, M. L.) *Saint Teresa of Avila.* Trans. from the French of Louis Bertrand by Marie Louise Hazard. New York: The Society of the Propagation of the Faith, 1929. XVIII. 301 pp.

Breen, P. *Compendious Critical Life of St. Teresa.* 205 pp.

Brice, CP (Pseud. of Frank Bernard Zurmuchlen, CP). *Teresa, John and Thérèse.* A family portrait of three great Carmelites: Teresa of Ávila, John of the Cross and Thérèse of Lisieux. New York: Pustet, 1946. 336 pp.

Bruno of J. M., OCD. *Three Mystics: El Greco, St. John of the Cross and St. Teresa.* Ed. by Fr. Bruno de Jesús Marie, OCD. New York: Sheed and Ward, 1947.

Butler, Alban. *The Life of St. Teresa, Foundress of the Reformation of the Barefooted Carmelites.* Dublin: J. Duffy and Co. 64 pp.

Carmel of Wheeling (cf. Mary Magdalene).

Carmichael, M. *Saint Teresa and Her Prior General.* (Apud: *Thought,* 7 [1932-1933], pp. 240-261.)

Castro Albarrán, L. de. *The Dust from Her Sandals.* Reminiscences of St. Teresa of Ávila. 250 pp.

Chesterton, C. *Saint Teresa,* by Mrs. Cecil Chesterton. London: Hodderon's Strighton, 1928. VI. 288 pp.

Colvill, H. H. *Saint Teresa of Spain,* by Helen Hester Colvill, with twenty illustrations. 5th ed., London: Methuen and Co., 1909 (6th ed., 1910. XIII. 343 pp.).

Crisogono, P., OCD (Stanislaus, P., OCD). *St. Teresa of Jesus: Her Life-Story and Her Ascetico-Mystical Doctrine.* Adapted from the Spanish of Rev. Fr. Crysogonus of

J. E., by Fr. Stanislaus of Jesus, OCD. Prof. of the Ap. Sem., Alwaye. Alwaye, India: 1939. XII. 312 pp. (Cath. ed., 1942. *Ibid.* 309 pp.)

Cunninghame, and Graham G. *Saint Teresa of Avila.* Some accounts of her life and times, together with some pages from the history of the last great Reform in the religious orders. London: Adam and Ch. Black, 1894. 2 vols. X. 463. VI. 452 pp. (2nd ed., London: Eveleigh Nash, 1907. XIX. 792 pp.)

Gabriel of St. Mary Magdalene, OCD. *Saint Teresa of Jesus.* Trans. from the Italian by a Benedictine of Stanbrook Abbey. Westminster, MA: The Newman Press, 1949. XII. 123 pp.

Goodier, A. *Saint Teresa and the Dominicans.* (Apud: *The Month,* 163 [1936], pp. 247-257.)

Joly, H. *Saint Teresa.* Trans. by Emily M. Waller. London: 1903. (2nd ed., 1912; 3rd ed., 1918; 1922, 1929, etc.)

Kelly, J. *Meet Saint Teresa.* An Introduction to "La Madre" of Ávila, by Mgsr. Joseph P. Kelly. New York: F. Pustet Co., 1958. XII. 212 pp.

Kennedy, M. M. *The Holy Child Seen by Her, Saint Teresa.* With illus. by Lindsay Smygnton. London: B. Oates, Ltd., 1913. 115 pp.

Life of Saint Teresa. With a short account of the Foundations which she made. Abridged from her own writings. London: 1957.

Lockhart, E. *The Life of Saint Teresa of the Order of Our Lady of Mount Carmel.* Edited with a Preface by the Arch. of Westminster (Card. Menning), London, s.d.

Lovat, A. *The Life of Saint Teresa.* Taken from the French of a Carmelite Nun. With a Preface by Msgr. R. H. Benson. London: 1911. 662 pp. (2nd ed. London: Plymouth, 1914. 629 pp.)

Mary Magdalene of Jesús (Potts) OCD. *Saint Teresa of Jesus.* Wheeling, WV: Carmel of Wheeling, Elm Grove, 1914. 16 pp.

Mullahey, K. *Teresa of Avila, the Woman.* A study by Katherine M. 1929. 115 pp.

Nevin, W. *Teresa of Avila,* by Winifred N. Milwaukee, WI:
The Bruce Publishing Co., 1956. XII. 169 pp.

Nigg, W. *Great Saints.* Trans. by W. Stirling, IL: 1948.

—— *Warriors of God.* The great religious orders and their
founders. Trans. from the German by Mary Ilford. New
York: A. Knoff, 1959. VII. 358-XVI pp. *(St. Teresa and
Carmel,* pp. 280-314.)

O'Brien, K. *Salute to Saint Teresa,* by Kate. (Apud: *Woman's
Journal,* London: 1946. Cond. in *The Catholic Digest,* 10
[1946], pp. 35-38.)

—— Teresa of Avila. New York: Sheed and Ward, 1951. 96
pp.

Osgood, M. *Saint Teresa and the Devotees of Spain.* Boston:
1849.

Parkinson, F. K. *The Land of Stones and Saints,* by Frances
Keyes. New York: Doubleday Co., 1957. Illus. XXVI.
357 pp. (About St. Teresa, pp. 63-124.)

Peer, E. Allison. *Studies of the Spanish Mystics,* by Edgard A. P.
New York: The Macmillan Co., 1951. 2 vols. (1st ed.,
London: Sheldon Press, 1927-1930; 2nd ed. of vol. I,
London: SPCK, 1951.)

—— Handbook to the Life and Times of St. Teresa and St.
John of the Cross. London: W. Clowes and Sons, 1954.
227 pp. (Westminster, MD: The Newman Press.)

Pius XI. *Apostolic Letter* of Pope Pius XI. 1922.

Sackville-West, V. *The Eagle and the Dove.* Contrasts St. Teresa of Avila and St. Thérèse of Lisieux. New York:
Doubleday and Co., 1944. VIII. 175. (Spanish version
by S. Santaines. Barcelona: 1945. Id. Ital. by
M. Gallone. Verona: 1946. IV. 311 pp.

Sheed, F. J. *Saints Are Not Sad.* Forty biographical portraits.
New York: Sheed and Ward, 1949. 441 pp. (St. Teresa,
p. 334.)

Silverio de Sta. Teresa, OCD. *Saint Teresa of Jesus.* Trans. by
Sister Teresa of the Heart of Jesus. London: Sands and
Co., 1947. XII. 191 pp. (Dist. in America by The New-
man Press, Westminster, MD.)

Sisters of Notre Dame. *Saint Teresa and Her First English Daughters.* London: Sands and Co., 1919. IV. 276 pp. 7 illus.

Swainson, W. P. *Teresa of Avila.* London: 1903. (Coll. "Christian Mystics.")

Trench, M. *The Life of Saint Teresa.* London: 1875. 64 pp.

Walker, H. Helen: *My Favorite Saint: Saint Teresa of Avila.* (Apud: *The Sign,* 38 [1959], n. 11, pp. 17-19.)

Walsh, W. Thom. *Saint Teresa of Avila.* A biography. Milwaukee, WI: Bruce Publishing Co., 1943. XII. 592 pp. ("Best-seller" sixth print., 1943; 8th ed., 1946; 1954, etc. Spanish version by M. de Alarcon, Buenos Aires: 1945. 586 pp. Barcelona: Espasa, 1946.)

Wortham, H. E. *Three Women: St. Teresa, Mad. Choiseul, Mrs. Eddy.* Boston: L-Brown and Co., 1930. VI. 318 pp. (About St. Teresa: "St. Teresa and the Ideal," pp. 1-114.)

Whyte, Rev. Dr. A. *Santa Teresa: An Appreciation.* With some of the best passages of the Saint's writings. Edinburgh: 1897. (2nd ed., New York: 1899.)

III. Studies

Alphonsus of the M. of Sorrows. *Practice of Mental Prayer and of Perfection, According to Saint Teresa.* Trans. by Fr. Jerome O'Connell, OCD. Bruges-Rome: desclée de Br., 1910. 1st vol., XVI. 459 pp.; 2nd vol., IX. 424 pp.; 3rd vol., 444 pp.: 4th vol., 373 pp. (1913); 5th vol., 390 pp. (1914); 6th vol., 535 pp. (1920).

Brandsma, Blessed Titus, O. Carm., *Carmelite Mysticism, Historical Sketches.* Chicago, IL: the Carmelite Press, 1936. 113 pp.

Carmelo de J. M., OCD. *The Missionary Spirit of St. Teresa.* (Apud: *Charitas,* Alwaye, 5 [1937], pp. 19-24.)

Cassidy, J. F. *The Common Sense of St. Teresa of Avila.* (Apud: *Irish Ecclesiastical Record,* 41 [1933], pp. 128-135.)

Farges, Msgr. Albert. *Mystical Phenomena.* A treatise on ascetic theology according to the principles of St. Teresa, declared by the Carmelite Congress of Madrid, 1923.

Frassinetti, G. *Saint Teresa's Pater Noster.* A treatise on prayer. Trans. from the Italian by William Hutch. London: Burns and Oates. (Other ed., New York: Benziger Bros., 1887; 7th ed., 1887. XX. 368 pp.)

Gabriel of St. Mary Magdalene, OCD. *Saint Teresa of Jesus, Mistress of the Spiritual Life.* Trans. from the Italian by a Benedictine of Stanbrook Abbey. Cork: The Mercier Press, 1949. XII. 123 pp.

Hoornaert, R. *Saint Teresa in Her Writings.* Trans. by Rev. J. Leonard, CM. New York: Benziger Bros., 1931. X. 410 pp. (4th ed., London: 1933.)

Kaiser, A. *Saint Teresa's Hymn in the Light of Her Autobiography.* (Apud: *The Ecclesiastical Review,* Philadelphia, 91 [1934], pp. 159-169.)

Lucas de S. José, OCD. *Saint Teresa's Book-Mark.* A meditative commentary. Trans. by a friend for Carmel of St. Louis. St. Louis, MO: H. S. Collins Print Co. XVII. 130 pp.

Marie-Eugene, Rev. F., OCD. *I Want to See God.* A practical synthesis of Carmelite Spirituality. Trans. from the French by Sr. M. Verda Clare, CSC. Chicago, IL: Fides Publ. Assoc., 1953. XXII. 549 pp.

Mary of the Bl. Sacrament, OCD. *A Retreat Under the Guidance of St. Teresa, Drawn from Her Writings.* With a letter of commendation from the Card. Mercier. London: Burns and Oates, 1929. XXVIII. 316 pp. (Dist. in America by Benziger Bros.)

Maw, M. B. *Buddhist Mysticism.* A study based upon a comparison with the mysticism of St. Teresa and Juliana of Norwich. Cambette-Bordeaux: 1942. 235 pp.

Otilio del N. J., OCD. *The Marian Spirit of Saint Teresa of Jesus.* Trans. (Apud: *Mount Carmel,* Washington, D.C., 22 [1942], pp. 4-5; num. 4, pp. 18-20; num. 5, pp. 22-24, etc.)

Rohrbach, F. Peter-Thomas, OCD. *Conversation with Christ.* An introduction to mental prayer. Chicago, IL: Fides Publ., 1956. XIV. 171 pp.

IV. Literature

Clarke, W. F., SJ. *Martyr of Love.* Poem. (Apud: *The Church Calendar of West Virginia,* 26 [1922], pp. 6-7.)

Crashaw, Richard (1613-1649). *Poems of Saint Teresa.* Printed many times, v. gr. edit. by Leonard Martin. New York: Oxford Press, 1927, etc. Trans. into Spanish by Muñoz Rojas, A. *Los Poemas de Crashaw a Santa Teresa.* Estudio y versión. (Apud: *El Escorial,* n. 26 [1942], 447-468.) Ferrer Rovira, J. *Santa Teresa de Jesús de Crashaw* (Apud: *La Anunciata,* Habana, 37 [1959], p. 60; and in *Aromas del Carmelo, ibid.,* 1959, etc.)

Joyce Keenan, Cecile. *The Pride of Spain.* Poem. (Apud: *The Church Calendar of West Virginia,* 26 [1922], pp. 3-4.)

Waggaman, Mary T. *To Saint Teresa of Jesus.* Poem. *(Ibid.,* p. 2.)

V. Sermons and Devotions

Alexis L. of St. Joseph, OCD. *Novena to the Seraphic Virgin Saint Teresa of Jesus.* Trans. from the French by Peregrinus. New Orleans, LA: M. F. Dunn and Bro., 1882. 26 pp.

Alphonsus M. Liguori, St. *Novena in Honor of Saint Teresa.* With a Preface by Card. Gibbons. Philadephia: McManus Press, 1914. VIII. 115 pp. (Other ed., Buffalo, NY: The Holling Press, 1926. 12 pp.)

Balfe, K. M. *Thoughts of Saint Teresa for Every Day.* 1925. 133 pp.

Bossuet. *Panegyric of St. Teresa.* pp. 130-147. (Apud: Panegyrics of the Saints from the French of Bossuet and Bourdalue. Ed. by the Rev. Dr. O'Mahony. London: B. Herder, 1924. XXIII. 249 pp.)

Carmel of New York. *Novena to St. Teresa of Avila in Thanksgiving for Peace.* New York: 1945. 4 pp.

VISIT, WRITE or CALL your nearest ST. PAUL BOOK & MEDIA CENTER today for a wide selection of Catholic books, periodicals, cassettes, quality video cassettes for children and adults! Operated by the Daughters of St. Paul. We are located in:

ALASKA
750 West 5th Ave., Anchorage, AK 99501 **907-272-8183.**

CALIFORNIA
3908 Sepulveda Blvd., Culver City, CA 90320 **213-202-8144; 213-397-8676; 213-398-6187.**
1570 Fifth Ave. (at Cedar Street), San Diego, CA 92101 **619-232-1442; 619-232-1443.**
46 Geary Street, San Francisco, CA 94108 **415-781-5180; 415-781-5216.**

FLORIDA
145 S.W. 107th Ave. Miami, FL 33174 **305-559-6715; 305-559-6716.**

HAWAII
1143 Bishop Street, Honolulu, HI 96813 **808-521-2731.**

ILLINOIS
172 North Michigan Ave., Chicago, IL 60601 **312-346-4228; 312-346-3240.**

LOUISIANA
423 Main Street, Baton Rouge, LA 70802 **504-343-4057.**
4403 Veterans Memorial Blvd., Metairie, LA 70006 **504-887-7631; 504-887-0113.**

MASSACHUSETTS
50 St. Paul's Ave., Jamaica Plain, Boston, MA 02130 **617-522-8911.**
Rte. 1, 450 Providence Hwy., Dedham, MA 02026 **617-326-5385.**

MISSOURI
9804 Watson Rd., St. Louis, MO 63126 **314-965-3512; 314-965-3571.**

NEW JERSEY
561 U.S. Route 1; No. C6, Wicks Plaza, Edison, NJ 08817 **201-572-1200; 201-572-1201.**

NEW YORK
150 East 52nd Street, New York, NY 10022 **212-986-7580.**
78 Fort Place, Staten Island, NY 10301 **718-447-5071; 718-447-5086.**

OHIO
616 Walnut Street, Cincinnati, OH 45202 **513-421-5733; 513-721-5059.**
2105 Ontario Street (at Prospect Ave.), Cleveland, OH 44115 **216-621-9427.**

PENNSYLVANIA
168 W. DeKalb Pike, King of Prussia, PA 19406 **215-337-1882; 215-337-2077.**

SOUTH CAROLINA
243 King Street, Charleston, SC 29401 **803-577-0175.**

TEXAS
114 Main Plaza, San Antonio, TX 78205 **512-224-8101.**

VIRGINIA
1025 King Street, Alexandria, VA 22314 **703-549-3806.**

CANADA
3022 Dufferin Street, Toronto, Ontario, Canada M6B 3T5 **416-781-9131; 416-781-9132.**